Professor Christopher McMahon centers his ecclesiology firmly on the Paschal Mystery, and rightly so. Drawing on cutting-edge scholarship in Scripture, history, liturgy, systematics, and ethics, he provides a contemporary, ecumenically sensitive, and practical vision of the Church that will challenge students' minds and inspire their imaginations. *Called Together* is a terrific textbook!

William P. Loewe, PhD
Associate Professor of Historical and Systematic Theology
Catholic University of America, Washington, DC

Reading Christopher McMahon's book *Called Together* reminded me of the restoration work on the Sistine Chapel. Beneath layers of accumulated dust and grime, the artists showed a magnificent, bright, colorful work that challenged sensibilities and elicited deep thinking on the nature of God, and on creation, life, death, judgment, and resurrection. Chris has done similar work in helping us think about the Church. Recent years have made us keenly aware of the "grime," but he has shown us that underneath it is something beautiful, dynamic, and challenging. I recommend this substantive, erudite, and yet very readable book to both students and others interested in a basic question: who does Jesus call us together to be for the world?

Tim Muldoon
author of "Seeds of Hope: Young Adults and the Catholic
Church in the United States"

D1567964

Author Acknowledgments

Many people deserve thanks and praise for their assistance in seeing this project to its completion. First, the current and former editors and staff at Anselm Academic Press have been incredibly generous and supportive. Leslie Ortiz first introduced me to Anselm Academic and provided me with the initial encouragement for the project. Jerry Ruff and his team of editors have worked diligently to improve the text at every step, and Brad Harmon, along with the promotion and sales team at Anselm, has provided encouragement along the way. A special word of thanks to the anonymous readers and reviewers whose feedback helped to reshape the final product; their insights were invaluable.

This project would not have been possible without the support of the Saint Vincent College Community. Father Rene Kollar, OSB, the Dean of the School of Humanities and Fine Arts, and Jason King, the Chair of the Department of Theology at Saint Vincent College, have supported my work through regular conversation and through a course release during the spring semester of 2009. Kimberly Baker and Father Nathan Munsch, OSB, my colleagues in the Department of Theology, along with Tim Kelly and Gil Bogner in the History Department provided helpful suggestions and feedback; particularly helpful were their insights on the historical portions of the text. Several students at Saint Vincent College also assisted me in the course of my research and writing: My research assistant Katie Macioce devoted two semesters to this project, providing excellent feedback on the text and helping with research assistance along the way. Students Nick Pityk and Claire Alessi provided able assistance at various stages in the development of the text.

I would like to thank Joseph Komonchak, William Loewe, and the faculty at Catholic University for their years of service to the Church and their patience with me during my years as a graduate student. They have provided ongoing encouragement and advice, and all that is right and true in these pages has its origin in their scholarship and instruction. Lastly, I would like to thank my wife, Debra Faszer-McMahon, my families (the McMahons, the Clemmons-McMahons, the Faszers, the Garlocks), and my church families (the Benedictines of Sacred Heart Monastery in Yankton, SD; Annunciation Priory in Bismarck, ND; and Saint Vincent Archabbey in Latrobe, PA; as well as the people of Scottdale Mennonite Church in Scottdale, PA) for their constant witness to the gospel that is reflected in the pages of this book. As always, the invaluable assistance of those mentioned above does not diminish my responsibility for the book, and any shortcomings or errors are my own.

Publisher Acknowledgments

Thank you to the following individuals who reviewed this work in progress:

Donna Proctor, MA,
Marian University, Indianapolis, Indiana

Father John Sajdak, SM, STL,
Madonna University, Livonia, Michigan

CALLED
together
AN INTRODUCTION
TO ECCLESIOLOGY

CHRISTOPHER McMAHON

ANSELM
ACADEMIC

Created by the publishing team of Anselm Academic.

Cover image royalty free from PHOTOS.COM

Printed in the United States of America

7030

ISBN 978-1-59982-005-7

A Debra, eres mi mera mera

Contents

Introduction

CALLED TOGETHER

When my siblings and I were growing up, our mother became something of a neighborhood legend. Almost every night at dinnertime, she would stand in front of our house and ring a gigantic handbell. Her voice would ring out with the bell as she called us kids (in the order of our birth), "Maureen, Jim, Sean, Christopher! Dinner is ready!" When we were little, this was a comforting call, and an effective means of summoning us from various parts of the neighborhood. As we grew older, however, the sound of the bell and the tone of our mother's voice became, shall we say, less endearing, and our response became correspondingly less eager and less prompt. My sister, four years older than I, had to endure this humiliating "cattle call" far longer than she deserved. Memories of this custom often come up at family gatherings these days, and we find it amusing how parenting sensibilities have changed. The image of young kids roaming around the neighborhood unsupervised and unprotected makes today's parents as uncomfortable as the clanging bell once made us children. Yet, the experience of the bell and my mother's voice resonates strongly as I consider what it means to be Church, because to be Church is to be "called together," and I wonder

how much of the human response to such a call echoes the experience of being called when we were children—a little resistant but nonetheless assured by its ringing call.

"Called together" is the root meaning of the Greek word *ekklesia*, which the translators of the New Testament render as "church." Within the world of Judaism and early Christianity, the call of God was associated with the people of Israel and their experience as a nation, a people set apart, constituted by God's call. In fact, as many historians of ancient Israel have long noted, however the origins of Israel were connected with the patriarchal figures Abraham, Isaac, and Jacob, by the time of the Exodus and the entry into the land of Canaan, the Israelites were a patchwork of different tribes with a loose sense of corporate identity.[1] The common identity of the Hebrew people was solidified over the course of generations by the experience of being called together by God, for God's purpose. We see this unity in diversity being carried over into the New Testament, particularly in the Acts of the Apostles, when Jews of every nation and social standing, and Gentiles from around the world, come together through the power of God's call.

So it is with any account of the Church: God calls humans together, and out of this diversity, a common identity and common mission are discerned. However, this discernment is not

1

always easy; diversities endure, and the story of God's call and our response is uneven, fraught with struggles. In the current age, the very notion of being "called *together*" is in question. Rather, the call of God is often portrayed as intensely personal, even to the point of being an utterly individual and private experience. The present book seeks to offer a balanced and inclusive account of the Church, its shortcomings and its mission. Although written from the perspective of contemporary Roman Catholic theology, this book hopes to offer an account of the Church and its mission that resonates with Christians from other traditions and even with those who hold a wide range of beliefs and convictions.

An area of some concern for Protestant Christians when addressing Roman Catholic Christians on the subject of ecclesiology (the study of the Church) is that the Catholic approach seems to place too great an emphasis on the Church, almost deifying it.[2] As a sign of this excessive ecclesiology, Protestants may point to the Roman Catholic tradition's custom of capitalizing the word *church* when used in reference to the one Church of Christ as it subsists in the Catholic Church. Throughout this text, the word *church* will be capitalized in accordance with customary practice in Roman Catholic theology. This move should not be interpreted as a challenge to, or a repudiation of, an ecumenical ecclesiology. Obviously, there will be occasion when "the Church" clearly refers uniquely to the Catholic Church, but readers should also learn to apply the use of "the Church" beyond those boundaries, notably in reference to the one, holy, catholic, and apostolic Church as expressed in the Nicene Creed. This includes the broader community of Christians, including Orthodox, Protestant, Roman Catholic, and evangelical churches. While learning to think about the Church so broadly may challenge some readers, discomfort and confusion often accompany theological discussions of the Church.

In the theological education of the laity, few areas are more important and yet more neglected than ecclesiology. Undergraduate courses on scripture, ethics, Christology, and even world religions tend to proliferate, while ecclesiology often takes a backseat. Theologians, on the other hand, have devoted considerable effort to this study, especially in the post–Vatican II era (since the mid-1960s). They argue powerfully about the connection between ecclesiology and the history of the Church, the structures of the Church, and the way authority is exercised by the Church's hierarchy (e.g., Roger Haight's recent multivolume study, *Christian Community in History*, and Hans Küng's post-conciliar manifesto, *The Church*).[3] Richard Gaillardetz's recent book, *Ecclesiology for a Global Church*, nicely blends all of these concerns in an effort to summon the Church to a self-understanding that will enable it to engage a new globalized world.[4]

The present text does not seek to duplicate these efforts. Rather, it seeks to address the apparent marginalization of ecclesiology as a focal point of theological education. It does this by focusing on the nature of the Church and its mission in the world from a soteriological perspective—the perspective of how the Church promotes salvation by participating in the saving work of God in Jesus Christ. In short, this book will focus on both what the Church does, as well as what it is, without letting the history of the Church or its power structures dominate the discussion. *Called Together* articulates a theological understanding of the Church primarily in terms of its soteriological mission. This is but one manner, one pathway, for introducing students to ecclesiology as a theological discipline, and it must be pursued without excluding other approaches. However, this orientation will help to center the conversation about the Church on the work of God in Christ.

Certainly the issues confronting the Church are myriad, and ecclesiology must be capable of addressing these issues. This book seeks to function as an introduction to, or an initial frame of reference for, ecclesiology. In other words, it seeks to provide a theoretical and practical basis for thinking about the Church, what it is, and what it does. With this foundation in place, conversations about power, ministry, structures, globalization, and enculturation may be more fruitfully pursued, and both readers and instructors are invited to make these issues part of their approach through incorporating supplementary materials as well.

THE PLAN FOR WHAT FOLLOWS

Ecclesiology is both descriptive and prescriptive. From a descriptive perspective, ecclesiology must address how the Church actually works in the life of believers within history, what some would call *ecclesiality*.[5] Yet, ecclesiology also makes certain claims about how the common life of believers *ought* to unfold. It is within this prescriptive dimension of ecclesiology that the soteriological mission of the Church will find its place, particularly in the two opening chapters.

Chapter 1 presents the story of Jesus as a narrative of diverse and complex people—the people of Israel. The diversity of Gospels within the New Testament suggests that the Christian tradition understands that the story of Jesus is sensitive, deep, and inexhaustible. This chapter sets forth a theological and historical reading of the Jesus story in a manner that will highlight the communal and redemptive dimensions of that narrative. While some of this material may already be familiar to readers, such a review is often helpful in introducing a new subject. In chapter 2, the focus moves to the soteriological tradition and how it has reinforced various understandings of the Church and its mission, particularly from the Middle Ages through the

Counter-Reformation. That chapter concludes with the soteriological reflections offered by Bernard Lonergan and the model of the Church his soteriology informs.

Chapters 3–5 briefly describe the Church, its practices, and its self-understanding over the course of history. Chapter 3 provides an overview of the development of ecclesiology from the early Church through the early twentieth century. While this snapshot of developments is necessarily selective, it helps to highlight the connection between the form the Church has assumed in history and the sociocultural location of the Church. In other words, it shows how the Church's social setting has affected its understanding of itself and its mission. Chapter 4 treats the Second Vatican Council as a watershed in the life of the Church, particularly in its account of the Church and its relationship to the world. The chapter treats the events at the council, the context of those events, and the two major ecclesiological documents produced by the council itself. Chapter 5 bridges the descriptive accounts of the Church in chapters 3 and 4 and the recommendations for Church practice outlined in chapters 6 and 7. Chapter 5 extends the conversation about the Church and the world that was started at the council by addressing the post-Christian, globalized marketplace culture of the twenty-first century. The chapter briefly discusses the emergence of small-group structures and new ecclesial movements as a response to a growing dissatisfaction with parish life, and the way these movements present alternative models of believing and acting as Church. The chapter includes a cautionary note suggesting that Christians must avoid the temptation to retreat from a world that has become increasingly post-Christian, and instead focus on the Church's vocation to be an instrument of redemptive recovery in world history. Such a vocation requires critical engagement and cooperation with those outside Church boundaries.

The final two chapters outline proposals for what it means to be "called" and to be "sent" by God as a community that embodies and promotes conversion and redemptive recovery in history. Chapter 6 focuses on the dynamism of being "called" to conversion, to life with God (*communio*), through the celebration of the liturgy. The liturgy constitutes the Church and gives it its orientation to the world. Chapter 7 then addresses the dynamics of being "sent" into the world (*missio*). The social teaching of the Church, in particular, the tradition of Catholic Social Thought provides the framework for the discussion. Two issues, in particular, focus the conversation: war and family. These two issues may not be the most urgent or relevant for some readers, but they provide good examples of the mission of the Church in the world, and they resonate with the experiences (and failures) of local parish living. Many readers may relate to these issues, and their impact on the world and on history is evident.

Each of the chapters includes several pedagogical features designed to promote classroom discussion. First, every chapter includes two sets of questions: "Questions for Understanding" and "Questions for Reflection." "Questions for Understanding" asks basic questions about content; it is designed to highlight some of the more important aspects of each chapter. "Questions for Reflection" asks students to engage the material in a way that takes them beyond the text and even beyond the classroom. Instructors may use or ignore these questions and exercises as they see fit. Second, each chapter includes a brief selection of books "For Further Study." These books, along with those cited throughout the chapters and in the chapter endnotes, while by no means exhaustive or even representative, should nonetheless lead readers to discover additional resources for thinking about the Church. Finally, throughout the text are sidebar presentations intended to supplement and advance those issues most central to the text.

The text may be judged a success if readers and instructors find here resources that will help to animate a conversation about the Church that resonates with their experience and challenges their assumptions about what the Church is and what it is called to do. Those who find the scope of the book somewhat narrow are again encouraged to make use of supplemental material to move the conversation in other directions. In the end, it is hoped that *Called Together* will provide a helpful orientation to the Church via the fundamental theological claim of the Christian tradition, namely, that in Christ God is reconciling the world to himself (2 Corinthians 5:19).

Endnotes

1. John Bright, *A History of Israel*, Fourth Edition (Louisville, KY: Westminster John Knox, 2000), 133–137. Bright is not alone in this assessment, and his account of Israel's history is still a standard work in the field. See also Mark S. Smith, *Memoirs of God: History, Memory, and the Experience of the Divine in Ancient Israel* (Minneapolis, MN: Fortress, 2004), 7–27.

2. For example, see Mark Noll and Carolyn Nystrom, *Is the Reformation Over? An Evangelical Assessment of Contemporary Roman Catholicism* (Grand Rapids, MI: Baker, 2005), 237–251.

3. Roger Haight, *Christian Community in History*, 3 vols. (New York: Continuum, 2004, 2005, 2008); Hans Küng, *The Church* (New York: Sheed and Ward, 1967).

4. Richard Gaillardetz, *Ecclesiology for a Global Church: A People Called and Sent* (New York: Orbis, 2008).

5. See Paul Lakeland, "Maturity and the Lay Vocation: From Ecclesiology to Ecclesiality," in *Catholic Identity and the Laity*, College Theology Society Annual Volume, 54, ed. Tim Muldoon (New York: Orbis, 2009), 241–259.

The Story of Jesus

Some years ago, many Christians started wearing bracelets or pins inscribed with the initials WWJD—"What Would Jesus Do?" The question was meant to provoke one to consider how everyday choices were to be modeled after Jesus. "Should I tell a lie to protect my friend?" "Should I ask the kid sitting alone in the cafeteria to join my friends and me at our table?" "Should I go on a mission trip to Guatemala, or should I take a vacation instead?" Well, what would Jesus do? Although the industry that grew up around WWJD was widely criticized, and some suggested that the question itself grossly oversimplified moral reasoning, the sentiment behind the question has merit, even if the application of the biblical narrative is not always readily apparent or even advisable. If Christians are not formed by the story of Jesus, what it means to be "Christian" becomes convoluted and hopelessly abstract. Accordingly, one needs the story of Jesus, but one might fairly ask—Which story? How does one put the story together? Is it simply a matter of picking up the Gospels and reading?

Anyone can simply read the Gospels, but it is important to recognize that one always reads selectively, with certain predispositions and with certain ends or purposes in mind. Of course, reading with a purpose is a good thing, but by doing so, one necessarily limits one's field of vision. In what follows, this text does not pretend to present *the* story

5

of Jesus or even a normative account. Rather, what this text offers is *a* reading of the story of Jesus—one of many possible readings. In doing so, it hopes to highlight aspects of the story that will contribute to a well-formulated sense of Jesus' mission and the nature of the Church. As such, it is a story that will resonate with other readings of the Jesus story and, above all, with the contemporary expression of the Church's tradition. For it is through the story of Jesus that Christians are formed and called to union with God and fellowship with one another, so learning to narrate this story is crucial to an understanding of what it means for a Christian "to do" and "to be" Church.

JESUS AND THE STORY OF ISRAEL

The story of an individual is also the story of a community. A person cannot be fairly understood or rightly appreciated without an awareness of the family, friends, and culture(s) that have formed the individual. The story of Jesus is no exception. Without an adequate appreciation of the people and cultures that informed Jesus' life and ministry, one cannot understand him or his destiny. The author of the Gospel according to Matthew makes this point emphatically in his opening chapter.

Matthew opens by narrating the family tree of Jesus. Although this list of generations (*Toledot* in Hebrew) may look like a fairly straightforward account of Jesus' ancestry, the device is actually quite complex. *Toledot* are found in several places throughout the Old Testament, especially in the opening chapters of Genesis in which they provide the transition between various narrative cycles (e.g., the transition from the creation narrative to the story of Noah and from Noah to the Abraham cycle of stories; see Genesis 6 and 11).[1] As such, Matthew signals a transition from the

story of Israel's return from exile, the latest episode in the ongoing story of Israel, to the story of Jesus. Matthew provides a link between Jesus and the story of Israel, and without that connection, the story of Jesus would be lost or distorted.

The basic contours of Israel's story, particularly as it pertains to the story of Jesus, may be summarized in three interrelated themes: covenant, monarchy, and eschatology. Each of these themes, though rich and complex in its own right, nonetheless resonates strongly with the contemporary experience of Church and provides an important backdrop for the struggle to understand the Church and its mission today.

The Story of Israel: Covenant

Stories are integral to how one understands the nature of the universe and one's place within it, what is often called one's worldview. The stories of Israel's ancestors and especially the recurring themes of covenant and mercy need to be understood, not as pious fairy tales, but as the embodiment of Israel's worldview. Of special importance in the story of Israel, and therefore integral to Israel's self-understanding, is the call of Abraham in the book of Genesis.

As the story goes, Abraham is called, or chosen, by God in Genesis 12, and Abraham responds to this election with trust, or *emunah* (the Hebrew word for "faith"). A key point in the story is that although Abraham is described as responding to God with faith and trust, God's call, or God's election, precedes Abraham's trust. In other words, God's election of Abraham is utterly gracious; Abraham has done nothing to deserve his election.[2] At this point, one may rightly ask about the fairness of this election. Such an election may sound like favoritism and an affront to the common understanding of God's love for all of humanity. An accounting of the covenant ceremony in Genesis 15 might help respond to this question.

Jesus' Family Tree

The genealogies of Jesus in the Gospels of Matthew and Luke are quite interesting. In Matthew, the genealogical list begins with Abraham and continues through David and his descendants—the kings of Judah (note the famous names, such as Solomon, Hezekiah, and Josiah). The list ends with the generations from the Babylonian Exile to Jesus. The author contends that the list from Abraham to David, from David to the Exile, and from the Exile to Jesus contains fourteen generations in each. This is not entirely accurate (the generations from the Exile to Jesus only number thirteen), but the number fourteen has more than literal significance. First, it is a play on the name of David, as each of the Hebrew characters in *David* has numerical values that add up to fourteen:

David — דוד (ד=4, ו=6, ד=4)

Some scholars suggest, however, that the significance of the number fourteen rests in that it is a multiple of seven—the perfect number. All of this signifies the timeliness of Jesus' birth: he is a descendant of David, the long-awaited king, who comes at the appointed time.

Additionally, Matthew's genealogy includes mention (directly or indirectly) of four women: Tamar, Rahab, Ruth, and Bathsheba. Each of these women forms an important link in the story of Israel and the ancestry of David, yet none of them is an Israelite. Moreover, the women enter into the ancestral lineage in unconventional ways. Tamar is a neglected widow who seduces Judah, the father of her dead husband(s) (Genesis 38). Rahab, a prostitute in Jericho, survives the bloodletting that followed that city's destruction because she cooperated with a pair of Israelite spies (Joshua 2:14; 6:22–25). The story of Ruth includes a journey to the home of her deceased husband, accompanying her mother-in-law, where she seduces a new husband, Boaz (Ruth 3). Finally, the story of David's seduction (rape?) of Bathsheba and murder of her husband is well known (2 Samuel 11).

In Luke, the genealogy runs back from Jesus through David and Abraham to Adam. Luke includes none of the kings of Judah in his list. Luke's genealogy is nonroyal, and in some ways nonmessianic. Jesus is a child of Adam, not just a child of Abraham—Jesus' lineage has a universal quality. The story of Jesus is still intimately bound with the story of Israel, but Luke narrates that story from the perspective of the poor and the dispossessed—the *anawim*.

God does not call Abraham in Genesis for Abraham's benefit, but to make Abraham into a great nation, a goal that requires the possession of land and the proliferation of Abraham's descendents. God promises Abraham, "I will make of you a great nation, and I will bless you; I will make your name great, so that you will be a blessing. I will bless those who bless you and curse those who curse you. All the communities of the earth shall find blessing in you" (Genesis 12:1–3). Given that God's plan is for the salvation of the world, a nation that is chosen and formed by God will be able to make known God's love, mercy, and fellowship. Yet, from the very moment God gives Abraham these promises, circumstances conspire to frustrate their fulfillment. In fact, Abraham finally becomes somewhat incredulous, and he questions God's ability to deliver on the promises. At that point, God intervenes, and in a ritual quite strange to modern readers, God makes a covenant with Abraham.

The covenant ceremony that unfolds in Genesis 15:1–21 highlights the profound novelty inherent in the idea of a covenant between God and humans. To the people of the second millennium BCE, however, the ritual made perfect sense. God passes between the two halves of a series of animal carcasses, and as this action unfolds, God swears an oath, saying that Abraham will inherit the land that was promised earlier: "from the river of Egypt to the Great River, the Euphrates." This ceremony appears to have been borrowed from the ancient Hittites, who used it as a means of ritually binding an overlord to someone of inferior social standing [3] The idea was that the overlord, who was beyond the grasp of those beneath him, would walk between the carcass halves that had been set out (such a scene no doubt invoked the image of a horrible and painful death). As the overlord passed through the bloody mess, he would pronounce an oath and outline the specific terms of the promise. For example, he would guarantee that a particular piece of land was to be given to the inferior party. If the overlord failed to deliver on the promise, the deity who was the witness to the promise would then rip the overlord in half (note the similarity with the ceremony in Jeremiah 34:18–22). Given this cultural-historical background, the scene becomes even more remarkable — God freely chooses to be solemnly bound to the promise made to Abraham without "needing" anything in return. Certain signs of the covenant, or election, appear later in the story, and these are meant to reinforce the special relationship between God and the descendents of Abraham (e.g., circumcision in Genesis 17). The covenant with Abraham becomes the point of reference in the dramatic story of Israel's foundation, the Exodus from Egypt and the journey to the land God had promised to Abraham and his descendents.

The story of Moses and the Exodus is the foundational narrative for the people of Israel. The experience of enslavement in Egypt and of God's power to bring liberation from the pharaoh, the god-king of Egypt, colors all aspects of Israel's life. The story narrated in the Pentateuch describes not only God's power to defeat enemies and liberate those who are oppressed, but it also describes the failures of the Hebrew people to remain faithful to God and to trust in God's promises. In the familiar scene at Mount Sinai, as God draws near to seal the covenant, Israel turns away (Exodus 32:1–14). The golden calf incident, the wandering in the wilderness, the danger of famine and death, all capture the dynamic of the covenantal relationship between Israel and God — God reaches out to humanity, while humanity turns away to embrace its own destruction. This pattern is pivotal in the Old Testament because it accentuates two ideas central to covenant: humanity's weakness and God's *chesed*, (fidelity, love, and mercy). Even though humans will not live up to the covenant, God always will live up to it and more. God goes beyond the boundaries of a normal covenantal agreement in order to secure Israel and preserve the people from utter destruction. Thus, the story of Israel is not the story of a nation, but of a people formed and sustained by God's fidelity, expressed in his *chesed*.

The Story of Israel: Kingship

Leadership within the People of God has always been a major concern. In Israel, the story of David stands out as a beautiful and tragic example of the glories and the dangers of institutionalized leadership within a community constituted by God. It is noteworthy that in the New Testament Jesus is given the title "Christ" or "messiah" — a title that ties him directly to

David, the one who was anointed king in Israel. There was a hope, an expectation within Israel, that just as God had raised David up to lead the people in obedience to God's covenant, so too would God raise up a new messiah, a new king, to do the same. But as messiah, or anointed one, Jesus reminds the people that God is their king and that institutionalized leadership can only survive so long as God's kingship and God's *chesed* are kept front and center. The story of David serves as an important point of reference on this issue.

The books of First and Second Samuel narrate the story of King David and his rise to power. Even though the narrative is intended to celebrate the achievements of David and honor him as Israel's greatest king, the text also includes those voices in ancient Israel that thought the establishment of a monarchy was a bad idea (1 Samuel 8:1–22; 12:1–25). According to those voices, the true ruler of Israel could only be the God of Abraham, the God who led Israel out of slavery in Egypt (1 Samuel 10:17–19). If a single human was to rule Israel, that human would have to be a special kind of person, an agent of God who did not rule in the same manner as the kings of other nations. The first king of Israel, Saul, presumably had many qualities that made him a good king, though these are not mentioned in the text, as well as many weaknesses (1 Samuel 15:1–35). His successor David, regarded by the people of Judah as the greatest king of Israel, was also a man with great talent as well as many flaws. It is in the story of David, however, that the Old Testament sets forth the paradigmatic example of what it means to exercise authority over God's own people.

Contemporary scholars debate about the character of David and the extent to which he really does provide an appropriate example of how a king of Israel should act. In particular, David Bosworth has highlighted some of the recent scholarship on David—both sensational and modest—and concludes that although there are many forces at work in the biblical narrative, the Deuteronomistic narrative in first and second Samuel is reasonably reliable.[4] David is described as a hero in the wars against the Philistines (1 Samuel 18:6–12). His victories are credited to him rather than to God, whereas in Exodus and the book of Joshua, neither Moses nor Joshua is credited with winning military victories. Many saw David's personal charisma as a threat (1 Samuel 18:1–30): it was certainly a political threat to other tribes that wanted power and those who believed that Israel had no king, but God saw it as dangerous.

Perhaps the most familiar story of David's failure to be a good custodian of God's people involves his hubris—but not on the battlefield. While his generals are in the field, along with the Ark of the Covenant, that great sign of God's presence with Israel, David stays home and takes advantage of Bathsheba, the wife of Uriah, one of his best and most devout soldiers. The prophet Nathan, in a remarkable scene in 2 Samuel 12:1–14, denounces David's adultery and subsequent murder of Uriah. Nathan publicly unmasks David's dark deeds and pronounces judgment upon him. In almost any other kingdom, the monarch would have made short work of Nathan and his supporters, as a traditional monarchy could not endure such a public challenge. Because God is the real ruler of Israel, however (David is only a custodian), God will hold David accountable through the words of the prophet (the Greek word *prophētēs* means "one who speaks on behalf of another"). David recognizes that he must submit to the judgment of God, even though it puts him in a difficult political position.

In the words that come from Nathan, one hears a delicate balance among the personal integrity of David, the collective identity of Israel, and the covenantal *chesed* of God. Like the patriarchs, especially Jacob, David exhibits a character that is at once noble and frail. Such moral paradoxes characterize the people of God and their leaders from the very beginning. Only when the people and their leaders are obedient to God, when they fully embrace God's *chesed*, can authentic leadership be exercised. This is precisely the challenge issued by Jesus in his ministry, and it is the point that arouses stern and even deadly opposition among the leaders of the people.

The Story of Israel: Eschatology

The custodians of God's people, the anointed kings of Israel and Judah, often failed to live up to their lofty vocations. In the centuries that followed the reign of David, the political situation of Israel deteriorated with internal weakness and the rise of great regional powers such as the Assyrians and the Babylonians. Eventually, the Northern Kingdom of Israel was destroyed and subsequently, the Southern Kingdom of Judah went into exile in Babylon. With the return from the Babylonian Exile, one sees the emergence of a distinct religious identity centered in Jerusalem and the rebuilt Temple (the Second Temple). The many forms of Judaism that emerged over the centuries after the Babylonian Exile reflected the political, cultural, and social developments that took place with successive foreign powers controlling Jerusalem (587 BCE–70 CE). The dominant theme of this period is the tension between Israel's covenantal vocation to be a people set apart as "a light to the nations," and the fact that Israel's destiny now seemed to be determined by the whims of a pagan empire (the Greek Seleucid Empire and then the Roman Empire). There was a sense among the people that God would intervene and resolve this situation, and it was this sense of impending intervention that modern scholars identify as the eschatological worldview of first-century Judaism.

N. T. Wright, the eminent Anglican New Testament scholar, nicely summarizes first-century Jewish eschatology as a response to four basic questions: Who are we? Where are we? What is wrong? What is the solution? Though various sects, or strands, of Judaism (e.g., Pharisees, Sadducees, Essenes, etc.) might disagree with particular answers to these questions, the general parameters are consistent as they deal with Israel's basic worldview.

1. **Q:** Who are we?

   A: We are Israel, the chosen people of GOD the creator.

2. **Q:** Where are we?

   A: We are in the land promised to our fathers, but we are still in exile because of the oppression we suffer at the hands of the pagans (and lax Jews).

3. **Q:** What is wrong?

   A: We endure suffering and oppression at the hands of foreign rulers and our own rulers.

4. **Q:** What is the solution?

   A: All problems will be resolved when God intervenes and establishes his kingly rule.[5]

As God works to bring about this solution, Israel becomes more keenly aware of just who God is. As such, the monotheism of Israel, the centerpiece of God's identity for Israel (Deuteronomy 4:6), undergoes significant development. Many Jews of the late Second Temple period were able to read such texts as Daniel 7 and the description of "one like a son of man" standing before God and acting on behalf of God as suggesting that God encompassed a plurality of divine beings. In fact, the first-century Jewish philosopher and theologian Philo argued that God's Word, through which the world was created (Genesis 1) and though which the prophets were called and the Torah was given, was actually "another God."[6] Such speculation regarding God's Word (or Wisdom) and the "son of man" figure in Daniel are evidence of a growing twofold concern in Judaism after the Babylonian Exile: (1) God must be understood as separate from the world in which evil and sin reign, and (2) God is not remote but is active in the history of Israel and the world in order to combat and defeat the power of evil. Apropos of the latter, God had elected Israel, made a covenant with Israel, continued to bless Israel in the course of history, and was as the Word (Wisdom) or as "the son of man" entering into history at the *eschaton*.

The *eschaton* for which Israel hoped was not the end of the world; instead, Israel's stories, symbols, and practices, and especially its propensity for revolution, suggest that its hope was very earthy, very political. For many Jews of the first century, the hope of the *eschaton* was also a hope for resurrection, and this hope did not represent a desire to flee from the world, to escape into some distant space away from the political turmoil that was engulfing Israel. Rather, resurrection was an important symbol that affirmed the belief that God was going to transform the present reality and not destroy it. According to N. T. Wright, the resurrection was not simply a pious hope about the deliverance of the righteous who suffered in this world; it was the indispensible way of expressing the hope of future vindication of the righteous amidst the suffering Israel had been undergoing since the time of the Exile. As such, it was an integral part of Jewish apocalyptic expectations.[7] The resurrection was the primary means by which Israel expressed their hope for a "return from exile," the forgiveness of sins (the cause of its continuing exile), and the reestablishment of Israel as the true humanity intended by God.[8] If first-century Jews literally expected the world to end at the *eschaton*, as so many interpreters of New Testament apocalyptic literature have suggested, then there would be no resurrection—it would make no sense. Wright,

rather, speaks of Israel's apocalyptic literature as envisioning a renewal of the created order established by God. That order would supplant the current order in which pagans dominated; in the new order, the true Israel would dominate.

What constituted the *true* Israel would be a cause for debate within Judaism in the two centuries before the time of Jesus. There was, in fact, substantial room for differences at the level of what one might call secondary beliefs, and these differences would create rival descriptions of who could be counted as part of the true Israel and, therefore, would be saved from destruction.[9] The existence of rival sects within Judaism testifies to this reality. For the Pharisees, the true Israel would be those Jews who embraced their renewed emphasis on Torah observance; for the Essenes, the true Israel would be defined by those who had adhered to the Teacher and abided by the rules of the community. One could go on through the list of various first-century movements and find issues that helped to redefine the boundaries between the true Israel (those who would see resurrection) and God's enemies (those who would be destroyed). The sectarian literature from Qumran, the early rabbinic literature, and even the Gospels themselves testify to these attempts to define boundaries. In trying to create boundaries, first-century Jews were not just speculating about future salvation—who would receive rewards at the resurrection and who would be destroyed; rather, these boundaries were manifest in the present. Faithfulness to the covenant in the present time of distress would be vindicated in the future with resurrection and participation in a new world that God would soon usher in with the *eschaton*.

Jewish eschatology highlights God's fidelity, God's *chesed*. The covenant and the monarchy both point to a consummation of God's saving plan whereby Israel's exile comes to an end, the kingly rule or reign of God is established, and the nations are brought into fellowship with

God. None other than God has promised this and none other than God will accomplish this for Israel. It was into this context that Jesus was born, and it was this context that the Gospel of Matthew highlighted in its use of the *Toledot*.

THE "KINGDOM" STORY

The story of Jesus, as told by Mark, begins with Jesus' announcement, "This is the time of fulfillment. The kingdom of God is at hand. Repent, and believe in the gospel" (Mark 1:14). Such an announcement, while familiar to most Christians, remains obscure. Yet, the preceding section should help to bring this announcement into clearer focus through its connection to the story of Israel. The announcement of the "kingdom of God" powerfully binds the words and deeds of Jesus in the Gospels. Modern readers, however, are often tempted to dismiss or domesticate this symbol simply as a description of heaven, yet careful attention to the text will yield some intriguing results. If the story of Jesus is narrated as the "kingdom" story, it may be reengaged in a powerful way. In what follows, this text makes no pretense that this is the only way to tell the story of Jesus but insists that it generally reflects a reading of the story of Jesus from the perspective of contemporary New Testament criticism and theology.

Jesus and John the Baptist

Any discussion of Jesus' life and ministry must include mention of John the Baptist. In fact, all four canonical Gospels agree that John's ministry provides the basic context for understanding Jesus and his own proclamation. In short, Jesus' proclamation about the in-breaking of the kingdom rests on John and his ministry of baptism and repentance.

The synoptic Gospels portray John the Baptist as an antiestablishment figure who conducted his ministry in the wilderness near the Jordan River (Luke 1:80). Many have speculated about the connection between John and the sect known as the Essenes, whose main settlement was nearby at a place called Qumran. Of particular interest is John's baptizing activity, which is remarkably similar to Essene water purification rituals. Such parallels are not unheard of in first-century Judaism, but the geographic proximity of John and his antiestablishment message raises interesting questions about how much John borrowed from the Essenes (see 1Q pHab, the commentary on Habakkuk from the Dead Sea Scrolls, which were probably produced by an Essene community).

In Matthew 3:7–10, John the Baptist calls those who have approached him for baptism (a sign of repentance in the face of impending eschatological judgment) a "brood of vipers." He challenges them not simply to come to him out of fear of God's judgment but in *metanoia*, or repentance. John demands a swift decision to be baptized and a radical reformation of both inner attitudes and external conduct. In Matthew 3:11–12, John looks to the future when someone "stronger than me" will come and exercise judgment. The righteous will be spared if their repentance is sincere, and their baptism is the appropriate sign of sincere repentance.

American New Testament scholar John Meier believes that Jesus was actually a follower of John the Baptist.[10] Such a suggestion rests largely on the testimony of the Fourth Gospel (John), often regarded by biblical scholars as the least historically reliable of the four Gospels. In John, one finds the only explicit evidence regarding Jesus' direct association with the Baptist. For example, in John 3:22, Jesus spends time with his disciples baptizing, while at the same time, John the Baptist continues his ministry of baptism nearby. Meier suggests that the so-called criterion of embarrassment helps to substantiate that Jesus and his first disciples came from John's circle. The criterion of embarrassment operates by identifying those stories or sayings in the Gospels that might have caused difficulty for the early Church's missionary efforts, yet remain in the Gospels even though often thinly veiled. The Fourth Gospel tends to suppress any direct connection between the ministry of John and the ministry of Jesus (notice that this Gospel does not narrate the baptism of Jesus), yet such evidence remains.

Although others would not necessarily agree with Meier on this point about the historical reliability of the Fourth Gospel, most would agree that there is enough evidence to suggest a close relationship between the ministries of John the Baptist and Jesus. This relationship reinforces the notion that Jesus grew and developed in his self-understanding and in his ministry through contact with other members of the Jewish community in the first century. Moreover, the eschatological dimensions of John the Baptist's preaching are echoed within the ministry of Jesus. While the claim that Jesus developed his ministry in conjunction with John the Baptist undercuts the excessively individualist accounts of Jesus many Christians have taken for granted, the fundamentally communal dimensions of Jesus' self-identity and mission become even more evident when one looks at the Gospel accounts in light of his relationship with the Baptist.

The Advent of God's Kingdom

As noted in "The 'Kingdom' Story" section, the central symbol in the proclamation of Jesus was the kingdom of God. Yet the Greek expression *hē basileia tou theou* (the kingdom of God) ought to be read and translated in a way that minimizes spatial or temporal notions, as if the kingdom of God has delineated boundaries. Translators of the New Testament often insist on rendering

the phrase as "reign of God," which they suggest better articulates the relational aspect that the symbol expresses. Other scholars, such as the members of the controversial Jesus Seminar, have moved in the opposite direction, emphasizing the political aspects of the symbol and insisting that the image of a kingdom was meant to challenge the "empire" of Rome, which was oppressing the region. They argue that translating *basileia* as "empire" brings out the politically and socially subversive character of Jesus' ministry.

When the kingdom of God is interpreted against the backdrop of first-century Palestinian Judaism, one gets a good sense that Jesus was evoking the story of Israel and its hope for God's decisive intervention in history. The Old Testament provides the basic plot within which the kingdom fits. Israel always knew that God was their real king and that the earthly custodians of Israel (the Gentile powers that ruled Israel since the Babylonian Exile) had to recognize and enforce such knowledge, as David had for the most part. Throughout the Old Testament, the priestly and prophetic institutions of Israel announced that God's kingship is a past, present, and future reality. Following the demise of the monarchy and the Babylonian Exile, the hope for God's kingship becomes bound with Israel's hope for liberation from Gentile oppression and the establishment of a people as God's own. At that time, the Gentile nations would come to Jerusalem and worship the God of Israel because Israel would effectively and faithfully announce this reality to the world.

Debates have raged for decades concerning how Jesus understood the kingdom of God. As noted in the section, "Exile and the First-Century Worldview," N. T. Wright has provocatively suggested that any sense of an otherworldly event (an event that somehow ends space and time) would have been nonsensical to first-century Jews. To them, end-of-the-world language addresses that radical transformation of this world by the decisive intervention of God. While some may challenge Wright on this point, his insight has great merit. Rather than argue extensively over how precisely to understand the reference to the kingdom of God within the worldview of first-century Judaism, it might be best to take the lead from William Loewe, who has suggested that taking a functional approach to this symbol might be more fruitful.

Loewe synthesizes the various temporal and political approaches to the kingdom by asking the question, "What does the kingdom accomplish?" or "What is it for?" The answer: the kingdom of God is meant to bring human and cosmic fulfillment and an answer to the problem of evil.[11] The solution to the problem of evil is not a cosmic, mythical battle but a response to God's love and mercy uniquely present in Jesus. Loewe argues that Jesus' proclamation of the kingdom invites a response of faith and conversion at the personal and communal levels. This response occurs at a fundamental level of one's being, at the level of one's knowing and valuing. Loewe suggests that all have a worldview or horizon. Worldviews or horizons are imparted through both explicit and implicit means and help to structure a relatively coherent set of meanings and values that are both implicit and concrete in our dealings with the world. Loewe states that the horizon of human experience is an experience of mistrust, abuse, and exploitation. What Jesus offers is a shake-up of that worldview, a reformation of a horizon that has been malformed by sin, fear, and violence. He does so by making the unrestricted love of God available as the source of acceptance, healing, and liberation, thus transforming one's worldview, one's horizon of meaning and value.

The worldview of Israel understood that God was going to provide liberation from sin and death. Furthermore, they knew that liberation was simply an extension of what they experienced of God's *chesed* in creation and throughout the story of the covenant. Wright

contends that Jesus understood himself as the very embodiment of God, the Incarnation of God, who was now doing what God had always promised—conquering evil and liberating creation. In the person of Jesus, God holds nothing back and brings together all that God is and all that humanity has been created to be. In the experience of encountering Jesus, God fully communicates who and what God is. As a result of this communication and to the extent that one is enabled to receive it, one experiences God's love flooding the heart (Romans 5:5). As such, the person who encounters God's love in Jesus is transformed by unrestricted love and has no need to feel threatened by any force or power. There is no longer any need to pile up possessions or condemn others. In short, one is empowered by the love of God to forgive and bear another's burdens. The heart of Jesus' life and ministry is this call to conversion, this transformation of the horizon of sin, fear, and violence. As such, it is at the heart of Jesus' teaching and his practice.

The Kingdom in Words and Deeds

Most scholars would argue that even if it is difficult to trace any particular Gospel parable back to Jesus himself, parables were nonetheless central to Jesus' ministry. However, many still argue about the precise approach one should take to the interpretation of parables. In this discussion, two positions regularly emerge. First, parables are often interpreted allegorically. In other words, they are interpreted in such a way that each and every element in the story stands for something else. Although parables themselves often permit such interpretations, the thoroughgoing allegorization of parables can make their meaning hopelessly obscure. The second approach to interpretation moves in the opposite direction. Instead of focusing on each and every element in the story, the interpreter seeks to reduce the story to some basic moral. This moralizing tendency makes the parable itself rather inconsequential—merely a means for delivering a moral command that otherwise could have been given directly.

C. H. Dodd, a noted biblical scholar from the middle of the twentieth century, offered a memorable definition of a parable that steers a middle course between allegory and simple morality lesson. He describes a parable as "a metaphor or simile drawn from nature or common life, arresting the hearer with its vividness or strangeness in order to leave the mind in sufficient doubt about its precise application to tease it into active thought."[12] As such, a parable is not easily deciphered. Rather, the audience is encouraged to engage and even play with the material as they seek to interpret it. At the same time, however, the audience experiences the depth and challenge of the parable. Moralizing (getting down to the "bottom line") is not easily done. Meaning is both revealed and concealed at the same time. The arresting quality of the parable provokes a dynamic response from hearers by challenging their assumptions either by reversing expectations or through vividness of narration.

Luke's parable of the Lost Son, often called "The Parable of the Prodigal Son," provides a good model of the dynamics just discussed (Luke 15:11–32). Whether this parable can be traced to the actual words of Jesus remains obscure. Nevertheless, the parable reflects some basic aspects of Jesus' ministry, and it poignantly lays out the fundamental dynamic of Jesus' parabolic proclamation. This parable is the third in a series of parables of loss in Luke 15. These parables were delivered to an audience of pious Jews who were objecting to Jesus' frequent associations with sinners and other marginalized figures. Although all three parables deal with loss, only the third parable expressly makes the loss that of a beloved child. As each of the parables unfolds, the audience (the pious Jews who were questioning Jesus' fellowship with public sinners) is invited to identify with those who are not lost.

In the case of the parable of the Lost Son, the pious Jews identified with the elder brother, the one who did his father's bidding and who seemed to be neglected upon the return of his younger brother. In fact, the younger brother's original rejection of his father and brother is made all the more sharp when one realizes that his desire to return home arises not out of sorrow for his misdeeds but because his father's servants had good food.[13] In other words, the younger brother comes home simply because he is hungry! There is no sense of remorse or contrition at this point, and when the father sees him at a distance, he runs to greet his son without any expectation that the outstanding issues between them be resolved before reconciliation. Rather, the father embraces and celebrates the son's return without question. It is a story of unbounded love. The reaction of the older brother in this context is quite understandable, but one must take notice that he refuses to be part of the celebration. His sense of justice has been so badly shaken that he cannot see his way to fellowship with his brother or with his father. At the end of the story, the elder brother risks being lost. Just so, those who question Jesus' fellowship with sinners risk assuming the role of the elder brother; they risk being lost in their intransigence and in their attempt to "box in" their relationship with God in terms of a rather feeble account of justice. In the course of the parable, the audience is being summoned to conversion and repentance, to see the world anew and to discover a God who loves them and who does not allow their sensibilities about fairness and justice to hamstring the offer of new life and new fellowship.

This offer of new life and new fellowship was not only proffered through the parables, but also through various practices of Jesus, including the practice of mighty works, or miracles. Like the parables, the miracles of Jesus provoked onlookers to acknowledge God's love and mercy in the lives of those who were on the margins of society: the possessed, the sick, the dying. The

Magic versus Miracle

For many years, reputable scholars, such as Burton L. Mack and John Dominic Crossan, have debated the relationship between magic and miracles in the ancient world. In fact, some New Testament scholars have characterized Jesus as a magician. John Meier, the eminent American Jesus scholar, thinks that Jesus stands out in sharp contrast to the tradition of magic in the ancient world (*A Marginal Jew*, vol. 2, pp. 535–616). Meier argues that magic tends to involve the manipulation of a deity or a manipulation of natural forces to bring about a desired result. The magic is performed on behalf of a petitioner for a fee. In other words, the magician "works" for someone else, a client. Meier suggests that the ideal type of miracle, as presented in the Gospels, has seven characteristics that make it distinct from magic. The seven characteristics are as follows:

1. There is a relationship of faith and love between the human and the deity/divine agent.
2. The person in need is a disciple, worshipper.
3. The miracle is performed with a terse but intelligible set of words.
4. There is no reason to think that the deity is coerced into acting on behalf of the human.
5. Miracles are done in obedience to Jesus' Father and in the context of his "mission."
6. Miracles are understood as symbolic representations of the kingdom.
7. Miracles do not directly punish or hurt anyone.

In contrast, magic tends to be petty; it involves the manipulation of the deity; there is no church or community of magic; and its rituals are often unintelligible. To call Jesus a magician is to ignore the evidence, especially the absence of any charge of magic leveled against him. Meier believes that the collapse of miracle and magic into a single phenomenon is not helpful and is not attentive to the nuances of the evidence. Moreover, attentiveness to subtleties of the miracle tradition helps one to interpret their religious significance more readily; there is always an emphasis on relationships, on community, and on conversion in the miracle tradition.

marginalized population is the focal point and the prime exemplar of "kingdom living" in the ministry of Jesus. When Jesus healed, expelled demons, or raised the dead, he was redefining the boundaries of Israel in the eyes of many onlookers. Such was the kingdom of God, a kingdom inaugurated in the person and ministry of Jesus and in the response of conversion he makes possible. Jesus' dramatic parables in action empowered onlookers with a kind of love that is possible when people understand and experience themselves as loved unrestrictedly. However, this conversion is never quite complete, for people are always looking for ways to exclude others.

A NEW COMMUNITY

Jesus' proclamation of the kingdom in words and deeds evoked a response of faith and conversion, as well as of fear and hostility (Mark 3:1–6). The response of faith and conversion made possible a new, unique, and inclusive communal fellowship, a fellowship uniquely mediated by Jesus. Against those who would see Jesus as a radical individual, a countercultural gadfly, the Gospels offer a thoroughly communal account of Jesus as the catalyst for the formation of a renewed Israel. While somewhat spontaneous, this renewed Israel also seemed to have structure and form.

Crowds, Disciples, and the Twelve

Several New Testament scholars, including John Meier, have suggested that the community that grew around Jesus during his lifetime was not as amorphous and spontaneous as many would suppose.[14] Among the wide range of people who were intrigued by Jesus and who followed his work with interest, one can discern at least three concentric circles that would define these followers. First, there were the "crowds." The crowds (*ochlos* in Greek) were comprised of those who had heard of Jesus and who, as occasion warranted, showed up at any given moment to hear Jesus and witness his wondrous deeds. Many were undoubtedly transformed by their encounter with Jesus, while others remained confused and unsure about the man from Galilee. However, it was out of these crowds that some were drawn to become disciples.

From an early age, most Christians are taught that a disciple is anyone who follows Jesus. As such, all those who responded positively to Jesus within the crowds would be considered his disciples. However, in the pages of the New Testament, we see that the group known as the disciples (*mathētai* in Greek) was more restricted. Only those who met certain criteria were named disciples. First, they were called by Jesus and designated by him as disciples. Becoming a disciple did not rest on one's initiative but on the initiative of Jesus. Second, Jesus' call to discipleship required a radical break

from personal and social ties that defined one's place in society—including family, friends, and livelihood. Third, disciples needed to accept the possibility of hostility, suffering, and even death. Jesus also gave his disciples several distinguishing marks, or practices: baptism, special instructions about simplicity in prayer, and feasting rather than fasting. These marks, along with the modeling of Jesus, helped to form a new community, a kinship among Jesus' followers. Scholars often use the expression "fictive kinship" to describe this new set of relationships; the term refers to the process of granting someone who is not a member of a family the title, rights, and obligations normally given to family members.[15] This family, the obligations it engendered, and the social order it seemed to threaten, made the situation of the earliest followers of Jesus rather tenuous.

The call to discipleship subverted societal and religious norms of the first century and included both those who were impoverished or were public sinners as well as those who were pious and more respected members of society. This inclusiveness may also be inferred from other figures closely associated with Jesus but who were not called disciples. For instance, the Gospels cite a number of well-to-do individuals including Zacchaeus the publican, Lazarus and his sisters, and the anonymous host of the Last Supper. Although the Gospels do not use the word *mathētēs* to describe the many women who followed Jesus (probably because there was no feminine form of the word in Aramaic), there is little doubt that they were in fact disciples.[16]

One may cite Jesus' designation of a group known as the Twelve as evidence that he did not call into question Israel's chosen status; rather, through this symbolic act, Jesus sought to renew or reconstitute Israel. This group, though we know little about them as individuals (note that the lists of the Twelve differ somewhat in the Gospels), symbolized a reconstituted Israel around the ministry of Jesus as they embodied what it meant

PERSON OF INTEREST

Mary Magdalene

Recent scholarship and popular literature have focused much attention on one of the most interesting and important figures in the early Church—Mary of Magdala. She is among Jesus' closest followers. In fact, she appears to satisfy the qualifications of a disciple, though she is never explicitly designated a disciple in the Gospels. She is one of the women who stood by Jesus during the crucifixion (Mark 15:40), she is prominent among the women who found the empty tomb (Mark 16:1 ff.), she is the first to be addressed by the risen Christ (Matthew 28:9; John 20:11–18), and she is famously sent as "the apostle to the apostles" to announce the Resurrection (John 20:18). It is strange and interesting how such an important figure in the pages of the Gospels could have her legacy so distorted in subsequent generations. The Gospels only report that Jesus cast out seven demons from her (Luke 8:2), but other than that information, we know nothing about her past. However, it became a matter of convention in the early Church to identify her as a prostitute or adulterer. As such, she became less important as an example of discipleship even as the Blessed Mother, Mary, became increasingly identified as the ideal disciple. Much of the current scholarship on Mary of Magdala has been an attempt to portray her to modern audiences as an example of how the Christian tradition has wrestled with, and even distorted, the role of women within the Church.

to be a disciple. For Jesus and his Jewish contemporaries, any understanding of God's rule over the world—the kingdom—was unthinkable without the fulfillment of the hopes of Israel. While Jesus and his followers radically redefined these hopes and expectations, he nonetheless acted within the framework of first-century Judaism.

Within that framework, however, Jesus also stretched some social and religious boundaries, particularly in his practice of eating with outsiders, or table fellowship. In first-century Judaism, those with whom one eats is a matter of great religious and political importance. One either shares a blessing or a curse, depending on the company one keeps at the dinner table. That Jesus chose to eat with outsiders (public sinners and tax collectors) raised eyebrows among his coreligionists. Yet the practice of table fellowship is more than just an example of Jesus keeping dangerous company

or his propensity to shock and annoy "the establishment"; rather, through table fellowship Jesus signaled an offer of community, forgiveness, and salvation to those who were on the margins. A remarkable feature of this practice was that Jesus' offer of forgiveness and fellowship precedes the call for repentance and conversion—in fact, the fellowship is what makes such conversion possible. Thus, Jesus' practice of table fellowship signaled the breaking in of the kingdom in ways that many in Israel would have found familiar as well as challenging and even scandalous.

Community of Conflict

As mentioned time and again in this chapter, the ministry of Jesus must be understood as a ministry that took place within Israel. Because Jesus was a first-century Jew, his ministry is only intelligible as a religious renewal or reform movement within the context of first century Judaism. Some scholars have registered concern regarding this interpretation of Jesus' sayings; they suggest that portraying Jesus as a reformer or renewer of Judaism necessarily implies something was amiss with Judaism in the first century. While concerns over Christian misinterpretations of Judaism are well founded, calling Jesus a religious reformer does not imply a dismissal of Judaism and certainly does not lead to anti-Semitism. Rather, traditions are vital to the extent that they can inspire reformers, and reformers are to be located within the traditions they reform. Jesus had certain convictions about Israel's identity and mission, convictions that were born of his understanding of the covenant itself and an understanding of his identity, role, and mission within that covenant.

The center of Jewish life in the first century was the Torah, the first five books of the Bible, and its observance. After all, the Torah contained the foundational stories of Israel and the covenant. Also in the Torah are the commandments of God, the statutes and the decrees to which Israel was bound as God's chosen people. The narratives and the commandments found in the Torah cannot be divorced from one another. If such a divorce were to take place, the commandments would take on a life of their own; unbounded by the narratives, the commandments would have the potential to become violent and capricious. With this in mind, many of the disputes between Jesus and the religious authorities of his day can be put into perspective: Jesus sought to contextualize

and deepen the interpretation of the Torah by keeping it powerfully connected to the narratives of God's loving and merciful election of Israel.

A good example of Jesus' work is the story of healing and pronouncement found in Mark 3:1–6. In this story and several others like it in the Gospels, Jesus is confronted by religious authorities (here it is implied that they are Pharisees) as he heals a man with a withered hand on the Sabbath. Additionally, in Mark 3:2, the onlookers are watching Jesus in order to find some transgression, something that might help them bring accusations against him for violating the commandments. Instead, Jesus places the issue within a broader theological context by asking,

Christian Anti-Semitism

Within the pages of the New Testament, we often find Christian faith seemingly contrasted with the practices of Judaism. "The scribes and Pharisees," or worse, "the Jews" in John's Gospel, tend to be portrayed as narrow-minded, loveless, vain, and merciless. In Paul's letters, the observance of Mosaic Law by early Gentile Christians appears to be denounced and seen as at odds with the grace of Christian faith. Moreover, the Christian writers and preachers have used this material to attack Judaism as a religion as well as the Jewish people themselves. Unfortunately, even many of the great theologians of the Christian tradition were complicit in this trend, even through the early and middle part of the twentieth century.

The Holocaust was a watershed event in Christian self-reflection on anti-Semitism; however, scholars such as G. F. Moore had identified the problem decades earlier. Scholarship on early Judaism began to flourish after World War II and by the 1970s people such as Jacob Neusner, Krister Stendahl, E. P. Sanders, and others inaugurated a new era in which a more balanced, sympathetic, and historically accurate picture of first-century Judaism began to emerge.

"Is it lawful to do good on the Sabbath rather than to do evil, to save life rather than to destroy it?" Jesus is also invoking the principle—one known to the Pharisees—that the observance of the Sabbath cannot be used to justify the loss of life that otherwise might be saved. This principle is clearly stated in the Mishna, a collection of rabbinic teachings from the first and second centuries, "[W]henever there is doubt whether life is in danger this overrides the Sabbath."[17] The conflict involves Jesus correcting a distortion in the interpretation of the Torah, certainly not abrogating the Torah. As such, the stories of Jesus in conflict with religious authorities provide examples of how Jesus, acting out of fidelity to the best prophetic and rabbinic traditions, sees the story of God's love and the value of humanity as the determining factor for the interpretation and application of any commandment.

The conflict Jesus and his followers provoked or endured was even more pointed with those whose motivations did not arise from zeal for God's commandments. Jesus ran afoul of the governing authorities in such a way as to become an object lesson for the masses. The authorities were making a statement by executing Jesus, and that statement would have been obvious to all onlookers: don't become entangled with Jesus and his call to conversion. Some, no doubt, tried to portray Jesus as a libertine, as someone who played fast and loose with Israel's traditions and its identity (Luke 7:34). However, Jesus was no libertine, and his threat to the established order only emerged from his conviction that the demands of the covenant are properly understood and lived when interpreted as part of the story of God's love for Israel.

Death, Discipleship, and Salvation

The death of Jesus was not accidental; it was not a mistake or an oversight. The life and ministry of Jesus led to his execution. He was executed in public, and his body was displayed before onlookers as a warning. Those disciples Jesus called to follow him were cautioned about such an act to come. In fact, Mark, Matthew, and Luke recount Jesus' threefold prediction of his own suffering and death and his promise that those who would follow him would suffer the same rejection (and the same resurrection). What sense can one make of this in the context of what has been observed throughout this chapter on the story of Jesus?

As N. T. Wright has correctly observed, Jesus embodied and enacted Israel's hope that God would visit and restore his people. This is apparent in Jesus' proclamation of the kingdom and from the earliest days of his ministry when he is portrayed as conscious of his status as Messiah, yet reluctant to embrace the "baggage" associated with that title.[18] Instead, Jesus preferred the provocative self-designation, "Son of Man." In fact, when Jesus used this self-designation at his trial before the high priest Caiaphas, it caused dismay within the Sanhedrin, the Jewish legal council in Jerusalem. The dismay erupted because the Son of Man figure was best situated and understood within the context of Israel's nationalistic hope for restoration (the expulsion of Gentile oppressors like the Romans). Within the conventional sensibilities of first-century Judaism, however, Jesus' proclamation of the kingdom and the dangerous community it created amounted to a subversion of Israel's story and symbols and placed it under the scrutiny of the Roman authorities. In short, almost no one in power was prepared to acknowledge the claim of Jesus (Nicodemus and Joseph of Arimathea are two possible exceptions); thus, the rejection of Jesus seems to be the logical outcome.

That Jesus understood and accepted his death is evident from all four Gospels. Each recounts a last supper, a symbolic meal that blended elements of the table fellowship practiced throughout his ministry and elements of Jewish ritual meals, including the imminent celebration of the Passover Seder. It is within this context that Jesus' attitude toward his death is best grasped. During the course of the meal, Jesus provocatively blends his own story with that of Israel as he proclaims a new covenant made in his blood. His life, thus, becomes the very climax of Israel's story, the *eschaton* for which so many longed and hoped. [19] Additionally, the "cleansing of the Temple," an event three of the four Gospels record as happening only a few days prior to Jesus' arrest and execution, made clear Jesus' attitude toward the Temple and the sacrificial system. In the course of the Last Supper, Jesus replaces the system of sacrifice with himself; his death was to bring about an end to Israel's exile and oppression.[20] Jesus' life would be the symbol of a renewed Israel, a people defined by their suffering and the suffering of Jesus.

N. T. Wright provocatively and persuasively argues that Jesus went so far as to see his death as vicarious substitution—Jesus would embody the suffering of Israel and even suffer in place of the people of Israel. As such, Jesus was interpreting his death in terms set forth in the Maccabean literature of the second century BCE and celebrated in parts of the so-called Suffering Servant of Isaiah.[21] Wright states:

> Jesus believed it was his [G]od-given vocation to identify with the rebel cause, the kingdom cause, when at last that identification could not be understood as [an] endorsement [of violent nationalism] . . . He would go ahead of his people, to take upon himself both the fate that they had suffered one way or another for half a millennium at the hands of pagan empires and the fate that [many of] his contemporaries were apparently hell-bent upon pulling down on their heads once for

all. The martyr tradition [as embodied in the Maccabean literature in particular] suggested that this was the way in which Israel would at last be brought through suffering to vindication.
>
> —*Jesus and the Victory of God*, 596

Jesus was bringing vindication to Israel through the purification of the Temple and the inauguration of God's kingdom. Yet his inauguration of the kingdom, with its summons to faith and conversion, was redefining Israel's enemy even as it was reshaping Israel itself. The enemy was not Rome, or "the nations." Rather, the enemy was Satan, whose power was manifested throughout Israel and Rome, and who threatened to seduce Israel with violent and self-destructive nationalism. Jesus, in his triumph, confronts the power of Satan, the power of sin and evil, with the love of God. The outcome of such a confrontation is cruciform, yet that form is also the life of the world.[22] Thus, the cross becomes the form, the pattern, and the life of all those who would come after Jesus. The cross is not something that Christ carries alone; for Christians, it is a life to which all humans are called. (More will be said about this in chapter 2.)

CONCLUSION

Over and against those who would insist that Jesus is best understood as a heroic individual who bucked the trends and traditions of the establishment, the reading of Jesus' story given in this chapter contends that the first and last words in the story of Jesus center on community. Jesus is part of the community of Israel; his ministry finds its meaning within Israel's stories, symbols, and worldview, specifically within the matrix of

Old Testament themes such as covenant, kingship, and eschatology. Jesus is the expression of God's covenantal *chesed*, God's superabundant love; he is the one through whom God's rule is inaugurated; he summons Israel to conversion and faith as the ultimate response to God's covenant for the salvation of the world. Jesus' ministry inaugurates a renewal of Israel, which, in time, becomes a distinct community determined to announce to the world the saving significance of what the God of Israel has done in Christ. As one seeks to understand what the Church is and what it does, one needs to make sense of Jesus' story and examine the relationship between that story and the people whom it forms, the Church. Additionally, the story of Jesus will help to focus one's understanding of what we will call "the work of Christ," or soteriology, in the next chapter. The story of Jesus' life and ministry, his proclamation and his practice, focuses on the call to conversion, repentance, and new life in God. Yet, the question remains as to whether this has been the heart of Christian accounts of Christ's saving work.

Questions for Understanding

1. What is the meaning of the strange story in Genesis 15, "The Covenant of the Pieces"? How is this story relevant for understanding the story of Israel?

2. What is *chesed*, and why is it important for understanding the covenant?

3. Summarize Wright's account of the Jewish worldview in the first century. How does Israel see itself? What is their situation?

4. How does Wright interpret first-century Jewish eschatology? Is it focused on the end of space and time or on the end of the universe? Explain.

5. How do the parables and miracles of Jesus function in relationship to his proclamation of God's kingdom?

6. Who were the followers of Jesus? How did this group represent a challenge to some of Jesus' contemporaries?

Questions for Reflection

1. How has your life been integrated into the lives of your family and larger community? Have these communities been life-giving or have they been destructive?

2. Jesus adopted a practice of embracing the outsiders of his day. Does this practice of Jesus inform current Christian practice as you witness or understand it? Should it? Explain.

3. The last part of this chapter connects the death of Jesus and the fate of his disciples, both the historic disciples and those who would call themselves disciples of Jesus today. Does such an emphasis on "dying" seem appropriate? Fanatical? Dangerous? Explain.

Suggestions for Further Study

Getty-Sullivan, Mary Ann. *Parables of the Kingdom: Jesus and the Use of Parables in the Synoptic Tradition.* Collegeville, MN: Liturgical Press, 2007.

Getty-Sullivan offers a clear and highly readable account of Jesus' parables.

Gnilka, Jaochim. *Jesus of Nazareth: Message and History.* Translated by S. Schatzmann. Peabody, MA: Hendrickson, 1997.

Gnilka, an eminent German biblical scholar, provides an excellent overview of historical Jesus research. He offers an approachable account of the historical Jesus, one that is similar to that of John Meier's multivolume work, *A Marginal Jew.*

Lohfink, Gerhard. *Does God Need the Church? Toward a Theology of the People of God.* Translated by L. Maloney. Collegeville, MN: Liturgical Press, 1997.

Lohfink connects the story of Israel, the story of Jesus, and the story of the Church in his presentation of ecclesiological dimensions of salvation.

Maloney, Elliott C. *Jesus' Urgent Message for Today: The Kingdom of God in Mark's Gospel.* New York: Continuum, 2004.

Maloney offers a reading of Mark's account of Jesus' proclamation that resonates with contemporary culture.

Wright, N. T. *Jesus and the Victory of God.* Minneapolis, MN: Fortress, 1996.

Wright offers a powerful and provocative reading of Jesus' life and ministry, one that focuses on the religious as well as the social and political dimensions of Jesus' proclamation.

Endnotes

1. While the term *Old Testament* has often been replaced with the term *Hebrew Bible* in contemporary Christian writing, a decision has been made in this text to use the older and more customary term. This decision has been made, in part, for the sake of (1) consistency—within official documents of the Catholic Church, the term *Old Testament* is still used; (2) accuracy—the title *Hebrew Bible* does not adequately capture that Roman Catholic canon is not co-extensive with canon used by Jewish people; and (3) clarity—students are often perplexed by the use of the term *Hebrew Bible*. Readers should not infer from the use of the term *Old Testament* that there is any attempt to suggest that God's covenant with Israel has been abandoned or superseded.

2. In later Jewish tradition, Abraham's faith became the reason why God chose him and his descendants. It was understood as the way Abraham deserved his election. See 4 Ezra 9:7; 13:23; *Mekilta*, Exodus, 14:15.

3. Delbert Hillers, *Covenant: The History of a Biblical Idea* (Baltimore, MD: Johns Hopkins University Press, 1969), 41.

4. David Bosworth, "Evaluating King David: Old Problems and Recent Scholarship," *Catholic Biblical Quarterly* 68 (2006): 191–210.

5. N. T. Wright, *The New Testament and the People of God* (Minneapolis, MN: Fortress, 1992): 243; hereafter *NTPG.*

6. Philo, *de Somniis* 1: 229.

7. *NTPG*: 332.

8. *NTPG*: 332.

9. *NTPG*: 336.

10. John Meier, *A Marginal Jew: Rethinking the Historical Jesus*, vol. 2, *Mentor, Message, and Miracles* (New York: Doubleday, 1994): 116–129.

11. William P. Loewe, *A College Student's Introduction to Christology* (Collegeville, MN: Liturgical Press, 1996): 47–48.

12. C. H. Dodd, *Parables of the Kingdom* (New York: Scribner, 1936): 16.

13. This reading of the parable is given by Michael J. Himes in his book *Doing the Truth in Love: Conversations about God, Relationships, and Service* (Mahwah, NJ: Paulist Press, 195): 11–15.

14. Most of the material in this section is derived from John Meier, *A Marginal Jew: Rethinking the Historical Jesus*, vol. 3, *Companions and Competitors*, (New York: Doubleday, 2001): 19–252.

15. N. T. Wright, *Jesus and the Victory of God* (Minneapolis, MN: Fortress, 1996): 430–432; hereafter *JVG*.

16. The discussion of female disciples does not touch directly upon the Catholic Church's argument against the ordination of women. Part of that argument involves that women are not numbered among "the Twelve" or the contention they were not "apostles" (cf., Romans 16:7 which some see as a reference to women apostles in the early Church). See John Paul II, *Ordinatio Sacerdotalis* and The Congregation for the Doctrine of the Faith, *Inter Insigniores* for the arguments against women's ordination.

17. *Mishna Yoma* 8. 6, from H. Danby, *The Mishna* (Oxford: Oxford University Press, 1933).

18. *JVG*: 487–488; Wright cites Wrede and Bultmann as two influential figures who advocated the identification of Jesus as Messiah as a postresurrectional event.

19. *JVG*: 553–563.

20. *JVG*: 558.

21. *JVG*: 576–592. In early Judaism, there were stories that envisioned salvation from the present evil age through the sufferings of certain figures that embodied the sufferings of Israel.

22. *JVG*: 606–609.

CHAPTER 2

The Work of Christ and the Nature of the Church

The Jesus story in chapter 1 highlights the communal dimensions of that story as well as Jesus' call to repentance and conversion. Yet, for many Christians, these dimensions of the story are often circumscribed by theological positions on the saving work of Christ that tend to emphasize the death of Jesus as *the* saving event, to the exclusion of all else. Such a one-dimensional emphasis diminishes the larger Jesus story and suggests the death of Jesus, *of itself*, effects a cosmic transformation that simply permits some (all?) humans to enter into the beatific vision (heaven) upon their death.

As an example of this tendency, consider Mel Gibson's controversial 2004 film, *The Passion of the Christ*, which provoked movie critics and theologians alike. Many issues came to the fore in response to the film, but perhaps the most salient is the film's exclusive focus on the suffering and death of Jesus. Although Christianity teaches that the suffering of Jesus is an indispensible part of the mystery of salvation, it likewise holds that his suffering and death are unintelligible apart from Jesus' life and the life of the disciples who came after him. Imagine, for example, the following scenario: the soldiers who were sent to kill the infants of Bethlehem in Matthew's Gospel are successful; they locate the baby Jesus and kill him in his crib (Matthew 2:16–18). If Jesus had been executed as a newborn baby, would his death have the same meaning, the same significance? Would the murdered infant still save the world through his death? Although Christians have never made such an argument, considering it nonetheless may help to frame a discussion of the Christian tradition's tendency to emphasize Jesus' death apart from his life and ministry and to understand why this is problematic. Additionally, if the mandate "to make disciples of all nations" and promote salvation in Christ is at the heart of the Church's mission, then the Church's understanding of how that salvation comes about may factor importantly in the form the Church takes and the practices it adopts.

An understanding of Jesus' saving work is decisive for understanding ecclesiology. The Church identifies itself as an instrument of Christ's redemptive work. Cyprian of Carthage stated it this way: "*extra ecclesiam nulla salus est*" (outside the Church there is no salvation). While the danger of misconstruing this famous maxim in a narrowly exclusivist way is readily apparent, the statement also expresses a basic conviction of the Christian faith — God's gift of salvation in Christ is mediated through the witness of the believing community. In order to get a better handle on the redemptive mission of the Church, a sound understanding of soteriology is needed — an understanding grounded in the story of Jesus rehearsed in the previous chapter.

EARLY CHRISTIAN APPROACHES TO SOTERIOLOGY

In the early Christian Church, the dominant approach to soteriology was defined by the way in which the Jerusalem Temple functioned in the first century. The Temple cult (the word *cult* here simply refers to any public act of worship) revolved around the sacrifice of animals and other rituals that were structured to promote purity and freedom from sin. The rituals associated with the Temple influenced the presentation and interpretation of Jesus' death in the New Testament and fostered the emergence of what one might call the cultic approach to soteriology. The cultic approach proved highly influential in the early Church, and it eventually provided the basis for the emergence of the approach to soteriology that has become normative in conservative Protestant communities under the form of "penal substitution" (more about this development later). Yet, one might rightly ask whether the imagery and the theology associated with the cultic approach to soteriology really generate an adequate theory of salvation, or is the imagery used to express the religious meaning of Jesus' death limited to the culture and practices of first-century Palestinian Judaism? Somewhat related to the cultic interpretation of Christ's death are the economic or transactional images of redemption and ransom. These images were also used in the New Testament and by many of the early Christian writers, and while these images are occasionally rooted in sacrificial or cultic language, they take on a different meaning over the course of the centuries.

Christ's Sacrifice and Saving Work in Paul and Hebrews

A focal point in the interpretation of the death of Jesus is the ritual of sacrifice associated with the expiation of sin on the Day of Atonement (in Hebrew, *Yom Kippur*). Leviticus 16 describes the ritual that was constructed by the priestly tradition and probably does not antedate the Babylonian Exile (586–532 BCE), yet the ritual does incorporate many ancient elements. We read in Scripture that the high priest had to orchestrate a number of rituals in order to regularly remove the sins of the people of Israel.

The ritual of Yom Kippur outlined in Leviticus 16 revolves around two important elements: blood and expulsion.[1] First, the high priest offers a bull and a goat as sacrifices before entering the most sacred place on Earth—the Holy of Holies (the inner sanctuary of the Temple), where the Ark of the Covenant was kept. Here, the high priest was to apply the blood of the sacrificed animals on the *kapporet* (the covering of the Ark, where God was enthroned). Second, the high priest was to go outside of the Holy of Holies where a goat was presented to him—the scapegoat. This goat symbolically received the sins of the people from the high priest. The goat was then driven out of the community and into the desert, where it would die. Thus, the sins of the community were carried away by the scapegoat while community impurities were eradicated by the blood offering.

Blood was a sacred substance because it contained the power of life and death, the power to destroy as well as to cleanse or sanctify—power that properly belongs to God alone. As such, it was dangerous for humans to handle blood. In this context, blood has the force to cleanse the sanctuary of impurities. In addition, there is a transference and expulsion of sin from the community so that through a combination of ritual actions Israel may be both purged of sin and cleansed. Some New Testament authors will play with, or perhaps combine, these rituals as they explore the religious significance of Christ's death.

PERSON OF INTEREST

René Girard, Violence, and Sacrifice

René Girard, an important French literary critic, is perhaps the most celebrated and popular critic on the origin of violence and theories of sacrifice.[2] He offers a sweeping and comprehensive account of the origins of violence that resonates with common experience; this, in part, accounts for the popularity of his theory.

Girard understands the origins of human violence in terms of "mimetic desire." The Greek word *mimēsis* means "imitation." Girard hypothesizes that humans actually learn to desire what their peers, and especially their elders, teach them to desire. It logically follows that if all desire the same things, and the things desired are limited, anxiety and violence result. This anxiety and violence is regulated through the scapegoat mechanism—a society will transfer its guilt and anxiety onto an innocent individual, who is then driven out and destroyed. The scapegoat thus restores balance within a society and, paradoxically, becomes an object of worship, invested with supernatural or even divine power.

Societies develop moral codes, rituals, and myths that serve to both mask foundational violence and perpetuate the "benefits" of that violence. Girard argues that Jesus is the perfect scapegoat, the one who lays bare all of the violence inherent in religious systems and throughout human culture. Raymund Schwager and James Alison, among others, have been influential in appropriating Girard's ideas for a Christian soteriology, notably through helping convene The Colloquium on Religion and Violence to explore the implications of Girard's thought for a variety of fields.

Although the ritual of Yom Kippur remains an important factor in the development of the soteriological language of the New Testament, the concept of sacrifice that Leviticus presupposes undergoes substantial development in the centuries following the Babylonian Exile. In fact, as one looks at the letters of the apostle Paul, one sees that Israel's sacrificial system has been substantially spiritualized. In other words, these rituals were beginning to be interpreted metaphorically or analogously in order to give expression to a drive toward personal interaction with God. While sacrifices were still being offered in the Temple in Paul's day, and all Jews (including Paul) saw these sacrifices as religiously important and effective, the meaning of these rituals had developed considerably.

Romans 3:25 provides us with a good example of this spiritualization of the sacrificial system. Here, Paul interprets the meaning of Christ's death by using the Greek word *hilastērion*, a translation of the Hebrew word *kapporet* (the New American Bible translates *hilastērion* as "expiation"). The *kapporet* was the focal point of the rituals of Leviticus 16 and the Day of Atonement even though the actual Ark of the Covenant had been lost since it was taken as plunder after the Babylonian destruction of Jerusalem in 586 BCE. As such, the *kapporet* became invested with great symbolic and metaphorical power for Paul and other Jews of his time. The Jewish-Christian readers of Romans would have been keenly aware of this and would have disabused Gentile Christians of any possible literalist misinterpretations. In Paul's writings, cultic terms such as *hilastērion* are used to express the unrivaled power of Christ's death and Resurrection for achieving forgiveness of sins and reconciliation with God.

The author of Hebrews takes Paul's argument even further: Christ's death represents the sacrifice that ends the Temple's sacrificial system. That author stands within the tradition

of Hellenistic Judaism, the form of Judaism that emerged in the Greek-speaking world beyond the land of Israel (as opposed to Palestinian Judaism), and embraces a dualistic outlook, emphasizing dichotomies of matter and form, old and new, perfect and imperfect. Thus, in Hebrews, the Temple simply foreshadows and prepares for the death of Christ, so it makes perfect sense to explain the meaning of Christ's death via the Temple. Hebrews 4–10 develops an elaborate typology in which the Temple service is dismissed as ineffectual and banal in light of Christ's death. The death of Christ becomes then the sacrifice par excellence. Christ is the true high priest descended from the order of Melchizedek (the idealized universal priest from Genesis 14:18 and Psalm 110:4), and he offers himself as the perfect sacrifice. This sacrifice is definitive and totally effective.

In sum, the New Testament authors who use cultic metaphors to explore the meaning of Jesus' death are continuing to place the story of Jesus in the broader context of Israel's story. As one recognizes this dynamic in the work of the New Testament authors, one is empowered to reread these cultic metaphors in a manner that does not mystify the properties of blood or characterize God as a bloodthirsty father. Rather, these cultic metaphors are then given a privileged place within the Christian tradition, precisely because they keep the stories of Israel and Jesus intertwined. One story is unintelligible without the other.

Ransom and Redemption

New Testament accounts of Christ's saving work are not limited to sacrificial metaphors. In fact, Paul's thought on soteriology is not confined to the sacrificial language explored in the previous section. Among several other images, Paul uses an economic or social metaphor when he employs the terms *redemption* or *ransom* (*apolutrōsis*) to express the believer's freedom from sin (Romans 3:24; 1 Corinthians 1:30). Slavery was a social and political institution that was embedded within both the Roman Empire and the Ancient Near East, making it a reality with which far too many people had experience. Within this context, a ransom was the price paid to free or "to redeem" a slave from bondage. For the early Christians, ransom from slavery became an apt metaphor for the experience of sin—in Christ, Christians saw themselves redeemed or ransomed from slavery to sin.

It is obvious from even a cursory reading of his letters that Paul was not limited by cultic language in his theology. Yet, it is also true that his use of cultic language as well as the slavery metaphor discussed here emphasize the death of Jesus as decisive for understanding how Christ saves. This emphasis, however, is also open to interpretation. For example, the notion of ransom or redemption was used in connection with the deaths of Jewish martyrs in the Seleucid Period, two centuries before the time of Christ. From this perspective, the death of righteous Jews at the hands of their oppressors was understood as a ransom for the nation:

> These, then, who have been consecrated for the sake of God, are honored, not only with this honor, but also by the fact that because of them our enemies did not rule over our nation, the tyrant was punished, and the homeland purified—they having become, as

Paying Ransom to the Devil

In the early centuries of the Christian Church, several writers extended the images of ransom and redemption found in the pages of the New Testament. The images began to take the form of a narrative containing a certain logic. Within the narrative, Adam was seen as selling himself and his heirs into slavery to the devil. Christ became the ransom paid for the emancipation of humanity. Origen was perhaps the most famous proponent of this approach, though it was criticized by other theologians of the time, especially Gregory Nazianzen (*Orations* 45, 22). Gregory of Nyssa, in chapters 22–24 of his *Catechetical Orations*, elaborated on this basic narrative by comparing the death of Christ to an angler using a fishhook. The sinless Jesus was offered as payment to the devil for the release of humanity. But Jesus' human nature, the bait, masked the hook—the divinity of Christ—so that when the devil seized Jesus in death, the divine nature of Christ was revealed. Like a fish that swallows the hook along with the bait, the devil was thus caught in a trap and forced to give up his claim on humanity and on Christ. Other theologians played with this image and used the analogy of a mousetrap. So popular was this image that the mousetrap became an important detail in late medieval art (e.g., Robert Campin's *Annunciation Triptych* at the Cloisters Museum in New York).

it were, a ransom (*apolutrōsis*) for the sin of our nation.

— 4 MACCABEES 17:21–22; RSV

The author of this passage suggests that these deaths were the means by which Israel was released from its enslavement to foreign domination. Although the deaths are holy, they are not necessarily understood as a sacrifice. Rather, the emphasis here is that the deaths of these righteous Jews were not simply a testimony of their faith; these deaths were "for the nation." In this sense, then, the deaths were vicarious; they brought about liberation of the nation held captive by foreign oppressors. The New Testament, however, enlarges the narrative so that Jesus, through his vicarious death (a death he endures "for us") brings liberation from the oppression of sin and death. Once again, the New Testament language is rooted in the life, experience, and theology of Israel, thus binding the interpretation of Jesus to the community of Israel.

Throughout the New Testament a range of images and ideas are presented that control various attempts to understand the meaning of Christ's death. Reflection on the meaning of Christ's death used a variety of symbols and narratives at the heart of Jewish life, and no single approach was canonized. One is well advised then to keep in mind that the biblical language is often analogous or metaphorical (such as sacrifice, ransom, and redemption). The New Testament uses a variety of cultural and social metaphors to express what has been achieved in Jesus, without attempting a grand synthesis.

TWO DOMINANT SOTERIOLOGICAL APPROACHES

The influence of biblical images of sacrifice and ransom helped to focus attention on the death of Christ as the salvific moment par excellence. Such focus is quite understandable given the cultural and theological context of the biblical authors, but it also seems appropriate given the importance Jesus places on his death by his words and actions at the Last Supper.

With the rise of scholastic theology in the High Middle Ages, around 1100, there emerged more systematic approaches to understanding the saving work of Christ. These, in turn, have focused the attention of the Christian tradition for almost a millennium. Anselm's account of vicarious satisfaction and the Reformation emphasis on penal substitution have been the most influential of these soteriologies; yet both approaches raise serious ecclesiological questions, because each has significant implications for how one understands the Church and its mission in the world.

Anselm and Vicarious Satisfaction

The great Benedictine monk, Anselm of Canterbury (1033–1109), is credited with offering a definition of theology as "faith seeking understanding" (*fides quaerens intellectum*) and for using a sharp sense of reason to explore the truths he affirmed through faith. One of his most important contributions to the Christian tradition is his account of soteriology offered in his famous and often misunderstood work, *Cur Deus Homo?* (*Why Did God Become Human?*). In this work Anselm articulates "the necessary reasons" for the Incarnation, death, and Resurrection of Jesus. Although Anselm's project was to be a formal investigation of the basic principles behind the work of Christ, his writings betray his particular location: medieval Europe. Thus, *Cur Deus Homo?* presupposes a medieval worldview. That fact, however, does not necessarily mean that Anselm's work is to be neglected as outdated or irrelevant. His work establishes some important, and even classic, themes within the Christian tradition.

Anselm's Europe was governed by a series of reciprocal obligations between different classes of people that helped to form the social bonds that held medieval society together. One of the most basic relationships in medieval society was that between the lord of an estate and the people who worked on that estate. The lord had rights to his land either by virtue of birth or by exercise of power, and he had a type of ownership over the people on the land. He provided the means by which the people made a living; he also provided security and protection against criminals and other rogue elements in society. The lord's power to govern was ultimately sanctioned by God. For that reason, the people of the land owed the lord respect and honor. If someone failed in these obligations, the very fabric of medieval society would be threatened and, thus, the social order on which everyone relied. In such instances, the offending party was required to make satisfaction. That is, some act had to be performed whereby the honor (the right relationship between servant and master) could be restored.

Although Anselm's medieval context is essential for understanding his interpretation of Christ's death, one must not fall into the trap of supposing that Anselm sees God as a medieval lord. In fact, Anselm characterizes God as "One than whom nothing greater can be conceived,"[3] the creator of existence. Anselm explicitly rejects any notion that God is a petty medieval lord, and he rejects the idea that God's honor could actually be damaged or lost.[4] As the creator of all existence, God is owed obedience and love. Unfortunately, through their sin, humans have rejected God's lordship and violated God's honor. This violation threatens the very fabric of the universe, because it separates creature from creator. For Anselm, it would be utterly just and right for God to allow humans to reap the consequences of their sin—utter oblivion. But God's love tempers God's justice.

For Anselm, the solution to the problem of sin is to be located in the tension between God's love and God's justice. Anselm works this out through the following steps: First, humans already owe God everything, so they cannot offer anything to God that would make "satisfaction" for their offense and restore the order of the universe. Even if they gave their life to God in an act of self-giving, they would only be giving God what is already and always required. Second, God's justice seems to require the death of all humans. However, Anselm reasoned, if a sinless human, who was not required to die because of sin, were to offer his life, such an offering could make satisfaction, in part. However, a mere

human could not really make satisfaction for the sins of humanity because that sin is an infinite offense against God. If this sinless human is also divine (infinite), however, the death of that person would have infinite value. As perfectly human and perfectly divine, the God-man would make satisfaction for humans. This satisfaction has infinite value for others (it is a vicarious or "supererogatory" act and benefits others rather than the one making the sacrifice) and has the power to restore God's honor and bring harmony to the universe.

Anselm's soteriology has many features to recommend it: First, it seems to appropriately emphasize the divinity of God in relation to the universe. God transcends the limitations of the human condition and is to be worshipped and reverenced. God does not need to play tricks on the devil or to have his wrath appeased. Second, Anselm's approach to sin is cosmic. Sin threatens cosmic order precisely because it is a rejection of God, the creator and sustainer of the universe. Anselm's approach, however, also raises issues for many modern readers. For example, many theologians find Anselm's emphasis on God's "honor" inappropriate and out of line with the portrayal of God in the Gospels. Additionally, the death of Christ seems to be emphasized, while his life and ministry as well as his Resurrection seem to play a less significant role.

These theological and Christological issues also have important ecclesiological implications. For example, Anselm's understanding of sin and the need to make satisfaction corresponds to medieval and monastic practices of penance. Increasingly, in the Middle Ages, the sacraments of baptism and Communion were seen as the unique means by which one participated in the life of Christ and the Church. Sin threatened this participation, but penitential practices, and eventually a more regularized system of confession and penance, became the means through which one gained and maintained access to sacramental participation in Christ. So Anselm's approach to soteriology seems to reinforce a functional and administrative notion of the Church—the Church's job is to supply sinners with the appropriate means by which the problem of sin might be addressed.

In the worst case, Anselm's soteriology tends to make the Church the arbiter of various sacramental and penitential practices, or perhaps the organization that supplies human beings with the appropriate recipes, the appropriate "works" required in order to overcome sin. The authority of the Church to recommend or enforce these practices, as well as other practices the Church promoted in the later Middle Ages, became the target of the reformers in the sixteenth century. Although one might reasonably connect the soteriology of Anselm with the distortions of penitential practice identified by the reformers, it

---

PERSON OF INTEREST

Abailard against Anselm

Peter Abailard (1079–1142), often spelled *Abelard*, one of the greatest theologians in medieval Paris, publically challenged the adequacy of Anselm's approach to soteriology. According to Abailard, Anselm had utterly neglected the role that love plays in redemption. Abailard's rebuttal of Anselm's account of vicarious satisfaction emphasized the manner in which the crucified Christ enkindles the love of God within the hearts of believers—the crucified Jesus is the example of God's love for humanity. As such, humans, upon "seeing" the crucified one, are summoned to respond to the love of God and turn from sin. Abailard makes this point plainly in his commentary on Romans:

> Now it seems to us that we have been justified by the blood of Christ and reconciled to God in this way: through this unique act of grace manifested to us—in that his Son has taken upon himself our nature and persevered therein in teaching us by word and example even unto death—he has more fully bound us to himself by love; with the result that our hearts should be enkindled by such a gift of divine grace, and true charity [love] should not now shrink from enduring anything for him.
>
> . . . our redemption through Christ's suffering is that deeper affection [*dilectio*] in us which not only frees us from slavery to sin, but also wins for us the true liberty of sons of God (Romans 8:21), so that we do all things out of love rather than fear.

— PETER ABAILARD, *EXPOSITION OF THE EPISTLE TO THE ROMANS*[5]

Many modern accounts of the history of soteriology have dismissed Abailard's approach as theologically weak because it does not emphasize the necessity of Christ's death and because it emphasizes the subjective response of the believer. The condemnation of some of his ideas by various local councils and by Pope Innocent II diminished Abailard's influence. Additionally, his celebrated romance with Heloïse, the niece of the powerful churchman Fulbert, who had Abailard banished from Paris for years, has also eroded his credibility as a theologian, thus further valorizing only the so-called objective approaches to soteriology.

would be as unfair to attribute these distortions to Anselm as it would be to accuse the reformers of directly encouraging the distorted ecclesiologies their soteriologies also seemed to inform.

Penal Substitution and the Gratuity of Christ's Work

Soteriologies gradually developed over the course of the centuries following Anselm's death. Yet, it was the Protestant Reformation in the sixteenth century that helped to usher in a distinct soteriological theory, a theory that has exercised significant influence even to the present. This theory, called penal substitution, is commonly associated with the two great theologians of the Reformation, Martin Luther (1483–1546) and John Calvin (1509–1564).

Luther, in particular, articulated his soteriology in response to the array of dubious penitential practices that had developed in the late medieval Church. He sought to reinvigorate the Church with simpler practices more in line with biblical teaching as he understood it. Luther's main points of emphasis, points he shared with many other reformers, included a rejection of traditional ecclesiastical authority in favor of a less centralized and a comparatively (though not by contemporary standards) more democratic form of Church governance. He also insisted upon the autonomy of the believer in the interpretation of Scripture. Perhaps the central aspect of Luther's theology was his insistence on the essentially gratuitous nature of redemption—salvation is a gift, pure and simple. This assertion was directed, in large measure, against penitential practices that seemed to Luther and other reformers to reinforce the idea that human effort was needed to please God and to earn salvation. Such an interpretation ran contrary to what Luther read in Romans, namely, Christians are made right with God, i.e., they are justified, through faith and not works. This emphasized the gratuitousness

of God's work in Christ. One's salvation is given and must be received as a gift. This was at the heart of the soteriology that would grow out of the Reformation.

Luther's soteriology emerged from his reading of Scripture, and Scripture was considered the only legitimate authority in the theology of the Reformation. As such, Luther's approach to soteriology is often highly dramatic and echoes a wide range of biblical imagery and elaborate narration. Given the primacy granted to Paul in Luther's theology, it should come as no surprise that one of the central ideas in Luther's soteriology comes from Galatians and Romans. In commenting on Galatians, Luther notes that Paul "guarded his words carefully and spoke precisely,"[6] thus reinforcing his focus on the meaning and importance of the text he was about to consider. In this case, it is chapter 2 of Galatians. In this passage, Jesus has been cursed because he has become a representative of all humanity and thus taken on the suffering and death humans merit because of their sins. Luther calls this "a fortunate exchange"[7]—Christ takes on our punishment while we share in Christ's righteousness. Luther's *Lectures on Galatians* summarizes this soteriological theory commonly known as penal substitution.

> All the prophets of old said this, that Christ was to become the greatest thief, murderer, adulterer, robber, desecrator, blasphemer, etc. there has ever been anywhere in the world. He is not acting in His own person right now. Now He is not the Son of God, born of the Virgin. But He is a sinner, who has and bears all the sin of Paul, the former blasphemer, persecutor, and assaulter; of Peter, who denied Christ; . . . In short, He has and bears all the sins of [humanity] in His body . . . in order to make satisfaction for them with His own blood.
>
> — *LECTURES ON GALATIANS*, 277

For Luther, Christ became a curse inasmuch as he has taken upon himself the penalty that is due for sin. Christ has put himself into humanity's place and has borne humanity's punishment and "the wrath of God."[8] Because Christ suffered the penalty for sin, one does not need to suffer the penalty, provided one is united to Christ by receiving the gift of faith.

The founder of the second major branch of the Protestant Reformation (the Christian Reformed tradition), John Calvin, articulated a similar approach in his *Institutes of the Christian Religion*. Like Anselm four hundred years earlier, Calvin borrowed ideas from the social order of his day. As such, Calvin made use of the analogy of criminal law to understand the saving significance of Christ's death. For Calvin, Christ "was made a substitute and a surety in the place of transgressors and even submitted as a criminal to sustain and suffer all the punishment which would have been inflicted on them."[9] As the virtual dictator of Geneva for several years in the middle of the sixteenth century, Calvin understood the power of law and the necessity to attach sanctions to any violation of the law. Therefore, it is quite understandable that the criminal law analogy is more pronounced in Calvin than in Luther.

Luther and Calvin, perhaps somewhat unwittingly, contributed to what has become for so many contemporary Christians the default soteriology. Yet, at the same time, many theologians, both Protestant and Catholic, have come to recognize the danger of this approach and have sought to temper its influence in favor of a more biblically founded and socially relevant account of soteriology.[10] Some of the concerns scholars raise include neglecting the role conversion plays in this soteriology; righteousness is simply "imputed"[11] to the believer and conversion becomes merely the reception of Christian faith (this faith is often reduced to a proposition).[12] As one receives the grace of faith, one is given righteousness—one is justified or saved. In an effort to rightly emphasize the centrality of grace, proponents of penal substitution also attribute to God, or God's wrath, an active role in the suffering of Jesus. In this scenario, God is appeased, or "propitiated" (the preferred translation for *hilastērion* in many older Protestant translations of the New Testament), by the blood of Christ.

Additionally, penal substitution raises issues about ecclesiology. If salvation is simply received as the imputation of righteousness to the believer, then the Church's role becomes that of evangelizing community—giving people knowledge of Christ's saving work and calling upon them to accept this in faith and gratitude. Worship and mission center on the call to faith and on the reception of the gift of faith. While there are many aspects of this teaching that are laudable, like the emphasis on the gratuity of God's saving work in Christ, the role of the Church in the saving work of God may become limited and the broader dimensions of sin remain unaddressed, as sin is only a personal problem with a personal solution—a personal relationship with Jesus. At its most problematic, penal substitution has the propensity to underwrite an individualistic ecclesiology in which the Church exists for just two reasons: to perpetuate itself, and to provide people the occasion to accept Jesus as their own personal (individual) savior.

CONVERSION AND SUBJECTIVITY: THE HEART OF SOTERIOLOGY

While not exhaustive, Anselm's theory of vicarious satisfaction and the Reformation's theory of penal substitution have enjoyed a privileged status within the Christian tradition. Both approaches tend to emphasize the objective dimension of

God's work in Christ. In other words, these accounts emphasize that this work has been done "for us," and pay far less attention to what happens "to us" in the saving work of Christ. Dismissed as lightweight or relativistic, the subjective dimension of salvation often has been marginalized within many Christian churches.

Yet to neglect the subjective dimension of soteriology is to truncate the Christian account of salvation and to leave it open to misinterpretation and distortion. This may include the neglect of the proclamation and instruction of Jesus, the call to conversion, the creation of a new fellowship among followers of Christ, and the transformation of human living beyond the boundaries of the Church. Jesus' proclamation, as noted in chapter 1, centered on the call to conversion and faith (Mark 1:14). Throughout the Gospels, Jesus employs proclamation, parables, miracles, and a variety of practices to summon and provoke a response of faith and conversion of life. The early Christian Church understood this conversion of life as placing believers in a unique relationship with God through Christ and in a unique relationship with one another and the world around them.

This emphasis on the subjective dimension of salvation has been emphasized in the early witness of the biblical authors, in the writings of many Church fathers, and in the work of medieval theologians. Perhaps the most articulate advocate for the centrality of conversion

Divinization

Patristic soteriology was not exclusively wedded to biblical imagery or to the elaborate ransom narratives discussed in "Paying Ransom to the Devil." Rather, theologians such as Athanasius (293–373), the great champion of Nicea, Cyril of Alexandria (378–444), and the many other eastern Christians argued that the entire life of Christ brings salvation. Certainly the cross plays a special role, and sacrificial as well as redemptive language is used to describe its effectiveness, but coupled with such imagery is an emphasis on divinization (*theōsis* or *theōpoiesis*). Athanasius' classic phrase frames the idea well: "God became human so that humans might become God" (Athanasius, *On the Incarnation*, 54, 3). Divinization describes the saving work of Christ in terms of participation (*methexis*), whereby all that is human is taken into God so that God is not lowered, but humans are elevated.

Gregory of Palmas (1296–1359), a monk from the celebrated monastery of Mount Athos, emphasized such divinization in his cultivation of Christian spirituality (often called *hesychast* spirituality). For Gregory, divinization is to be cultivated in deep prayer of union with God. *The Catechism of the Catholic Church* quotes Athanasius' Letter to Seraphim: "[God] gave himself to us through his Spirit. By the participation of the Spirit, we become communicants in the divine nature. . . . For this reason, those in whom the Spirit dwells are divinized" (§1988). Gregory Nazianzen (330–390), the great Cappadocian theologian and archbishop of Constantinople, even argues that humans become more Godlike in divinization than when they were first created.

in soteriology is the great Canadian Jesuit, Bernard Lonergan (1904–1984). Lonergan's work demands attention, for he offers possibly the most comprehensive and robust account of what Christians mean when they claim that in Christ they have found the solution to the problem of sin.

Toward a More Adequate Account of Sin

Any discussion of sin must avoid the simplistic tendency, popular among many Christians, that understands sin primarily as "rule breaking." Such an approach makes sin rather arbitrary and portrays God as the enforcer of rules or laws, making God's power and sovereignty capricious. Christian accounts of salvation from sin often tend to emphasize the manner in which believers are forgiven rather than the manner in which they are healed of sin. For Lonergan, sin is a distortion of one's thinking and valuing (what one thinks is true and good is subtly and pervasively skewed). Lonergan explains this distortion as the result of several interrelated factors: original sin, actual sin, and social sin.

Original sin, the sin of Adam handed on to the rest of humanity, is not a genetic defect that all humans inherit. Although one might rightly identify the guilt of original sin in all humans, many theologians have moved away from the traditional emphasis on guilt and instead have emphasized the experience of victimization. For these theologians, original sin is the basic affirmation that humans have been, in some sense, victimized—even from the very moment they entered the world. Such victimization is not the result of some malignant divine being or alien force; rather, it has its roots in human action (Genesis 3). The effects of original sin are pervasive, leaving none untouched. As Sebastian Moore has described it, humanity finds itself inhabiting a world in which it has been sinned against, and this sin, or victimhood, exists before any deliberate sin on the part of the individual.[13] This victimhood gives humans a weakened sense of themselves and a distorted sense of their own self-worth. Such weakness becomes the foundation and even the catalyst for acts of desperation and distortion that may be identified as actual sin (consider the example of an abused child and the struggles that child faces as a result of that abuse—anger, difficulty in forging loving relationships, etc.).

Actual sin is the form of sin one can most readily identify in one's life. Yet, within the Roman Catholic tradition, the experience of sacramental reconciliation often highlights how frequently and repetitiously sins are committed. Within the celebration of the sacrament, penitents often confess the same kinds of sins month after month and year after year, even though with each celebration of the sacrament the penitent expresses the grace-aided resolve "to sin no more and to avoid the near occasion of sin." Perhaps no Christian author better captures this aspect of sin than Augustine. In his *Confessions*, Augustine laments his inability to turn his life over to God and recognizes that his sin is a habit, a compulsion. For Augustine, sin is like an addiction; it is a habit that when unchecked binds the individual and turns certain behaviors into a compulsion.[14] It is precisely this self-destructive dimension of sin that Lonergan seeks to emphasize. As in addiction, humans destroy what they should love and cherish and cherish what will destroy them. Humans are constantly hurting themselves and others, even as they are strangely convinced, even momentarily, that what they are doing is good.

Original sin and actual personal sin are projected into the world in social and cultural forms. What is often called social sin, or structural sin, is evident, and the examples are all too numerous. One example is that according to census data from the U.S. government, the median annual earnings for women in 2005 were only $.77 for every $1.00 earned by men. Black women ($.71) and Latinas ($.58) fared even worse.[15] To pay someone less for labor simply because that person is female is a form of sex discrimination—it victimizes women and those who are dependent on their income. Given that children are disproportionately raised in single-parent households headed by women, it would make more sense for women to have a higher average salary.

If one is inclined to push the question a bit further, one would quickly begin to unearth deeply seeded attitudes toward women that would serve to legitimatize such discrimination. Unexamined, these values emerge as part of a culture and help to reinforce social arrangements that leave people victimized. This is the cultural dimension of sin. Sexism, racism, materialism, and consumerism all stand out as obvious forms of cultural sin and help to reinforce a variety of social structures that envelope people around the world.

For Lonergan, sin is not "rule breaking," nor is it a purely spiritual problem. Sin is fundamentally a distortion in one's thinking and valuing; it has addictive properties that make escape and healing seem impossible. Sin is an encompassing and dynamic reality with personal, social, and cultural expressions. Thus the solution to sin needs to be articulated in a manner that addresses the many dimensions of sin. For Lonergan, the solution to the problem of sin rests in the experience of religious conversion.

The Law of the Cross

Lonergan has written extensively on the dynamics of conversion, and his interpreters have extended his project to cover a variety of forms conversion might take (intellectual, moral, psychic, etc.). For the purpose of this book, the focus will be on Lonergan's understanding of religious conversion—"the Law of the Cross" as William Loewe has elaborated it—and in particular, the manner in which religious conversion is tied to the story of Jesus. [16]

Although Lonergan frames his soteriology with the language found in Scripture and in the great theologians of the Middle Ages (Anselm and Aquinas), salvation from sin must go beyond the language of these earlier centuries. Rather

than portray the cross of Christ as "necessary," he takes his cue from Aquinas and investigates the cross of Christ as "contingent" (God could have redeemed us in a number of ways but chose the cross of Christ). The theologian's task, then, is to determine the intelligibility of the cross. Instead of asking why it was necessary for Jesus to die in order that humanity might be saved from sin, the theologian asks, how does God, in fact, solve the problem of sin through the cross of Christ? Lonergan's response is the Law of the Cross.

Put simply, the Law of the Cross is a principle of transformation that is presented in the life, death, and Resurrection of Jesus. The principle itself highlights three important and distinct moments: The first moment is enshrined in the biblical maxim, "Sin yields death." Sin kills. It is a distortion of one's knowing and valuing, and Lonergan uses the word *bias* to reflect this.[17] When one's horizon of meaning and value is skewed, truncated, or myopic, one acts out of bias. Such bias is not limited to personal matters but has social and cultural dimensions as well, as noted in the previous section. On a personal or individual level, bias reduces the truly good to what is good for the individual, while on the level of a group or class, what is truly good is limited to what is good for this or that particular group. More insidiously, what is good can be reduced to what is simply pragmatic or useful. Such a field of moral vision brings about violence and suffering. However, while sin is death, if the death and suffering caused by sin is confronted in love, it can be transformed.

This transformation is the second movement in the Law of the Cross. When one is injured by the thoughtlessness, the bias, or the sin of others, one can respond out of love. Though one experiences violence and alienation (the death of sin), one has the capacity to see sin as the product of disvalue and can embrace the suffering that has been inflicted upon one, not passively, but proactively. This point is often quite difficult to grasp and is prone to dangerous misunderstanding. The confrontation between the power of death and the love of God entails rupture and difficulty. Yet this difficulty is not to be equated with the passive and quiet suffering that enables violence and injustice to persist, nor is it to be understood as a just counter-violence. Rather, God's gift of love in Christ and the union that comes with it (religious conversion) is experienced as suffering—a consequence of that union in a world of sin. As one lives out this conversion in one's life and through a confrontation with the powers of sin, one will experience suffering that has the power to be transformed in love.[18]

Transformed dying leads to the blessing of new life—the third moment in the Law of the Cross. With transformed dying, the power of death and sin is overcome in the love of God so that death and sin no longer hold sway in one's world. The expansive power of sin and death are arrested, and grace abounds. In faith, with the love of God, Christians anticipate full union in the life of God here and now—they are born anew individually, socially, and culturally.

Martin Luther King Jr., Civil Rights, and Transformed Dying

The story of Dr. King and the American civil rights movement stands out as an example of the redemptive practice of which Lonergan and his interpreters speak.

Sin Yields Death

Personal, social, and cultural dimensions of sin are obvious. Racism exists on a personal level. This is the personal dimension of sin. This personal sin is furthered by a social system. In Dr. King's day, real estate brokers would refuse to sell properties in white neighborhoods to black families, and there was no law against this (the Fair Housing Act had not yet been passed). Lunch counters and hotels regularly barred black

patrons, and the legal system was stacked against any challengers. This is the social dimension of sin. Finally, the ideology that saw black Americans as dangerous, lazy, and intellectually inferior was so pervasive that the social practices just mentioned could only be undone by the force of law and federal intervention through the Civil Rights Act. The persistence of such ideology is the cultural dimension of sin.

Love Can Transform Death

Dr. King and other civil rights leaders understood all too well the suffering of black Americans in the South and across the nation. The violence exercised against black citizens who dared to challenge the status-quo racism of the day is well known. Beatings, lynchings, executions, and the day-to-day drumbeat of common racist practices made violent rebellion seem almost inevitable and even justified. However, the organizers of the Southern Christian Leadership Conference, under the guidance of Dr. King, directly confronted the insanity of American racism with nonviolent protest and civil disobedience. Writers such as Dietrich Bonhoeffer, Mohandas Gandhi, and Ralph Waldo Emerson had greatly influenced King's understanding of the Gospel, and he was convinced that the violence of American racism had to be met head on. This confrontation, however, was to be an encounter between the violence of racism and the love of God. In such a confrontation, the love of God becomes cruciform, and the death wrought by sin rages against God's elect.

Transformed Dying Receives the Blessing of New Life

The suffering and death of so many black Americans in the cause of civil rights might appear in so many ways to be a defeat. Yet, these individuals underwent those sacrifices in the belief that those who suffered for justice were blessed, not only with the joy of heaven for them personally, but also with the new life of justice in America. Salvation from racism began to take a social and cultural form. Certainly racism still persists in the United States, but the social and cultural dimensions of that sin have been confronted, and at least partially redeemed. Dr. King and others gave their lives to Christ in faith, and they were conformed to the cross of Christ so that the evil of racism might be transformed. The first fruits of that social and cultural transformation have appeared in the years since Dr. King's death.

Transformed Dying and "Being in Love"

Thus the American civil rights movement and the death of Dr. King exemplify the Law of the Cross. They demonstrate concretely a principle of transformation that makes it possible for humans, living in a world dominated by sin, to achieve authenticity (to become fully what God has created humanity to be). Although the expression "transformed dying" is open to a range of misinterpretations, it is meant by Lonergan and his interpreters to convey the structure of Jesus' life and ministry. The material covered in chapter 1, Jesus' parables, miracles, his calling of disciples, his attitude toward Torah, and his confrontation with authorities, all point to this principle of transformation. Lonergan describes this transformation as "being in love in an unrestricted fashion," or as "a state of unreserved openness to value." It is this "being in love" that makes living the Law of the Cross possible, because "on this side of heaven" (the world in which one lives) one only shares in the life of God partially in anticipation of future glory.

Yet even as one shares in the life of God here and now, the life of love is structured by the Law of the Cross; this principle of transformation structures one's "being in love." Authenticity is, therefore, the result of God's self-gift in grace.

A key text for Lonergan is Romans 5:5, "the love of God has been poured into our hearts through the Holy Spirit that has been given to us." For Lonergan, the love of God is to be understood both as subjective (God's love for humanity) and objective (God's love through humanity). In other words, in the experience of conversion not only do humans experience God loving them in Christ, but also as they are healed, they understand that God loves through them. The love humans have for their enemies is really God's love for their enemies—through them. This self-gift of God in religious conversion is uniquely mediated to the world in the person of Jesus, in his life, death, and Resurrection. All aspects of the life and ministry of Christ, particularly his call to repentance and conversion, are thus given their proper place in Lonergan's soteriology. The parables, miracles, table-fellowship, and moral teachings of Jesus are all integral to this soteriology. The Church then continues to mediate this saving work through stories, symbols, and liturgies that form its life and practice.

William Loewe, in particular, has worked to bring Lonergan's soteriology forward to confront the experience of social and cultural forms of sin in today's world. Loewe's interpretation of the Law of the Cross thus stands out as a remarkable example of the drive within contemporary Christian theology to articulate a socially responsible soteriology that centers on the transformation of human character—how one thinks and values—not simply on an individual level but also at the level of the community. This soteriology has implications for the entire planet. For Loewe, making Christian claims of salvation credible in a world torn by sin and violence rests on the manner in which conversion is mediated through the work of the Church as it confronts not only personal sin but also social and cultural forms of sin and its roots in the experience of original sin.

Justification, Sanctification, and Conversion

The doctrine of justification plays a major role in the Christian tradition, and it is central to the theologies of atonement developed during the Reformation. For Protestant Christians, Paul's Letter to the Romans provides some key texts: the phrase "righteousness of God" in Romans 1:17 and the account of sin and justification in Romans 3–5. Oftentimes, under the influence of Philip Melanchthon (1497–1560) and subsequent Protestant theologians, justification has focused on the manner in which righteousness is "imputed," or given, to the believer. In other words, the believer is declared righteous by God because the righteousness that belongs to Christ has been credited to the believer. The actual transformation of the believer, what Melanchthon and other reformers called "sanctification," was another event, distinct from the justification that the believer received with the gift of faith.

While the appropriateness of this distinction between justification and sanctification is a difficult question, their intimate connection needs to be emphasized; for Roman Catholics, this is a particularly important point. At the remarkable meeting at Regensburg in 1541, Roman Catholic and Reformation theologians hammered out a consensus statement on justification. Among the theologians present at the colloquium were Philip Melanchthon, John Calvin (as an observer), and John Eck. Although the Regensburg statement did not hold sway in the sixteenth century (the doctrine was still in flux among the Protestant theologians and was extremely underdeveloped within Roman Catholic circles at the time), a consensus statement on justification was officially reached between the Roman Catholic Church and representatives of the Lutheran World Federation in 1999. For an excellent and detailed history of the doctrine of justification from a Protestant perspective, see A. E. McGrath, *Iustitia Dei: A History of the Christian Doctrine of Justification*, Second Edition (Cambridge: Cambridge University Press, 1998).

Communal Mediation of Conversion

Lonergan's account of soteriology emphasizes the communal dimensions of conversion, for it is the community that helps to give language and meaning to the experience of conversion. For the Christian, the experience of conversion takes place within a concrete historical community; this is the Church—the community of believers who, from east to west, gather as community formed by the narratives, symbols, and liturgies that make present the love of God in Christ. Moreover, Lonergan's account of sin, rooted as it is in his account of bias, will not admit any privatization. Individual, communal, and societal conversion can only be accomplished through the Law of the Cross. For Lonergan, the life of the Church centers on a systematic soteriology and ecclesiology that is embedded in human history. In this context, the Church functions as a practical instrument of redemptive recovery in the world, for sin is the problem to which the Church addresses itself. Sin is primarily a practical problem, one for which the solution requires collaborative practice involving scientific, logistical, liturgical, and theological contributions.[19] This collaborative practice is certainly the work of the Church, but it finds expression beyond Church boundaries as well. The experience of conversion and the adoption of practices that inaugurate recovery in history can only be described as redemptive, regardless

Soteriology and the Church: Three Models

Name of Model	Vicarious Satisfaction	Penal Substitution	Law of the Cross
Major Figures	Anselm	Luther, Calvin	Lonergan
Understanding of Sin	Sin violates God's very divinity. Anselm uses the notion of "honor" to convey this. Sin disorders the universe God has created.	Sin is a violation of divine law. The sanction for such violation is death.	Sin is destructive and alienating, yet it masquerades as virtue or progress. A dynamic and expansive system, it is perpetuated by individuals and by social and cultural systems.
Summary	The death of a sinless human is an offering to God that makes "satisfaction" for sin. Yet, sin is an infinite offense, requiring infinite satisfaction. Therefore, Jesus, as the sinless God-man, is able to make satisfaction for sin. The universe is set aright and the divinity of God defended.	Christ, being fully divine and fully human, is able to take the punishment of death for all humanity. He dies in the place of humans, so humans do not have to die as punishment for sin.	The life, death, and Resurrection of Jesus enshrine a precept: death, when accepted out of love, is transformed, and transformed dying receives the gift of new life. As humans encounter the proclamation of the Gospel, they are called to conversion, to participate in the dying and rising of Christ to new life as sin is confronted and transformed personally, socially, and culturally.
Some Strengths and Shortcomings	Anselm introduces a "theoretical" approach to soteriology, but both his search for the "necessity" of the Incarnation and his focus on the death of Jesus limit its value. In addition, the social setting for his theory raises questions, as does the minimal role played by conversion.	This approach emphasizes the complete gratuity of God's salvation but also makes God the origin of Jesus' suffering. (It is not clear what role conversion has in this approach.)	Salvation is a participatory event and a response to the gift of grace through repentance and conversion. This conversion is a participation in "transformed dying." As such, the Law of the Cross ties the entire story of Christ to our salvation and makes salvation concrete in history.
Form of the Church	The Church tends to become an assembly in which certain practices enable humans to share in the satisfaction that Christ makes on humanity's behalf. The sacraments become the centerpiece of the Christian life.	The Church tends to be the assembly that calls out people, bringing them to faith whereby they may receive the gift of salvation. The Church tends to focus on "seekers," on "finding the lost."	The Church tends to balance its call to conversion with its outreach into the world to promote concrete redemptive recovery in history.

of whether the visible Church sponsors those practices. This conviction, central to Lonergan's soteriological outlook, is evident within numerous Church documents, especially the documents of the Second Vatican Council.

Interpreters of Lonergan have highlighted his unique contributions to the contemporary problem facing the Christian Church in a world increasingly understood as postmodern and post-Christian. In sum, the problem of evil, a practical problem, is not solved through rationalization or brute force. Rather, the solution to the problem of sin is located in the effective, forgiving love by which Christ lived and disarmed the power of evil, even ultimately through his bodily confrontation of the evil wrought by human beings. In that way, a kind of death, transformed dying, became a way of living, and it became the law of the new life that God gave Christ in raising him from the dead. What was accomplished in Christ's life, death, and Resurrection, appropriated through the mediation of symbolic narrative (Scripture) and ritual that form the heart of the Church's liturgy, is also the law under which every Christian lives. This principle is put into practice as the Church is formed and reformed in response to the practical problem of sin, and the ecclesiology this soteriology informs is therefore necessarily dynamic and historical—the Church must constantly reappropriate the story of Jesus in light of the current experience of sin, the structures it creates, and the cultures it forms.

CONCLUSION

This chapter has addressed the question of soteriology: "How does Christ save?" While biblical imagery and theological contributions of past ages play an essential role in a Christian appropriation of Christ's saving work, that tradition has also been distorted at times, and those distortions have significant ecclesiological implications. Although there are many soteriologies offered by contemporary theologians, and some of these have been acknowledged in the sidebars in this chapter, the thought of Bernard Lonergan has been the focal point in the last part of this chapter for several reasons: Lonergan and his interpreters more adequately incorporate biblical data (as presented in chapter 1) and the experience of conversion shared by Christians. Lonergan's contribution also helps to inform an ecclesiology that better enlightens and incorporates Church practice by (1) offering a more appropriate account of sin, (2) emphasizing the role of conversion in the work of salvation, and (3) promoting the mediating role of the Church in the continuation of God's work of redemption in Christ. Lonergan's soteriology is not utterly unique. In fact, many forms of contemporary soteriology will find important points of resonance here. Lonergan's approach, however, provides important points, which will be reexamined in subsequent chapters as the Church's self-understanding and its work in the world is "fleshed out."

Questions for Understanding

1. Describe the importance of Yom Kippur for understanding soteriological language in the New Testament.

2. Describe Anselm's theory of atonement and explain his understanding of God's honor. What are the potential implications of Anselm's approach for ecclesiology?

3. How is penal substitution different from Anselm's soteriology?

4. What are the implications of penal substitution for ecclesiology?

5. How does Lonergan understand sin?

6. Summarize Lonergan's "Law of the Cross." What are its implications for ecclesiology?

Questions for Reflection

1. Attend a church service in a Christian tradition. How does it seem "salvation" is presented? How is the work of Christ presented in the context of worship? What comes across as most important to this church community as you observe their worship?

2. Ask a friend or acquaintance (someone you know who would self-identify as a Christian), "Is it your belief that Jesus saves you from sin? If so, can you explain this saving action?" Summarize that person's response. Does the person's response include an account of the Church or its role in this saving work?

3. This chapter begins by alleging that an excessive emphasis on the death of Jesus, understood apart from his life and ministry, distorts Christian soteriology. How do "transformed dying" and "religious conversion" connect to the life and ministry of Jesus and not just to his death? Cite specific examples discussed in this chapter.

Suggestions for Further Study

Crysdale, Cynthia S. W. *Embracing Travail: Retrieving the Cross Today*. New York: Continuum, 2001.

Crysdale integrates the insights of Bernard Lonergan and contemporary feminist theology to articulate an account of the "Law of the Cross" within modern culture.

Finlan, Stephan J. *Problems with Atonement: The Origins of, and Controversy about, the Atonement Doctrine*. Collegeville, MN: Liturgical Press, 2005.

Finlan provides an accessible overview of various atonement theologies and offers a trenchant critique of atonement theology in general.

Schmiechen, Peter. *Saving Power: Theories of Atonement and Forms of the Church*. Grand Rapids, MI: Eerdmans, 2005.

The author examines ten theories of atonement and assesses their impact on ecclesiology.

Schwager, Raymund. *Must There Be Scapegoats? Violence and Redemption in the Bible*. Translated by M. Assad. New York: Herder, 2000.

Schwager explores the theories of René Girard and adapts them for a discussion of violence and redemption in scripture.

Endnotes

1. See Stephen Finlan, *Problems with Atonement* (Collegeville, MN: Liturgical Press, 2005), 11–38.

2. René Girard, *Violence and the Sacred*, trans. P. Gregory (Baltimore, MD: Johns Hopkins University Press, 1977).

3. Anselm, "Proslogion," in *A Scholastic Miscellany: From Anselm to Ockham*, ed. and trans. by E. Fairweather (Philadelphia: Westminster John Knox, 1982), 73.

4. Anselm, *Cur Deus Homo?* I, 14–15.

5. Peter Abailard, "Exposition of the Epistle to the Romans," in *A Scholastic Miscellany: Anselm to Ockham*, trans. and ed. Eugene R. Fairweather (New York: Macmillan, 1970), 283–284.

6. *Lectures on Galatians*, Luther's Works, vol. 26, trans. J. Pelikan and H. Lehmann (St. Louis, MO: Concordia, 1962), 277.

7. Ibid., 284.

8. Ibid.

9. *Institutes of the Christian Religion*, trans. H. Beveridge (Grand Rapids, MI: Eerdmans, 1990), 441.

10. For an excellent critique of penal substitution from an evangelical perspective, see Joel Green and Mark Baker, *Recovering the Scandal of the Cross: Atonement in New Testament and Contemporary Contexts* (Downers Grove, IL: InterVarsity, 2000).

11. In Romans 4:3 "Abraham believed God, and it was credited to him as righteousness." Under the influence of Erasmus, the great humanist of the sixteenth century, Melanchthon and others translated the Greed word *elogisthē*, a word derived from the economic world meaning "to credit someone's account," as "imputed" (*imputatum est* in Latin). The term *imputed* refers to a legal notion whereby someone accepts what he or she in fact does not really accept or acknowledge. For more on this, see J. A. Fitzmyer, *Romans*, (New York: Doubleday, 1993), 374.

12. For a nuanced, balanced, and thoroughly evangelical approach to soteriology, see Paul A. Rainbow, *The Way of Salvation: The Role of Christian Obedience in Justification* (London: Paternoster, 2005).

13. Sebastian Moore, *Let This Mind Be in You: The Quest for Identity through Oedipus to Christ* (London: Darton, Longman, and Todd, 1985), 69–109.

14. *Confessions* VIII, 10.

15. U.S. Census Bureau, *Income, Earnings and Poverty Data from the 2005 American Community Survey*, 9–11.

16. William Loewe, "Toward a Responsible Contemporary Soteriology," in *Creativity and Method: Essays in Honor of Bernard Lonergan, S.J.*, ed. Matthew Lamb (Milwaukee, WI: Marquette University Press, 1981), 213–227.

17. See Bernard Lonergan, *Insight: A Study in Human Understanding*, Collected Works of Bernard Lonergan (Toronto: University of Toronto Press, 1992), 244–266.

18. For a discussion of the potential pitfalls and pathologies associated with an emphasis on "transformed dying," see Cynthia Crysdale, *Embracing Travail: Retrieving the Cross Today* (New York: Continuum, 2001).

19. While Joseph Komonchak has produced a number of articles and essays on the subject, for what follows, see Joseph Komonchak, "The Church and Redemptive Community," *Foundations in Ecclesiology, Lonergan Workshop* (Boston: Boston College, 1995), 167–189.

3

The Evolution of the Church's Self-Understanding

The Church's self-understanding, or what we call ecclesiology, grew slowly over the course of centuries. New Testament accounts of the Church tended to emphasize images in the Old Testament and continuity between the Church and Israel. Over time, more theoretical accounts of the Church emerged; these tended to reflect, quite naturally, the distinctive milieu of medieval Europe where the Church had taken root. The fragmentation of the Church during the Protestant Reformation and the rise of modern secular states in Europe tended to produce even more distinctive accounts of the Church.

Although the development of ecclesiology and its relationship to emerging social and cultural systems is by no means simple, one may discern some important correlations between the two. This chapter will explore how the Church's self-understanding has emerged over time by taking snapshots of the Church at key historical moments. While such an overview will be highly selective, it will also be helpful for understanding the possibilities and challenges this history represents for the Church today as it articulates its self-understanding and rededicates itself to its saving mission.

BIBLICAL ACCOUNTS OF THE CHURCH

As Scripture and history both testify, a new social and political movement (the Church) had emerged in the wake of Jesus of Nazareth, and this new reality was formed and maintained by the conviction that "In Christ, God was reconciling the world to himself" (2 Corinthians 5:19). It is unclear just how formal or structured this new movement was and how it was related to the people of Israel, but in the pages of the New Testament one finds ample evidence that the Church was no accident. In the letters of Paul and his followers and in the Gospel narratives an emerging ecclesiology is disclosed, one that is anchored in the experience of Jesus (Christology) and, therefore, in the experience of Israel.

The Church in the Letters of Paul

One of the most contentious issues within the early Church was the relationship between Christians and the people of Israel. Initially, there was no issue — the earliest Christians considered themselves to be part of the people of Israel. After all, they were "sons and daughters of Abraham"—they were Jews. The Christian gospel was understood to be a summons to Israel that claimed the promises made through the patriarchs and the prophets had been fulfilled in Jesus of Nazareth. However, as it became clear that the gospel was not widely accepted in Israel and as Gentile participation in the Christian movement increased, tensions between the emerging Christian and the early Jewish communities were exacerbated.

Within this context, the apostle Paul began to argue for an understanding of the Christian Church that more sharply distinguished itself from Israel. This distinction emerged as two factors began to define the Christian movement:

First, the rapid proliferation of the Christian message among Gentiles began to cause friction within the Jewish community, among those Jews who were part of the Christian movement and among those who were not. Second, there was a corresponding marginalization of Torah observance within the Christian movement. This marginalization did not necessarily apply to Christian Jews, but it did apply to Christian Gentiles, and over time, it became normative for all Christians.[1]

The Letter to the Galatians stands out as an excellent example of Paul's insistence that faith in Christ created a new reality and a new relationship with God (Galatians 2:19–20; 4:26). In this relationship of righteousness and rebirth, Torah observance no longer held center stage and social, religious, and economic distinctions no longer held importance for the believing community (Galatians 3:28). For non-Christian Jews, the change helped to mark the Christian community as separate from Israel, even while Paul and others insisted that faith in Christ was an extension and even a fulfillment of what had been promised by Israel's prophets. These tensions, along with the pressures exerted by those who were remaking Judaism following the destruction of the Jerusalem Temple in 70 CE, finally led to the separation of Judaism and Christianity. Exactly when this separation happened remains unclear (Christian participation in Jewish festivals and worship was reported even as late as the fourth and fifth centuries), but the fissures began as early as Paul's lifetime.

In Paul's First Letter to the Corinthians, he reveals some of his most thoughtful reflections on the Church and its importance within the lives of Christians. Here, as elsewhere in his letters, the earliest use of the term *ekklesia* to designate the Christian community appears. Although *ekklesia* was used as a generic term in ancient Greek to designate an assembly, the Septuagint (the Greek translation of the Hebrew Bible accepted by early Greek-speaking Jews and

Tensions between Judaism and Early Christianity

The Gospels often portray Jesus in conflict with the religious authorities of his time. In particular, the Pharisees are regularly represented in a negative light. Many modern New Testament scholars suggest, however, that the portrayals of the Pharisees shown in the Gospels are anachronistic. They reflect not Jesus' attitude toward the Pharisees but the antipathy that was growing in some sectors of the community between the early Church and the early Jewish community.

Before 70 CE, Judaism was a diverse religious movement. Like contemporary Christianity, Judaism in the first century was expressed in a variety of ways, and there were many internecine disputes that pitted one Jewish group against another. With the Roman destruction of the Jerusalem Temple in 70 CE, the variety of movements that had existed in Jesus' time began to give way to a normative form of Judaism. This normative Judaism emerged under the leadership of the Pharisees, the rabbis who sought to remake Judaism so that it reflected their concerns and practices. It is important to remember, however, that the Pharisees were not a homogenous group. In fact, the Mishna, and subsequently the Talmud, was a collection of disputed interpretations of God's commandments in the Torah. If one were to read parts of the Mishna, one could easily imagine hearing the voice of "Rabbi Jesus" arguing with Rabbi Hillel on some point. In other words, the disputes between Jesus and the Pharisees recorded in the Gospels occasionally reflect some of the disputes between rabbis (between Pharisees) so that Jesus might be located credibly within the pharisaic movement. After all, Jesus is called "rabbi" at several places in the Gospels.

Much of the antipathy between early Christianity and early Judaism stems from the manner in which the early Christian movement increased among Gentile populations. Given the heterogeneous character of the Christian movement, this antipathy necessarily posed a problem for the early Jewish community who had difficulty recognizing the movement as "Jewish." Additionally, the development of Christology within the Christian community challenged traditional Jewish sensibilities and, coupled with the drive to homogenization at the end of the first century, led to serious tensions between early Jewish and Christian communities. This tension gave way, in the course of centuries, to the anti-Semitism that came to define Christian attitudes toward Judaism in the medieval and modern periods.

Christians) utilizes both *ekklesia* and *synagōgē* to translate the Hebrew word *qahal*—the assembly of God. Paul, on the other hand, sets forth a distinctive account of the Christian *ekklesia* that is rooted in the experience of the Christian faith and the work of the Spirit, while also stressing the continuity between the early Christian community and Israel.

For Paul, Christian faith has a profound individual dimension that creates what one might even identify as a mystical union between Christ and the believer.[2] At the same time, to dwell in Christ is to be united with others, to become part of Christ's body in the world. It is this image of the body that dominates so much of 1 Corinthians in which Paul seeks to overcome factionalism, spiritual hubris, and elitism. Paul uses the image of the body to develop an understanding of unity in difference, because each part of a body possesses

PERSON OF INTEREST

Junia

In Romans 16, at the ending to the canonical letter, there exists what scholars often call a letter of recommendation on behalf of a woman named Phoebe, a deacon in the early Church. In this portion of Romans, which was probably an independent letter that was later incorporated into the canonical letter, a series of names are mentioned as Paul sends greetings to the Church in Rome. Prominent among these names is a certain "Junia" who is called "a person of note among the apostles." It is important to recall that the term *apostle* (*apostolos* in Greek) was an office within the early Church and not a title associated with the early followers of Jesus.[3] Paul thus places Junia on the same level as himself—as an apostle.

The issue many New Testament scholars wrestle with is whether Junia is a man or a woman. In the text, the name is *Iounian*, which could be the accusative singular form of either the feminine name *Iounia* or the masculine name *Iounias*. Until the twelfth century, the vast majority of commentators agreed that the name was feminine, and many assumed that Junia was the wife of Andronicus, the name mentioned with Junia (Origen, Jerome, John Damascene). It was not until the ninth century that Greek manuscripts began to accent the name to make it masculine (*Iounian* would have an accent over the *a* if it was masculine, but it would have an accent over the second *i* if it was feminine). The first commentator to explicitly identify the name as masculine was Giles of Rome (1247–1316). Thus, the debate did not start until more than one thousand years after the time of Christ. Many of the early critical versions of the Greek New Testament and many English translations of the Bible (RSV, NIV, NEB) made the name masculine. More recent versions of the Greek New Testament and English translations show *Junia* as a feminine name (NAB, NRSV).

The issue became increasingly important as questions of women's participation in Church ministry and governance moved to the fore. Many have reasoned that if a woman, Junia, exercised apostolic authority along with Paul in the early Church, why not permit women to exercise this authority today? Additionally, many contemporary scholars have attempted to reconstruct the life of the early Church in Rome and have argued that the role of women therein was much more prominent than many had assumed. All of these issues and questions remain the subject of intense debate.

certain gifts and certain limitations (1 Corinthians 12:12–26). Only together, animated by the indwelling of Christ and the Spirit (n.b., Paul also uses the image of the Church as a "temple" in 1 Corinthians 3:16–17 and elsewhere), can all of the parts function together. Out of this conviction, several important ecclesiological themes emerge, especially themes of fellowship and suffering.

The Greek word *koinonia* means "fellowship" or "communion." The believer has fellowship with Christ, but in Christ, one also has fellowship with other believers. This fellowship exists across space and time and includes the saints (or "holy ones" in some New Testament translations) who have "fallen asleep." For Paul, discerning this fellowship is decisive for the life of the Christian as an individual as well as for the Christian community. In 1 Corinthians, Paul develops "fellowship" as a foundational theological and ecclesiological theme (1 Corinthians 1:9). He cautions believers against using their freedom to violate or strain fellowship, and he implores Christians to overcome factions by recognizing their fellowship in Christ. In Christian worship, particularly in the sharing of the Lord's Supper, failure to "discern the body" (failure to engage in this worship as an act of fellowship with Christ and with one another) is to bring condemnation and suffering on oneself and the entire community (1 Corinthians 10:14–22).

Although Paul can view suffering as punitive, he more often sees it as the result of the Church's fidelity to the gospel. Above all, the suffering of the believer is the result of being conformed to Christ, or of imitating Christ (Philippians 3:10), and therefore, the cross plays a central role in Paul's theology and preaching. As he summons his audience time and again to "become imitators of me as I am of Christ" (1 Corinthians 11:1), he is calling upon them to embrace a form of redemptive suffering. In union with Christ, Christians assume a cruciform existence, and their treatment of one another is to reflect the cross (Law of the Cross). Perhaps the most poetic and powerful example of this idea occurs in Paul's Letter to the Philippians in which he exhorts the Church to put on the mind of Christ and adopt a kenotic, or self-emptying, ethos (Philippians 2:1–11). It is only with this mind of Christ, in imitation of Christ (and Paul!), that the Church can really constitute the Body of Christ and find fellowship amidst the wide variety of gifts and vocations (1 Corinthians 12:1–31; 13:1–13).

It is clear that Paul's experience of the risen Christ gives him a sense of deep transformative union with God, and this union has profoundly shaped all aspects of his theology, including his ecclesiology. However, not all of Paul's ideas about the Church are fully developed, and the task remains for unnamed theologians operating in the tradition of Paul to bring some of his ecclesiological ideas to fuller expression.

The Church in the Deutero-Pauline Letters

Not all of the letters attributed to Paul in the New Testament are actually written by the apostle. In fact, scholars generally agree that the Pastoral Epistles (1 and 2 Timothy and Titus) were not written by Paul, neither was the Letter to the Ephesians. Many, though not all, scholars also believe that Paul wrote neither Colossians nor 2 Thessalonians.[4] It is usually best to treat the Pastorals apart from the seven undisputed letters of Paul already discussed. This is particularly true when considering ecclesiology in the New Testament. For it is in the area of ecclesiology that one sees significant developments in comparison with the undisputed letters of Paul.

Colossians and Ephesians are mirror images of each other, and their respective ecclesiological insights are best treated in tandem. The image of the body of Christ plays a major role in the ecclesiology of both letters. Both Colossians and Ephesians draw on the material presented in Romans 12 and 1 Corinthians 12, yet both make clear what is perhaps implicit in Paul, namely that Christ is the head of the body (Colossians 1:18; 2:19; Ephesians 1:22–23; 4:15–16; 5:23). As the head, Christ vivifies, sustains, and directs the body. Additionally, the author of Ephesians makes use of the prophetic metaphor of the bride and the bridegroom. For the prophets, the union between Israel and God was to be understood in terms of a marriage. Hosea, for example, used the image of marriage to indict Israel for its "adultery" in following other gods. In Ephesians, Christ is the bridegroom and the Church is the bride (Ephesians 5:21–32). This nuptial image also has strong eschatological overtones—the wedding night is about to arrive, and with great joy and anticipation, the

Pseudonymity in the Ancient World

Pseudonymity, or using a false name, was a common practice in the ancient world. Many canonical books were not written by the people to whom they were attributed. The practice of using a false name can be interpreted in at least two ways: First, pseudonymity can be viewed as an act of deception whereby an author seeks to conceal his or her identity in order to give the text more credibility than it otherwise might have. For example, among heterodox Christian groups such as the Gnostic Christians, it was common to attribute sacred texts to a prominent disciple of Jesus. The *Gospel of Thomas* and the *Gospel of Mary Magdalene* stand out as two prominent examples of this phenomenon. Second, the act of concealing one's name may be an attempt to pay homage to a prominent mentor or leader. The actual author of the text may be extending the thoughts or the ideas of the more prominent figure in order to extend the leader's message into new contexts. Such is the case with the so-called Pauline pseudepigrapha. Most scholars do not think that Paul actually wrote the Pastoral Letters (1 and 2 Timothy and Titus) or Ephesians, and possibly not even Colossians or Second Thessalonians (there is no consensus on these last two). Many Christians find this notion troubling and will argue against any pseudonymity in the New Testament, saying that such a practice is deceptive and would be incongruent with a Christian understanding of Scripture.

The Pastoral Epistles are remarkable, not for their developed ecclesiologies, but for the evidence of a more developed polity (Church organization and governance) and more precise ministerial roles within the Church. It is in the Pastorals that the role of bishop (*episkopos*—"overseer"), elder (*presbuteros*—"elder"), and deacon (*diakonos*—"servant" or "minister") are first described, and the qualifications of the bishop are enumerated. As such, the Pastoral Epistles represent an interesting development in the life of the Church and in ecclesiology. Although it could be argued that all of Paul's writings are about the Church, the Pastorals provide readers with much evidence regarding the structure of the Church as an organization with a certain hierarchical order, or at least, with a functional structure. Following the close of the New Testament era, the office of bishop will prove decisive in establishing the structure and unity of the Church, especially in the writings of early bishops, such as, Cyprian and Augustine.

bride awaits her groom. A note of prolepsis, or anticipation, colors the ecclesiological image, for the union is anticipated but not fully consummated. This theme of nuptial anticipation is made more explicit in the book of Revelation in which the Holy City, the New Jerusalem, is identified with the Church as the bride of Christ. The wedding feast of the lamb (Christ) is something for which the faithful long and in which they will rejoice at the *eschaton* (Revelation 19:5–10; 21:1–14).

The Church in the Gospels and Acts

Given the frequency with which the word *ekklesia* occurs in the Pauline letters, it is remarkable, in some ways, how infrequently the word is used in the Gospels (Matthew 16:18 and twice in 18:17). Matthew and Luke, particularly in the latter's second volume, Acts of the Apostles, have strong and explicit ecclesiologies, while Mark and John have more implied ecclesiologies that emerge from their respective foci: discipleship in Mark and Christology in John.

Matthew is perhaps the evangelist most concerned with articulating a definitive sense of the Christian assembly.[5] In part, Matthew's concern stems from the perceived intransigence of Israel in the face of the Messiah's advent. Matthew's community is the new Israel, the new people of God, and they have adopted a distinctive polity. Throughout Matthew's Gospel, Jesus delivers five different discourses in which he instructs the community on several issues, including how to practice a higher form of righteousness than the Pharisees and how to order the community justly and appropriately. In short, Matthew's Gospel reads like a handbook for the Church. In Matthew, Jesus instructs the disciples on the practice of righteousness (Sermon on the Mount, Matthew 5:1–7:29) and how they are to treat wayward brothers and sisters in a judicious and loving manner (Church Order Discourse, Matthew 18:1–35). This material demonstrates the basic continuity between the Christian community and Israel even while it also signals the beginnings of a rupture and the emergence of a new identity among the followers of Jesus.[6]

Matthew and the Commissioning of Peter

"The Commissioning of Peter" in Matthew 16:13–20 has had a particularly significant impact on Roman Catholic ecclesiology. Matthew takes the basic story from Mark 8:27–30 in which Jesus and his disciples are traveling "in the region of Caesarea Philippi," the Roman city to the north of Galilee. Jesus asks the disciples, "Who do people say that the Son of Man is?" and Simon Peter eventually responds, "You are the Christ, the Son of the living God." After this response Matthew adds three verses (16:17–19). These verses stand out as significant for Matthew's understanding of the Church, and they

also provide a point of controversy between Roman Catholic and Protestant interpreters:

> (17) Jesus said to him in reply, "Blessed are you, Simon son of Jonah. For flesh and blood has not revealed this to you, but my heavenly Father. (18) And so I say to you, you are Peter [*petros*] and upon this rock [*petra*] I will build my church. (19) I will give you the keys of the kingdom of heaven, and whatever you bind on earth shall be bound in heaven, and whatever you declare loose on earth shall be loosed in heaven."

Various commentaries on the passage make clear that generally speaking, Protestant and Catholic scholars are in agreement on verse 17. Here, Jesus proclaims Simon blessed, "for flesh and blood has not revealed this to you but my Father who is in heaven." In this context, "flesh and blood" is contrasted with God in heaven. "Flesh and blood" is human, mortal, and limited. The heavenly Father of Jesus is divine, eternal, and unlimited, and only through the gift of God's revelation, the gift of faith, can one acknowledge Jesus as God's Son.

Verses 18 and 19 are the source of some controversy, however. Here, Jesus says, "And I tell you, you are Peter [*petros*] and on this rock [*petra*] I will build my church, and the gates of the netherworld will not prevail against it. I will give you the keys to the kingdom of heaven. Whatever you bind on earth shall be bound in heaven; and whatever you loose on earth shall be loosed in heaven." Among Roman Catholic scholars, the difference between *petros* and *petra* is simply stylistic. *Petra* is the Greek word for *rock*, and it is feminine. To call a man *petra* would make little sense. *Petros* is simply a stylistic accommodation, and Peter, or his statement of faith, is to be the rock on which the Church is built. Some Protestant scholars, however, insist that the two words are being contrasted by Jesus. *Petros* is a small stone, while *petra* is bedrock. For some Protestant scholars, "this rock" refers to the words of Jesus that follow in verse 19 where "the keys of the kingdom of heaven" are understood as the words or law of Christ. So in this context, Jesus is not referring to the man (Simon Peter) or his statement; rather, the Church is to be built on the words of Christ, the bedrock, for the words of Jesus alone have the power to bind and to loose.

Matthew 16:17–19 began to be used over the course of the centuries to support the emerging authority of the bishop of Rome in the early Church. As early as the third century, Christian writers in the West were making the claim that Peter had established his See, the seat of his authority as bishop, in Rome and that the subsequent bishops of Rome had an authority that went beyond the boundaries of the diocese and bound all bishops in the Church. In time, Matthew 16:17–19 became decisive in establishing the primacy and, eventually, the jurisdiction of Rome in relation to all other churches. Quite naturally, with abuses of papal power and the emergence of the Reformation, "The Commissioning of Peter" in Matthew began to be interpreted in a different direction.

There is yet another layer of controversy as well. Oftentimes in popular Roman Catholic piety of the past, this passage could give the impression that Peter has the power to control heaven. Such a notion is deeply troubling to all Christians, and a careful look at the words in verse 19 helps to clarify the issue. The Greek expression is in a construction that scholars call a periphrastic future perfect. Put simply, the verse should be translated "what you declare bound on earth *will have been bound* in heaven," etc. The influence, so to speak, does not run from Earth to heaven, as if Peter can command heaven, and heaven would obey; rather, heaven commands the Church on Earth. The power of binding and loosing is about the conformity between the judgments of heaven and the judgments of the Church on Earth. As is the case in the interpretation of the role of Peter in this passage, Protestant scholars often emphasize the power of binding and loosing is available to the Church as it is obedient to the Word, the law, of Christ.

Mark and Luke

Mark's Gospel provides a common link for the ecclesiologies of Matthew and Luke, as both of these Gospels use Mark as their basic source. Although the word *ekklesia* does not occur in Mark, one can discern the basic outlines of his ecclesiology amid his treatment of discipleship. In Mark, one finds Jesus having to constantly admonish and correct his confused and frightened disciples. Conflict, death, and suffering hang over the Gospel like a pall. In the midst of these, Jesus prepares his disciples for the very real possibility of rejection and suffering. In Mark, Jesus offers this instruction in chapters 8–10 while they are on the road to Jerusalem. To be a disciple of Jesus, to be counted among this community of believers, means picking up one's cross, putting aside riches, becoming servants of one another, and abandoning common practices such as divorce. These basic teachings form the heart of Jesus' instruction on discipleship in all three of the synoptic Gospels, even though they remain characteristic of Mark and his understanding of the Church as the community of disciples.

The Church plays a central role in Luke's narrative. Between Luke's Gospel and Acts, the word *ekklesia* occurs at least nineteen times, indicating the importance of the Church to Luke's theology. In his Gospel, Luke develops the continuity between Israel and the Christian community through the use of fulfillment passages and other devices. Although for Luke the Christian *ekklesia* is the reestablished people of God, the new Israel, he does not envision the Church replacing Israel. Rather, Israel is being reestablished as the Church.

Yet, Luke also signals the distinctive identity of the Christian community as the new people of God by emphasizing the Church's distinctive practices and its turn toward the mission to the Gentiles, a universal mission signaled even at the opening of Acts with the outpouring of the Spirit at Pentecost (Acts 2:1–13, though the mission to the Gentiles is not explicitly embraced until Acts 10). In other words, the eschatological mission of Israel, to be light to the nations (Isaiah 2:2–5; 42:6), is being fulfilled in the Church. As such, Luke describes the Church as living the life Israel has been called to lead: holding all things in common, enjoying fellowship, and ministering to the needy among them. For Luke, the center of this mission is Jerusalem, and the inclusion of Gentiles at Antioch is overseen by the Jerusalem Church, as is the work of their missionaries, Barnabas and Paul. We know from the letters of Paul that the life of the early Christian community was hardly as "unanimous" as Luke presents it—one has only to read Galatians and Corinthians to see just how contentious life was in the early Christian Church. Yet, Luke paints an idealized picture for a specific theological purpose: the Church is to be the "people of God," and it is to encompass even the most disparate elements of society in its fellowship.

John's Complex Ecclesiology

Like the other Gospels, John's ecclesiology is complex and subtle. John's approach, however, is perhaps even more subtle and even more mystical than that of the other canonical Gospels. Of particular interest is his use of the Greek word *menō*, or "abide." The word is used with striking frequency and power, and it provides a theological foundation for both Christology and ecclesiology.[7] *Menō* is used within the Johannine corpus to express permanency of relationship between Father and Son and also to describe the parallel relationship between the Son and the Christian believer. The use of the term is central

to the Christian understanding of the relationship between the Son and the Father; it connotes a sense of permanent relationship (John 1:32). As such, the use of *menō* to describe the relationship between the believer and the Son becomes all the more important (John 13:34). It is the verb *menō* that provides the foundation for the powerful imagery of Christ and the Church as a vine with branches in John 15, arguably his most powerful image of the Church, though not the only one he employs (see John 10 in which the image of the sheepfold is used). John, thus, nicely articulates some of the most developed ideas on the relationship between Christology and ecclesiology in the economy of salvation and provides an appropriate summation of the New Testament's theology of the Church.

New Testament ecclesiology hinges on the person of Jesus and the experiences of Resurrection and Pentecost. For the Pauline tradition as well as the Gospels, the Church is intimately bound with the experience of communion with God through Christ and in the power of the Spirit. All discussions of ministry seem to be governed by and subordinated to the deeply theological and Christological presentation of the Church. As the New Testament period came to a close, however, circumstances would cause many theologians to shift their attention to the visible structures of the Church and the Church's relationship to the world.

PATRISTIC AND MEDIEVAL ACCOUNTS OF THE CHURCH

The Patristic era (the centuries following the writing of the New Testament, c. 100–600) introduced ecclesiology as both a practical and theological matter. In the Patristic era, the threat of heresy and the decline of imperial Rome in the west made ecclesial organization and unity a central concern. In the Middle Ages (c. 600–1500), the absence of a robust political system placed a heavy burden on ecclesiastical structures. The emergence of Benedictine monasticism and the great monk-missionaries of the age helped to shape Western Europe for centuries to come. In sum, the Church grew in its self-understanding and in its capacity to engage, transform, and undergo transformation in order to promote the work of redemption. Yet, the story of the Church in this era (as in others) is not always appealing, for in this age the Church also demonstrated its failures as a human institution as it succumbed to various cultural and social systems that would impede or distort its redemptive mission.

Manuals of Church Discipline from Early Christianity

In the first centuries of the Christian era, while Church order and discipline were still nascent, several important collections of teaching and instruction for maintaining Church practice emerged. Four of the most important "manuals" were *The Didache*, *The Apostolic Tradition*, the *Didasclia Apostolorum*, and the *Apostolic Constitutions*.

The Didache: The full title of this work is *The Teaching of the Lord through the Twelve Apostles*. This is an early–second-century manual of Church discipline that probably came from a church in Syria. Its sixteen brief chapters on moral conduct, fasting, and prayer are divided into two sections, "The Way of Life" and "The Way of Death." The document is of great interest to those who study the liturgy because it contains the earliest Eucharistic prayers. *The Didache* is also remarkable for the place it affords Christian "prophets" in the life of the Church. In fact, prophets as well as bishops may preside at the celebration of the Eucharist.

The Apostolic Tradition: This document is usually attributed to Hippolytus, a third-century presbyter in Rome. This document provides a description of early Christian worship and the text of early Roman Eucharistic prayers. In the contemporary canon of the Mass, Eucharistic Prayer Number One is based on the prayers recorded in this document.

Didascalia Apostolorum: This early–third-century document probably comes from Syria. It is a rather disorderly presentation of liturgical guidelines, pastoral duties, and admonitions against the observation of Jewish rituals and laws. It recommends fasting as a means of reconciling repentant sinners before admitting them to communion.

Apostolic Constitutions: This late–fourth-century document is actually a collection of parts of the three documents mentioned above, as well as some additional material. It provides a valuable source for understanding the movement toward the regularization of Church life and practice.

Cyprian and Augustine on the Unity of the Church

Against those who would insist that Christianity is fundamentally a European religion, one must recall that the hotbed of Christianity was in northern Africa for the first three centuries of the Common Era. In the east, Egypt produced the greatest theologians and the most important early Christian practices, and in the west the Roman province of Africa—the area around the ancient city of Carthage—similarly saw the greatest theological and ecclesiastical development. Northern Africa would play an important role in the development of Latin theology for a variety of reasons, but perhaps the most significant is the manner in which two great thinkers, Cyprian and Augustine, addressed the question of the unity and universalism or "catholicity" of the Church over and against those who would divide it.

Cyprian lived in a tumultuous era, the third century, in which the great persecution under the Roman emperor Decius took place (c. 250–251). During this persecution many Christians denied their faith under the threat of torture or death, and in the wake of this persecution, Cyprian had to deal with many splinter groups (heresies) that had developed. On the one hand, some groups insisted the Church had no power to reconcile these apostates (those who had denied the faith)—they were lost, beyond the mercy of God and the ministry of the Church. On the other hand, a number of Christians did not consider the apostasy of Christians in the face of persecution a matter for the Church to consider one way or the other—the Church was not to pass judgment at all. Against these two extreme positions, Cyprian argued that through the ministry of the Church, even apostates could be reconciled but that reconciliation required penance. It was only through the ministry of the bishop that the penance could be undertaken, and the apostate would, thereby, find reconciliation with the Church and with God.

It was in this context of persecution, apostasy, and heresy that Cyprian authored what is perhaps his most famous work, "On the Unity of the Catholic Church" (*De unitate ecclesiae*), in which he sets forth some common and recurring principles that will guide ecclesiology in the West for centuries to come. For Cyprian, in the midst of struggles with imperial persecution and

From House Churches to Basilica

In the New Testament, one sees that Christians gathered in homes to celebrate the Lord's Supper on the first day of the week. In such a setting, the celebration, though obviously ritualized in many ways, would still have resembled a meal. With the legalization of Christianity in the fourth century under the Emperor Constantine (c. 288–337), and with the patronage of the Roman emperors, the Church was given imperial office buildings to use for worship. These buildings, called basilicas (the Greek word for king or emperor is *basileus*), were large and rectangular. Along the colonnade that supported the roof were niches where imperial officials would conduct business. Important officials would enter the basilica in a procession, led by a servant carrying a censor and other servants carrying candles and followed by attendants called acolytes (the Greek word *acoutheō* means "to follow"). Government officials wore stoles to signify their position and other outer garments appropriate for their duties. So as the Church came into possession of these buildings, their worship began to reflect imperial service with its garments, procession, and symbols. Even the liturgy was deeply impacted by this change of location.

heretical factions, the principle of unity within the Church rests in the authority of the apostles, an authority that comes from Christ and is now exercised by their successors, the bishops. Apart from this unity one is not "in Christ." It is within this context that Cyprian's most memorable ecclesiological maxims occur. He insists that "outside the Church there is no salvation" (*Salus extra ecclesiam non est*; *Letter*, 73. 21. 2), and "One cannot have God as Father if one does not have the Church as mother" (*Habere non potest Deum patrem qui ecclesiam non habet matrem*; *On the Unity of the Catholic Church*, 6). For Cyprian, the unity of the Church, its power in the face of persecution and schism, and its very identity revolved around the ministry of the bishop.

A little more than a century later, a similar controversy involving persecution and apostasy erupted that engulfed the bishop of a neighboring diocese, the great Augustine of Hippo (354–430). Following the last great persecution of the Church under the Roman emperor Diocletian, the question of what to do with apostates, and, in particular, the apostates who had handed over copies of Scripture to be burned by imperial authorities, took center stage. A group called the Donatists argued that the Christian bishops and priests who were guilty of surrendering these books (they were called *traditores*) were not able to validly celebrate the sacraments. The Donatists appealed to Cyprian's writings for support in this matter, for he had argued that unity in the Church was essential and that unity came through fidelity to the bishop. Those who were outside the Church because of their apostasy could not administer the sacraments; thus, all those who had been baptized by apostate clergy needed to be rebaptized. Augustine, on the other hand, argued that God was the actor in the celebration of the sacraments and that such rebaptism was not necessary. In fact, he argued that the Donatists were the ones who really threatened the Church, because they were busy setting up their own church apart from the catholic ("universal") Church. Augustine's arguments against the Donatists, including his assertion that sacraments such as baptism and ordination conferred a "character" on the soul that could not be erased even by sin, held sway. The Donatist movement eventually died out, and Augustine's writings on the Church and sacraments became widely influential in the centuries that followed.

Both Augustine and Cyprian contributed to an emerging Latin ecclesiology that privileged the unity of the Church, a unity that revolved abound fidelity to the bishop, and especially, the bishop of Rome. For both of these writers, the power of the Church is derived from God and manifested in the celebration of the sacraments and the government of the Church, both of which focused on the power of the bishop. The works of Cyprian and Augustine would prove decisive for the development of ecclesiology and Church practice through the coming centuries, especially during the era that followed the collapse of the Roman Empire and witnessed the disintegration of most political and social structures in the West. It was during the Middle Ages that the centralization of authority in the bishop, and especially the bishop of Rome, would define the Church and its relationship to the world.

Ecclesiology in the Middle Ages

The demise of the Roman Empire in the west paved the way for a more robust and independent Church. Two popes in particular made tremendous contributions to an understanding of the Church and its place in the world: Gregory the Great and Gregory VII. Also in this period, monasticism came to dominate the landscape of Europe, contributing much to the development of the Church's self-understanding and its mission in the world.

Gregory I (540–604), or Gregory the Great as he is often called, was the first pope from the Benedictine monastic tradition and the pope most responsible for establishing the parameters of papal power during the Middle Ages. Upon his ascension to the papacy, Gregory I found himself in a difficult position. On the one side, the Eastern Roman (Byzantine) Empire, with its representative in Ravenna (northern Italy), missed no opportunity to diminish the power of the pope through military, economic, or ecclesiastical machinations. The Byzantine Empire was the remnant of the old Roman Empire that had survived the various Germanic invasions that eroded and eventually destroyed the western empire. After the city of Rome fell in the fifth century, the Eastern (Byzantine) Empire attempted to secure domination over central Italy and sought to keep the city of Rome from regaining any of its previous power. On the other side, Gregory I faced a city and a countryside wrecked by economic and political blight. The invasion of the Lombards into the Italian peninsula exacerbated long-simmering problems that had been unfolding with the demise of the Western Roman Empire. Yet, within this fraught context, Gregory I was able to establish his independence from Constantinople (and Ravenna) and set forth a bold understanding of the Church and the bishop in relation to what would come to be called the temporal or civil order. Perhaps one of Gregory I's greatest theological achievements, after his *Moralia in Job*, is his treatise *Liber regulae pastoralis* (Pastoral Care) in which he establishes the standards for the ministry and authority of the bishop. The text was to be a classic example of what the episcopate was in the Latin Church throughout the Middle Ages. While Gregory extols the virtues needed for the appropriate care of souls, he is also keen to point out the responsibilities of the bishop to govern his territory effectively. He argued that because bishops were responsible for distributing food and defending cities, they were to be honored as rulers to whom "subjects" were to give respect and honor.[8]

Gregory I did more than any other individual to spread Benedictine monasticism throughout Europe. He popularized the Rule of St. Benedict, a more balanced and moderate form of communal, or cenobitic, monasticism than those developed in the early centuries of the Christian era, by sending monk-missionaries like Augustine to Canterbury, England. In turn, when the English missionary Boniface returned to the Continent a century later in 719, he brought with him the Rule, which he used to organize monasteries in the newly converted German lands. From Boniface's abbey in Fulda,

monasticism spread throughout the eastern part of the Frankish kingdom (now Germany). Through the work of various figures, including Alcuin, another English monk formed under the Rule of St. Benedict, monasticism spread into the western parts of the Frankish kingdom (present-day France and the Low Countries). These areas were helped to develop and flourish by the establishment of Benedictine monasteries, many of which had schools attached to them. These schools provided education for Europe's leaders for the next several centuries, until the founding of the universities in the thirteenth century.

The combination of Gregory I's emphasis on pastoral governance and the growth of monasticism as an anchor for Church and civil order helped to solidify the place of the Church in western society. This combination also helped to promote an understanding of Church in which there was no clear separation, and sometimes barely a distinction, between the temporal and the sacred realms. Bishops and abbots (or abbesses) controlled and governed large portions of Europe, and they did so with the approval of civil authorities just as often as they acted against those authorities.

As Europe began to emerge from what many historians used to pejoratively call the Dark Ages (c. 450–800), civil authorities began to be more effectively organized, and a struggle between civil rulers and ecclesiastical authorities ensued. The emergence of Charlemagne (c. 742–814) as "Holy Roman Emperor" in 800 marked an important turning point for the Church in Europe. Having united warring tribes and established a kingdom that stretched across Europe, he was viewed by many in the Church, including Pope Leo III, as a political savior. The pope aligned himself with Charlemagne against the Byzantine emperor and helped to establish a new relationship between the Church and the civil rulers of Europe.

Rulers such as Charlemagne were expected to bring Europe out of the chaos that had engulfed it for centuries following the demise of the Roman Empire, and these hopes were well founded. It was Charlemagne who helped to establish schools throughout his kingdom. Charlemagne also worked to define and regularize Church life, including sacramental life in the Church.[9] Yet, it was the prowess of Charlemagne and his successors that also began to subordinate the Church to the needs of the civil government, and this provoked a response from Church authorities, who sought to defend the Church against the state. There was perhaps no better defender of the Church over and against the claims of civil authorities in the Middle Ages than Pope Gregory VII.

Gregory VII (1021–1085) was one of the boldest and most capable popes of the Middle Ages. He observed how much the Church and civil authorities had become intertwined and how this situation increasingly enabled civil authorities to make use of the Church for their own purposes. Trained as a Benedictine monk in an austere setting, Gregory VII became wary of this situation and resolved to establish the Church's independence. He renewed the prohibition against simony (the buying and selling of Church offices) and forbade the appointment and the ceremonial investiture of Church officials by civil authorities, a practice commonly called lay investiture. The Church was comfortable with the idea that it was to work with civil rulers to find appropriate candidates for Church office, but the notion that Church officials (bishops and abbots in particular) were to be invested with their power from the civil authorities was highly problematic. It was this ban on lay investiture that caused Gregory VII many difficulties, because virtually no ruler in Europe was willing to cede such power to the Church. (Bishops and abbots had great influence and often great wealth in the Middle Ages.) The complex political machinations Gregory VII's efforts required are beyond the scope of this brief section, but it is sufficient to note that he was able to impose his will on many rulers of the day and thereby sow much resentment in the process.

Gregory VII's efforts at reform tended to center on the power and prestige of the papacy against all challengers. One famous document from the time of Gregory VII seems to aptly summarize his position. The *Dictatus papae*, (Dictates of the Pope on The Euchologion) although probably not written by Gregory himself, is placed in the papal registers of Gregory VII in the year 1075. Although it might not be attributable to him directly, the document does epitomize what Gregory repeatedly stated in a variety of letters and pronouncements during his pontificate, as well as material from his predecessors. Some of the highlights of the document include astonishing assertions of papal power. Examples include the following:

> [The pope] alone may depose or reinstate bishops.
>
> [The pope] may depose emperors.
>
> He himself may be judged by no one.
>
> The pope alone may absolve subjects from their fealty to unjust men [the pope may permit subjects to reject and disobey their rulers].[10]

In this collection of maxims, the papacy became the chief power in Europe, even to the point that subsequent popes could insist that kings were their feudal vassals (the most famous case is the complex maneuvering between Pope Innocent III, King John of England, and the nobility of England). The control the papacy was able to exert over civil rulers reached its height in the twelfth century and began to decline steadily over the next several centuries even as popes such as Boniface VIII tried to work against this

Simony, Nepotism, and the Business of Doing Church

The abuses of the Church in the Middle Ages and the Renaissance make today's scandals and abuses seem almost tame by comparison (though contemporary abuses are not tame in the eyes of those who have suffered from them). Given that the Church exercised enormous influence over medieval society, which in turn, exerted considerable influence over the Church, it is no wonder that money, politics, and the desire for dynastic succession should have emerged in the Church.

Simony, the buying and selling of Church offices or anything spiritual, was condemned in the New Testament. In fact, the term *simony* comes from the story of Simon Magus, a man who attempted to purchase spiritual powers from Peter and the disciples in Acts 8:9–24. Yet, in the New Testament, one also reads of the apostle Paul insisting that he and other apostles have a right to live off the Gospel. So, when is one receiving the wages for one's work for the Gospel, and when is one profiting from the "sale of spiritual things"? Often simony is combined with nepotism or the granting of benefices (offices or titles connected to "payments") to family members.

Perhaps the most infamous example of simony and nepotism from the history of the Church is that of the Borgias, a Spanish family embroiled in Italian and French politics. Alfonso, the family patriarch, was Pope Calixtus III (1454–1458). His nephew, Rodrigo, is perhaps the most controversial figure in the family. He became a "cardinal nephew" at a young age. This type of nepotism was becoming a common and disturbing practice in the Renaissance, and sometimes these "nephews" were really the illegitimate sons of a pope. Nonetheless, it appears as though Rodrigo Borgia really was a nephew of Alfonso. The elevation of Rodrigo to the rank of cardinal at the tender age of twenty-five was obviously the result of familial connections. In 1492, Rodrigo became Pope Alexander VI. It was rumored that in order to secure a key vote within a highly contentious conclave (a meeting of the College of Cardinals in which the pope is elected) he paid handsomely for the deciding ballot. While Rodrigo was, perhaps, not without virtue, his personal life was remarkable. He fathered many children, among them the noteworthy Cesare Borgia whose ruthlessness and political abilities made him the inspiration for Machiavelli's *The Prince*.

Church laws against nepotism made it impossible for an illegitimate child to receive holy orders. Cesare, however, was dispensed from any impediment to ordination or advancement by a papal letter. He was made a cardinal and given numerous benefices (he was made an archabbot, bishop, and archbishop of several places). These benefices brought him considerable wealth and power. Eventually, Cesare left the "ministry" to marry a French noblewoman.

The story of the Borgia family, however, is not only the story of power and scandal. Through the lineage of Rodrigo's eldest son, Juan, the family produced a saint. The great grandson of Pope Alexander VI, Francis Borgia, was a nobleman turned cleric. Like the rest of his family, Francis was an able politician, but he eventually set aside his political career to join the newly formed Society of Jesus (the Jesuits). He eventually became the leader of the order, and his virtue and diligence won many admirers. So great was his virtue that he was canonized less than a century after his death.

shift in power away from the papacy and toward emerging nation-states.

While the actual power of the papacy began to wane in the thirteenth and fourteenth centuries, the theology of that power was heightened through the work of several theologians, but none more important than Giacomo (James or Jacobus) of Viterbo (1255–1308). His work *De regimine Christiano* (On Christian Government) provocatively outlined the extent of papal power.[11] He argued that the pope was the author of all legitimate authority on Earth, both spiritual and civil or temporal. Spiritual power was wielded through the work of the sacraments performed by the ministers of the Church (priests and bishops) while temporal power was wielded on behalf of the pope by the civil government. For Giacomo, the pope is the supreme judge of the world in both spiritual and temporal matters, and civil rulers should understand themselves as the emissaries of the pope.

These ideas were embraced and amplified by Pope Boniface VIII in his famous bull *Unam sanctam* (One Divinity [1302]). Boniface had been in a contentious fight with the king of France, Philip IV, over the relationship between the Church and the civil government. Needless to say, the king did not share Boniface's interpretation of papal power, and the tide began to turn against the papacy. Papal claims to power were to be maintained in the coming centuries, but the rise of nation-states and their ability to wield power against the papacy (see the Avignon Papacy) created a significant disconnect and, in the long run, contributed to a new vision of the Church in the Protestant Reformation.

The Patristic era and Middle Ages both witnessed many important developments in the life of the Church—developments that shaped the Church's self-understanding and its mission. While Cyprian and Augustine contributed to the emergence of a Church united and universal under the leadership of bishops, the Middle Ages made that universal Church also a highly organized and powerful social and political institution. As tensions between the civil and the sacred realms became more intense, and as abuses in the Church's organization and governance structures continued to grow, a spirit of reform was in the air that would drastically challenge and change the Church's self-understanding.

DISPUTED ECCLESIOLOGIES IN THE REFORMATION PERIOD

Popular images of the Church in the late Middle Ages have left the impression that it was thoroughly corrupt and reprobate. While there were numerous examples of holiness and reform long before the sixteenth century, the glacial pace of these reforms, and the persistence of corruption and bad faith at the highest levels of the Church, helped to galvanize opposition to the Church's power, structures, and theology. This situation was acute in the states of the Holy Roman Empire in the early sixteenth century, and it was no accident that it was precisely there that the Reformation gained its earliest and most ardent supporters.

The Challenge of Conciliarism

The Reformation is a complex social, political, cultural, and theological reality. It is not easily narrated, and its theological diversity is always oversimplified. The Reformation was, at least in part, the outgrowth of the opposition to papal authority. In the late Middle Ages, many men with weak character and divided loyalties came increasingly to occupy positions of authority within the Church, including the papacy, and they were increasingly beholden to foreign rulers. In fact, the French kings even moved the papacy to southern France, where they could more easily control the pope (a period known as the Avignon Papacy, 1309–1378). In the wake of such developments, the Church's power and influence began to wane. At this time, there were many great reformers and even many popes and bishops who attempted to inaugurate much needed reforms, but these either did not gain wide acceptance, or as was the case with Jan Hus (1372–1415) and others, the proposed reforms were far too bold to be tolerated by either the Church or the state.

Of particular interest was the conciliarist movement in the fourteenth and fifteenth centuries. In the years following the Avignon Papacy (1378–1417), there were at least two and sometimes three men who claimed to be the bishop of Rome. Given the increasing emphasis on papal power and authority, such claims were serious and disturbing. In an effort to resolve this situation, a council was called by the Holy Roman Emperor Sigismund, in the city of Constance. The council met from 1414 to 1418 and among its actions deposed the various claimants to the papacy. The council even assumed the power to depose the pope, or at least someone who claimed to be pope. It was at this time that numerous figures in the Church began to reason that a general, or ecumenical, council of the Church must have power over the pope to exercise should the pope act contrary to the gospel or the good of the Church. Now, it appears as though the council's actual power was limited by pragmatic concerns—how to deal with three popes! Yet, among some, this position was based on principle and not merely on pragmatism, and these people would become known as conciliarists.

The conciliarists reasoned that the pope's authority derived from the Church as a communion. Therefore, a pope could be condemned or deposed by a general or ecumenical council that would exercise supreme authority over each and every member of the Church, including the pope. The difficulty that they needed to confront, however, was the emphasis on papal authority that had become entrenched over the previous several centuries. It was this point of emphasis that created an uphill battle for the conciliarists. Shortly after the Council of Constance, at which Jan Hus was condemned and executed for his beliefs about the Church, the Council of Basel (1433) convened, and many of the conciliarists used this council as an opportunity to solidify their position. At this council, however, the Dominican theologian Juan de Torquemada (1388–1468; not to be confused with his nephew, Tomás, the leader of the Spanish Inquisition) launched a vigorous defense of papal authority, a defense that later became the basis of his famous treatise, *Summa ecclesiastica* (published posthumously in 1489). Though the council was eventually dominated by the conciliarists, Juan de Torquemada's defense of complete papal authority (Latin *plenitudo potestatis*) later became the centerpiece of early modern ecclesiology.[12] Following the Council of Basel, the conciliarists were eventually defeated, and the prospects for reform were dimmed, though not lost. Subsequent councils, popes, bishops, clergy, and laypeople were devoted to the ongoing reform of the Church.[13]

The Challenge of the Reformers

The proximate cause of the Reformation was the intermixing of ecclesiastical authority and the politics of the state. Albert Hohenzollern, the younger son of the Margrave of Brandenburg, one of those officials responsible for electing the Holy Roman Emperor (for the most part, the ruler of Germany), was eager to secure a position of influence alongside that of his brother, the new Margrave of Brandenburg. As a twenty-two-year-old, he had secured the position of Archbishop of Marburg, a major diocese in the empire, and was maneuvering to become the

Archbishop of Mainz. With this latter position, he would become another of the electors of the Holy Roman Emperor (this had been an elected position for centuries, and the electors were a combination of bishops and princes from the empire). His family would then control two of the votes necessary to become emperor. In order to secure this position, he was required to pay a tax and other honoraria to church authorities in Rome. Although Albert was from a powerful family, he needed a sizeable loan in order to secure the See of Mainz. To pay off the loan, he arranged to have an indulgence preached in his diocese and agreed to split the revenues between his bankers and the pope, who was in need of funds to rebuild St. Peter's Basilica. The scandal this created was the impetus for Luther's famous "Ninety-five Theses."

When Martin Luther (1483–1546), an Augustinian monk and theology professor in Germany, posted his "Ninety-five Theses," he was engaging in a traditional form of academic disputation. He was advancing certain theological ideas and challenging those with contrary views to present their case. Luther wanted to make some arguments; he had no intention of splitting the Church or creating a new Church. He was demanding a reformation of the Church he knew and presumably loved, and he demanded to be heard. In fact, when one actually reads the text of Luther's "Ninety-five Theses" (1517) and the text of his "Letter to Pope Leo X" (1518), one is struck by the reasonableness of Luther's tone and his care when addressing the question of papal authority. Yet, as the political and social situation heated up, so did the polemics on both sides, and eventually Luther began to articulate a vision of the Church that was remarkably different from the Church in which Luther had been raised.

Luther's position on the Church echoed that of the conciliarists inasmuch as he saw papal authority, and the authority of all clerics, as devolving from the communion of the faithful.[14]

Ordination to the priesthood or to the episcopacy did not entail a change in status, only a change in duty. The priest and bishop function on behalf of the Church community—they express the priesthood all members of the Church enjoy by virtue of their baptism. With this ecclesiology in mind, Luther and the German nobility called for "a free council" to be held in German lands (lands sympathetic to reform and in which the local rulers would not cave in to papal pressures). It was this call for a council, and the thesis that a council was superior to the pope, that caused positions to become increasingly entrenched, and it is in connection to the challenge of the reformers that the Catholic Church begins to take a far more defensive posture.

Luther's call for a more "democratic" polity in the Church was fairly mild compared to the positions of some of his fellow reformers. Even though he rejected the claims to authority and power associated with the papacy and the office of bishop in the Catholic Church, Luther could begrudgingly admit that episcopal structures were not necessarily antithetical to the life of the Christian Church. The following quote from Luther's letter on the Anabaptists is a remarkable example of this sentiment:

> We confess that under the papacy there has been much, even all Christian treasure, and that it also came to us from there, because we confess that in the papacy there is the true holy scripture, the true baptism, the true sacrament of the altar, the true key to the forgiveness of sins, true preaching office. . . . I say that under the pope there is true Christianity, even the model of Christianity, and many devout saints.

> — *LETTER ON THE ANABAPTISTS*, 1528[15]

The conciliatory tone taken on this occasion against an enemy common to Luther and Roman

Catholics (the Anabaptists), however, gave way to more bitter polemic in the course of the Reformation, and although figures such as Philip Melanchthon (Luther's close associate and the author of the *Augsburg Confession*) were somewhat sympathetic to episcopal structures, the mood of the Reformation in Germany, established by Luther in his "Letter to the Christian Nobility of the German Nation," was decidedly more democratic, for the most part, and far more supportive of a subordination of the Church to the Christian state.

Although Luther and John Calvin (1509–1564), the two patriarchs of the Reformation, disagreed on many issues, including substantial ecclesiological issues, they both agreed with their predecessor, Jan Hus, on a theological emphasis on the primacy of an "invisible church," a church of true believers, a church of the elect. This church could not be known in the world, but it would be revealed only at the Last Judgment. The "visible church" was useful insofar as it aided people in identifying those who were true believers, the elect. Luther had written, "the church is hidden and the saints are unknown."[16] Calvin even devoted a section of his *Institutes of the Christian Religion* to this distinction:

> How we are to judge the church visible, which falls within our knowledge, is, I believe, already evident from the above discussion. For we have said that Holy Scripture speaks of the church in two ways. Sometimes by the term "church" it means that which is actually in God's presence, into which no persons are received but those who are children of God by grace of adoption and true members of Christ by sanctification of the Holy Spirit. . . . Often, however, the name "church" designates the whole multitude of men spread over the earth who profess to worship one God and Christ. . . . In this church are mingled many hypocrites who have nothing of Christ but the name and outward appearance. There are very many ambitious, greedy, envious persons, evil speakers, and some of quite unclean life. Such are tolerated for a time either because they cannot be convicted by a competent tribunal or because a vigorous discipline does not always flourish as it ought. Just as we must believe, therefore, that the former church, invisible to us, is visible to the eyes of God alone, so we are commanded to revere and keep communion with the latter, which is called "church" in respect to [human beings].
>
> — *INSTITUTES OF THE CHRISTIAN RELIGION*, IV, 1, 7[17]

Such a dichotomy between the visible and invisible church was a direct attack on the Catholic emphasis on the visible and even temporal aspects of the Church, especially the emphasis on hierarchy and papal power. The reformers, thereby, hoped to temper the triumphalism of medieval ecclesiologies. Yet, other voices in the Reformation, the "radical reformers," challenged this triumphalism by moving in an altogether different direction.

Many of the so-called radical reformers, such as the Anabaptists, were launching a broadside attack on both Catholic and Protestant accounts of the Church, particularly the unquestioned alliance between temporal and spiritual power. For the Anabaptists, the legalization of Christianity under Constantine in the fourth century and the empire's subsequent endorsement of Christianity as the official religion of the empire under Theodosius I caused the virtual disappearance of the Church on Earth, though there were always examples of the true Church among those Christians who were demonized and persecuted by the imperial Church. Only in the sixteenth century was God's Spirit being given anew, while the Church was being reconstituted, concretely and consistently. The radical

The Schleitheim Confession: A Statement of Anabaptist Principles

One of the most influential statements of faith to come out of the radical reformation (the branch of the Reformation that believed that neither Luther nor Calvin was radical enough in their reforms) was The Schleitheim Confession. Written by one of the most important Anabaptist leaders of the sixteenth century, Michael Sattler, the confession was accepted by the Swiss Anabaptists on February 24, 1527, at an assembly in the village of Schleitheim. It stands out as an example of Anabaptist theology and ecclesiology.

I. Baptism.

Baptism shall be given to all those who have been taught repentance and the amendment of life and [who] believe truly that their sins are taken away through Christ . . . hereby is excluded all infant baptism, the greatest and first abomination of the pope.

II. Excommunication [The Ban].

[T]hose who have been baptized into the one body of Christ, and let themselves be called brothers or sisters, and still somehow slip and fall into error and sin, being inadvertently overtaken. The same [shall] be warned twice privately and the third time be publicly admonished before the entire congregation according to the command of Christ. But this shall be done according to the ordering of the Spirit of God before the breaking of bread so that we may all in one spirit and in one love break and eat from one bread and drink from one cup.

III. Breaking of Bread.

[A]ll those who desire to break the one bread in remembrance of the broken body of Christ and all those who wish to drink of one drink in remembrance of the shed blood of Christ, they must beforehand be united in the one body of Christ, that is the congregation of God, whose head is Christ, and that by baptism.

IV. The World.

We have been united concerning the separation that shall take place from the evil and the wickedness which the devil has planted in the world, simply in this; that we have no fellowship with them. . . . From all this we should learn that everything which has not been united with our God in Christ is nothing but an abomination which we should shun. By this are meant all popish and repopish works and idolatry, gatherings, church attendance. . . . Thereby shall also fall away from us the diabolical weapons of violence—such as sword, armor, and the like, and all of their use to protect friends or against enemies—by virtue of the word of Christ: "you shall not resist evil."

Continued

The Schleitheim Confession *Continued*

V. Pastors.

The shepherd in the Church shall be a person according to the rule of Paul, fully and completely, who has a good report of those who are outside the faith. . . . He shall be supported, wherein he has need, by the congregation which has chosen him, so that he who serves the gospel can also live therefrom, as the Lord has ordered. But should a shepherd do something worthy of reprimand, nothing shall be done with him without the voice of two or three witnesses. If they sin they shall be publicly reprimanded, so that others might fear.

VI. The Sword.

The sword is an ordering of God outside the perfection of Christ. It punishes and kills the wicked and guards and protects the good. In the law the sword is established over the wicked for punishment and for death and the secular rulers are established to wield the same. But within the perfection of Christ only the ban [excommunication] is used for the admonition and exclusion of the one who has sinned, without the death of the flesh, simply the warning and the command to sin no more.

VII. Oaths.

The oath is a confirmation among those who are quarreling or making promises. In the law it is commanded that it should be done only in the name of God, truthfully and not falsely. Christ, who teaches the perfection of the law, forbids His [followers] all swearing, whether true or false.

—Selections translated by John Howard Yoder in *The Schleitheim Confession*
[Scottdale, PA: Herald Press, 1973] used with permission

reformers shared Luther's emphasis on the fellowship of the baptized but created an even more "horizontal" Church polity. This Church was to stand apart from the world, especially apart from civil authorities, and the community was to embrace the practice of nonresistance to evil. Such practices set them apart and made them dangerous in the eyes of both ecclesiastical and civil authorities from every camp.

Ecclesiology in the Catholic Counter-Reformation

Luther's call for an open general council of the Church went largely unheeded in the early years of the Reformation. After all, such a council would have been difficult to control, and its agenda would have included a wide range of disciplinary, political, and theological issues. The need for a consistent response to the charges of the reformers, however, did eventually coalesce into a council in 1545. This council was to meet in many sessions between 1545 and 1563 in the city of Trent, near the southern border of the Holy Roman Empire. The council's agenda was determined by the reformers insofar as Catholic theologians at the council felt obligated (1) to respond to the challenges of the reformers, (2) to clarify the teaching of the Church in relation to what they regarded as the misrepresentations of the reformers, and (3) to address the abuses identified by the reformers that had sown the seeds of discontent throughout Europe. Many Roman Catholic officials still harbored hope that the council could restore the unity of the Church, and to that end, great reformers such as Philip Melanchthon were invited to attend the council (though he was unable to reach Trent due to military and political upheaval).

The Council of Trent was remarkably successful in achieving its aims, but at the same time, the defensive and polemical tone of the Reformation left its mark on Roman Catholic ecclesiology for centuries. The reformers had proliferated and heightened a fundamental distrust of the institutional structures of the Church and anchored those suspicions at the heart of their ecclesiologies. In response, Roman Catholic ecclesiology in the Counter-Reformation moved decidedly in the opposite direction — affirming the priority of the visible and institutional elements of the Church.

Perhaps no theologian of the Counter-Reformation better exemplified the spirit of the times than Robert Cardinal Bellarmine (1542–1621). In his treatise, *De Controversiis* ("On Controversies"), Bellarmine treats the topic "of the Church militant diffused throughout the earth." It is here that we find his famous definition of the Church:

> Our view is that the Church is only one reality, not two, and that this single and true reality is the group of people linked by profession of the same faith and by communion in the same sacraments, under the governance of legitimate pastors and especially of the single vicar of Christ on earth, the Roman Pontiff. . . . [W]e do not think that for someone to be able to be said in some way to be part of the true Church of which the Scriptures speak any inner virtue

is required. . . . For the Church is a group of people as visible and palpable as is the group of the Roman people or the Kingdom of France or the Republic of Venice.

— *DE CONTROVERSIIS*, II, 3, 2

Bellarmine's definition is thus a challenge to the Protestant distinction between the visible and invisible Church, though Bellarmine admits that the Church has both a soul (the virtues of faith, hope, and charity) and a body. His definition focuses exclusively on the visible body, because these are the minimum requirements for someone to be identified as part of the Church.

The emphasis on the visible structures of the Church, and the idea that one can be part of the Church, though imperfectly and without virtue, reflect the experience of the Church in the late Middle Ages and the early modern period. The Church was not an assembly of the elect; rather, it assembled people so that they might *be* elected. In this view, all those who have been baptized have been called together and incorporated into the Church through the sacraments. Through the unity of faith and sacramental practice and under the responsible governance of bishops, the members of the Church might come to know virtue and find the gift of salvation promised in Christ. In Bellarmine's view, virtue is cultivated by the Church, but it is not a prerequisite for membership. For this reason, in Roman Catholic circles, moral failures are considered scandalous, but it is the violation of Church order and unity by espousing heresy or defying Church authority that most often incurs the sanction of excommunication. With the dawn of the Modern Age, the Church had wedded itself to an ecclesiology focused on visible structures and on governance, particularly on the power of the papacy, and it was precisely these issues that made the Church so antithetical to the spirit of the age. The stage was thus set for a major confrontation.

ECCLESIOLOGY AND THE AGE OF MODERNITY

Scholars will often remark that the flourish of theological activity within Roman Catholic circles in the century or so after the Council of Trent was followed by an abrupt demise. The eighteenth century saw the flourishing of the Enlightenment, a movement that emphasized the autonomy of human reason apart from any deference to religious authority, and the birth of many great nation-states. Of central importance is the French Revolution (1789), in which the Church was identified as part of the political establishment (*l'ancien régime*). This identification made the Church, specifically the clergy and other ecclesiastical institutions such as monasteries and universities, the target of the revolution's anger and violence. The disestablishment of the Church in France was soon followed by similar developments throughout Europe and the Americas in the nineteenth century. The rise of radical secularism with the French and other revolutions and the consistent and even violent attack on the Church were exacerbated by the general absence of powerful and creative theological voices in the eighteenth and early nineteenth centuries. The Church was in a difficult position, partly of its own making.

Perhaps indicative of the Roman Catholic Church's predicament was the rise of the French emperor, Napoleon Bonaparte (1769–1821), and that of Holy Roman Emperor Joseph II (1741–1790). Both of these rulers were determined to rein in the Catholic Church's claims to temporal authority, and Napoleon even went so far as to have the pope taken prisoner. Joseph, on the other hand, simply went about remaking the Catholic Church into an institution that would serve the state and the rationalistic sensibilities that dominated European culture at the time. It was not until the reign of Gregory XVI (pontificate 1831–1846) that there was a strong resurgence of papal authority and with it a theological resurgence that would lay the groundwork for an important shift in ecclesiology in the twentieth century.

Ecclesiology in the Nineteenth Century

Perhaps no theologian better exemplifies the flourishing of Catholic theology in the nineteenth century than Johann Adam Möhler (1796–1838). Although he died young, Möhler left a considerable mark on Catholic thought and helped to plot the course of theology well into the twentieth century.

Ordained a priest in 1819, Möhler quickly rose to prominence as a teacher and writer. In 1828, he earned a teaching position at the University of Tübingen, and in 1832, he moved to the University of Munich. It was during his tenure at Tübingen, however, that Möhler wrote his two most important and influential works.

In 1825, Möhler published a book titled *Unity in the Church* in which he departed significantly from the ecclesiology typical of Bellarmine and other Counter-Reformation theologians.[18] Instead of focusing on the institutional or visible aspects of the Church, Möhler emphasized the work of the Spirit in the life of the believer and the manner in which the Spirit worked to bring about the bond of love and communion that constitutes the Church. It was out of this bond that the need for pastors, bishops, and even the papacy emerged in the life of the Church. The merits of his approach are apparent. First, Möhler placed an emphasis on the concrete history of the Church and the development of its ministries over the course of time. Second, by doing so, Möhler was able to locate the divine institution of episcopal and pastoral authority beyond the explicit directives of Jesus in the Gospels. In other words, God mandated or instituted the ministry of bishops

The Catholic Tübingen School

One of the centers of Catholic theology in the nineteenth century was the University of Tübingen in Germany. This ancient university became the center of the new spirit in theology that was sweeping both Protestant and Catholic circles following the Napoleonic Wars (c. 1799–1815). In 1817, the university created a Catholic Faculty in the School of Theology, and this development created the opportunity for some of the most creative and important theological work of the nineteenth century.

The leading theologians from the Protestant Faculty of Theology were Ferdinand Christian Baur (1792–1860) and Albert Ritschl (1822–1889). Both Baur and Ritschl developed an historical-critical approach to the study of the New Testament and early Christianity. Echoing the thought of Hegel, Baur, and subsequently Ritschl, envisioned early Christianity as beset by some basic conflicts (Peter and Jewish Christianity versus Paul and Gentile Christianity), which found resolution in the emergence of a "catholic" tradition in the second century. On the Catholic Faculty of Theology, Johann Sebastian von Drey (1777–1853) was the early leader and was followed closely by his former student, Johann Adam Möhler. Like their Protestant counterparts, both Möhler and Drey incorporated an historical and developmental approach to theology, and this methodology became a powerful resource for the further development of theology into the twentieth century.

The ecumenical setting of Tübingen forced Catholic theologians to provide historical grounds for their theological arguments regarding Church authority. This necessity had a twofold result. First, Catholic theologians were forced to come to terms with the historical development of the Christian tradition and could not simply appeal to papal or magisterial authority in their theology. Second, the presence of an established and dynamic Protestant Faculty of Theology required that in doing their historical research, Catholic theologians had to be prepared to concede the historical development of some of their convictions and thereby change the way they thought about and characterized Protestant doctrine and practice. The freedom of inquiry the university setting provided both faculties and the historical-critical methodologies they perfected in this setting made the Tübingen theologians dangerous in the eyes of many Catholic and Protestant authorities, but the erudition and honesty of the theologians also won them great respect, even if their conclusions did not always receive wide acceptance. For the leaders of the Catholic Faculty of Theology, their work would suffer as a result of the Thomistic revival at the end of the nineteenth century, but it would be vindicated as that revival began to incorporate a more historical outlook in the labors of luminaries like Henri de Lubac and others.

and the pope in the course of history rather than through the direct command of Christ.

Most scholars will trace a trajectory of maturation from Möhler's earlier writings, through his *Unity* and finally through the various revisions of his major work, *Symbolism*.[19] In *Symbolism*,

Möhler wrestled with the basic issue raised in the Reformation theologies of the sixteenth century: the relationship between human freedom and divine grace. In doing so, he was compelled to expand his ecclesiology beyond the historically and developmentally oriented account articulated in

Unity. He now constructed an ecclesiology that placed greater emphasis on the role of human freedom as the locus, or the place, in which God's grace was active in the world. In order to accomplish this, Möhler moved from a Spirit-centered ecclesiology (the approach developed in *Unity*) to an ecclesiology based on the union of the divine and human natures in Christ, or Christocentric ecclesiology.

In his Christocentric ecclesiology, Möhler brought together the dichotomy of the visible and invisible Church emphasized by the reformers. No longer were the visible structures of the Church allowed to dominate ecclesiology, and the temptation to reject these structures in favor of an abstract and spiritualized account of the Church was also eschewed. Rather, Möhler's integrated approach emphasized that the visible Church was the body of Christ in human history, a body constantly being made present in history in the form of humans. Möhler reasoned:

> Had that Word descended into the hearts of [human beings], without taking the form of servant, and accordingly without appearing in a corporeal shape, then only an internal, invisible Church would have been established. But since the Word became *flesh*, it expressed itself in an outward, perceptible, and human manner; it spoke as [a human being] to [human beings], and suffered and worked after the fashion of [human beings] in order to win them to the Kingdom of God; so that the means selected for the attainment of this object, fully corresponded to the general method of instruction and education determined by the nature and needs of [human beings].
>
> — *Symbolism*, 258

The Church then represents an extension of the Incarnation, and it is all ordered to the transformation of humans. We thus see the inclusion of an anthropology that will later become crucial in the development of ecclesiology. Möhler does not sacrifice or downplay the invisible reality of the Church in this. Rather, its visible reality is united to the invisible reality that is analogous to the divine nature in Christ. Such language also resonates with the words of Paul in 1 Corinthians in which the primary image of the Church is Christ's body. Möhler thus signaled the direction Roman Catholic ecclesiology would take in the century to come. Ecclesiology was to be more historically centered on the work of the Spirit, it was to emphasize the bond of love created by the Spirit that constitutes the Church as a communion, and finally, ecclesiology was to recover the image of Christ's Body in order to integrate visible and invisible aspects of the Church.

The Resurgence of Papal Power

Möhler's theological achievements exerted significant influence in the nineteenth century, but it was not until the middle of the twentieth century that his contributions to ecclesiology would fully flourish in the work of theologians such as Yves Congar and Henri de Lubac. Meanwhile, the nineteenth century was defined by the increasing tension between thoroughly secularized nation-states and a reinvigorated papacy.

The emergence of overt hostility to the Church from kings and newly formed republics as well as from anarchists and socialists moved popes such as Gregory XVI (pontificate 1831–1846) into a reactionary stance. In particular, the political climate in Rome and throughout Italy in general helped to marginalize the pope's political influence and stature. In an unfortunate development in the early part of Gregory's pontificate, he was confronted by a priest named Félicité Robert de Lamennais (1782–1854).

Early in his career, Lamennais was a celebrated philosopher and theologian who had been an outspoken critic of those who supported two causes: (1) indifferentism, or the idea that the state should be neutral in matters of religion, and (2) those who thought that the Church should be subordinate to the state. He wrote so eloquently and passionately that Pope Leo XII (pontificate 1823–1829) almost made him a cardinal. But subsequently, when the political fortunes of the Church in France and in Italy changed, Lamennais made bold appeals for religious liberty, freedom of conscience, and freedom of speech against those governmental authorities who sought to destroy the Church. These views, which some thought threatened the Church's power, were condemned when Lamennais presented them to the pope in 1832. In his encyclical letter *Mirari vos* (On Liberalism and Indifferentism; 1832), Pope Gregory XVI condemned freedom of speech, freedom of the press, and freedom of opinion as antithetical to Catholic teaching. Such a position created a significant backlash against the Church in Europe and eventually forced Lamennais outside the Church. The affair is one of the saddest of the early nineteenth century and set the tone in the Church for those who would seek to adapt to the new circumstances it now faced.[20]

Although Pius IX (pontificate 1846–1878) began his reign as pope with the intention of establishing a more moderate and tolerant attitude toward those who wanted a more secular form of government in Italy, he was soon driven to extremism when his overtures were met with violence and derision. When he finally gained control of his See (with the help of the French army), he began to reaffirm his predecessor's hostility toward the new politics of Europe. In the opening paragraph of his encyclical letter *Quanta cura* (Forbidding Traffic in Alms; 1864), one can easily identify the hostility of the pope and the urgency of his task of defeating political liberalism and the philosophical premises on which it rested. *Syllabus errorum* (The Syllabus of Errors), issued along with the encyclical letter,

enumerates the propositions the pope found to be dangerous and worthy of condemnation. Most of the propositions in the Syllabus are not explicitly theological; the erroneous positions touch upon the relationship between Church and state. In fact, even in the section on marriage, the issues tend to involve the relationship between Church and state rather than any issues of sacramental theology. The spirit of the times seemed to call for a robust defense of the Church against the encroachment of a thoroughgoing secularism that would subvert the social order established over the course of centuries, a social order that in many ways was established by the Church itself.

In the decades following the French Revolution (1789–1799) and the emerging secularism of many states in Europe, a growing conservative movement took root in many sectors of Europe and the Americas. This movement led to a rebirth in Benedictine monasticism and a renewed flourishing of religious life and reform of the liturgy. Along with this conservative movement came an attitude of deference to the Holy See, to Rome. In France its adherents were labeled *ultramontane*, because they looked "beyond the mountains (the Alps)" to Rome for leadership and direction. With the rise of ultramontanism, a renewed flourishing of religious life, and the threat of militant and totalitarian secular states, there emerged an opportunity to define more sharply the role of the Church, and the role of the papacy, in modern society. This opportunity was seized when Pius IX called the First Vatican Council (1869–1870).

The initial draft of the council documents on the Church reflected the theological contributions of theologians, such as Möhler, who moved beyond the standard Counter-Reformation ecclesiology of Bellarmine. The use of language like "Mystical Body of Christ" in these initial drafts signaled the emergence of a new ecclesiology, even though most of the rest of the document went on to treat questions of papal infallibility and church-state relations. The council fathers (the bishops present at the council) were not well disposed to the new theological tone and opted to remove the language of "Mystical Body" and instead focused on the visible structures of the Church. In the political maneuverings at the council, and throughout subsequent drafts of the text, the council decided that an initial document on papal primacy and papal infallibility would be followed by a separate document on the Church. However, the council was quickly disbanded in 1870 with the outbreak of the Franco-Prussian War and the corresponding departure of French troops from Rome. In the end, only *Pastor aeternus* (The First Constitution on the Church of Christ), the document that focused on the papacy, was approved, thus reinforcing the centrality (or the eccentricity) of the papacy in Roman Catholic ecclesiology.

Although the intention of the council fathers was to locate the definition of papal infallibility within the nature of the Church itself, the contingencies that framed the document and the inability to draft and approve the subsequent document on the nature of the Church itself, hampered that intention. The bulk of *Pastor aeternus* treats the issue of papal power and jurisdiction, although it insists in chapter 3 that this power does not impede the power and jurisdiction of local bishops (an important point of discussion at the Second Vatican Council). In chapter 4, however, one finds the crucial teaching on papal infallibility.

> [W]hen the Roman pontiff speaks ex cathedra, that is, when, in the exercise of his office as shepherd and teacher of all Christians, in virtue of his supreme apostolic authority, he defines a doctrine concerning faith or morals to be held by the whole Church, he possesses, by the divine assistance promised to him in blessed Peter, that infallibility which the divine Redeemer willed his Church to enjoy in defining doctrine concerning faith or morals. Therefore, such definitions of the Roman pontiff are of themselves, and not by the consent of the Church, irreformable.
>
> — *PASTOR AETERNUS* 4. 9.[21]

The statement was devised, in part, as a response to the growing philosophical pessimism regarding human knowledge and authority: how can we know anything? Vatican I made important statements about the cultivation of right reason and the harmony between faith and reason, but it also made an appeal to the authority of divine revelation and the place of the Church, and especially the pope, in receiving and defining that revelation. The council was making a concerted effort to supply the faithful with a sure foothold on truth by grounding it in the ministry of the Church. According to the constitution, although the pope exercises the charism of infallibility by virtue of his office, the charism *belongs* to the Church as a whole.[22]

Unfortunately, the absence of the second constitution on the Church leaves the statement on papal infallibility somewhat uncentered, and some might even say that it is eccentric (out of the center). The legacy of this situation is an increased emphasis on papal teaching authority and an expansion of the role of the papacy in ecclesiology and in the practical life of the Church. In the age of emerging superpowers (all-powerful nation-states under the absolute leadership of a centralized bureaucracy), the Church had come to model itself on what it feared most. The Church thus became a counter-state, a counter-government. Its teachings were guaranteed by the power of reason and the charism of infallibility, a charism that, over time, seemed to creep beyond the tight definition offered in *Pastor aeternus*. Only in the course of the twentieth century would greater balance emerge in the discussion of the papacy in relation to bishops and the rest of the Church. This was accomplished through the work of theologians and bishops at the Second Vatican Council (1962–1965) and beyond.

CONCLUSION

The development of ecclesiology over the centuries has been far more complex and subtle than the presentation in this chapter might suggest. The rise and fall of the Church's power and influence over the course of two millennia has had a dramatic impact on ecclesiology and the Church's exercise of its mission in the world. In this chapter, a basic line of development has been plotted through the various epochs of Church history, and one should be cautious about valorizing or vilifying any one epoch or any set of developments. This history is both beautiful and ugly at the same time; every age has contributed something important to the discussion of what the Church is, how it works to promote redemption, and what it must become. Yet, each age has also fallen short, even the early followers of Jesus, for the Church recognizes itself as always a work in progress, a pilgrim on a journey. Perhaps it is this realization, articulated so well by Möhler, that begins to characterize reflection on the Church in the twentieth and the twenty-first centuries and that begins to renew the Church's focus on its mission in the world.

Questions for Understanding

1. How does Paul understand the Church? What is the importance of the word *koinonia* in Paul's theology of the Church?
2. Compare and contrast approaches to the Church taken by each of the four evangelists.
3. What were the contributions to ecclesiology made by Cyprian? By Augustine?
4. What factors contributed to the rise of papal power during the Middle Ages?
5. Compare and contrast the approach to ecclesiology in the Reformation with that of Robert Bellarmine.
6. What was Johann Adam Möhler's contribution to ecclesiology?
7. What political and cultural circumstances contributed to the definition of papal infallibility at Vatican I?

Questions for Reflection

1. From the Middle Ages to the present, the Church has always struggled with its relationship to the state. What, in your opinion, are the reasons for this struggle? Should the Church have a stake in the workings of the state? What limitations ought either the Church or the state put on the Church's relationship to the state?
2. Throughout the chapter, the Church is shown to adopt the social form, the social structures, in which it is located. For example, the Church begins to look a lot like the Roman Empire

in the early centuries. In the Middle Ages, the Church is organized along the lines of a feudal system. In the nineteenth century, the Church begins to look like a totalitarian state. What is the dominant social form today, and how does the Church reflect that form?

3. The emphasis placed on the power of the papacy within Roman Catholic ecclesiology often causes concern among Catholics and non-Catholics alike. Given some of the infamous popes in the history of the Church, is such an emphasis problematic, or does the virtue of the pope make any difference when discussing his authority or his power? Explain your response, and include examples from the text or from additional research.

Suggestions for Further Study

Dietrich, Donald J. and Michael Himes. Editors. *The Legacy of the Tübingen School: The Relevance of Nineteenth Century Theology for the Twenty-first Century.*

This collection of essays from renowned American and European scholars wrestles with the achievement of the nineteenth-century Catholic theologians from the University of Tübingen, especially Möhler, and assesses the significance of these achievements for understanding theology today.

Gonzales, Justo L. *The Story of Christianity.* 2 Volumes. Nashville, TN: Abingdon, 1984.

This work has become a standard introduction to Church history in many theology programs throughout the United States. It offers a consistent narrative of two thousand years of Church history.

Noll, Mark A. *Turning Points: Decisive Moments in the History of Christianity.* Second Edition. Grand Rapids, MI: Baker, 2000.

This book recounts twelve decisive moments in the history of the Church; written by an eminent evangelical scholar.

Prusak, Bernard. *The Church Unfinished: Ecclesiology through the Centuries.* New York: Paulist, 2004.

Prusak offers a remarkably concise yet thorough overview of Church history and ecclesiology. It is well documented but accessible.

Endnotes

1. For an excellent discussion of the emergence of the Christian community and its relationship to early Judaism, see James Dunn, *The Partings of the Ways between Christianity and Judaism and Their Significance for the Character of Christianity*, Second Edition (London: SCM, 2006). For an alternative view, see Mark Goodman and Annette Yoshiko Reed, eds., *The Ways That Never Parted: Jews and Christians in Late Antiquity and the Early Middle Ages* (Minneapolis, MN: Fortress, 2007).

2. This was the point of emphasis in works such as Albert Schweitzer's seminal work, *The Mysticism of Paul the Apostle* (Baltimore, MD: Johns Hopkins University Press, 1998). It is echoed in contemporary Pauline scholarship in James Dunn's *The Theology of Paul the Apostle* (Grand Rapids, MI: Eerdmans, 1998), 390–412.

3. John Meier, "The Circle of the Twelve: Did It Exist during Jesus' Public Ministry?" *Journal of Biblical Literature* 116 (1997): 635–672.

4. For a discussion of the deutero-Pauline character of these documents, see Werner G. Kummel, *Introduction to the New Testament* (Nashville, TN: Abingdon: 1975), 340–345; 357–363; 370–384.

5. Graham Stanton, *A Gospel for a New People* (Louisville, KY: Westminster John Knox, 1992). Although

Stanton does not offer an overriding theme in his interpretation of the Gospel, his studies reflect concern for Matthew's new and distinctive community and its relationship to the synagogue and to the world.

6. Frank Matera, "Theologies of the Church in the New Testament," in *The Gift of the Church: A Textbook on Ecclesiology in Honor of Patrick Granfield, OSB*, ed. Peter Phan (Collegeville, MN: Liturgical Press, 2000), 3–21, at 6.

7. For what follows, see the classic study by Raymond Brown, *The Gospel according to John*, vol. 1, Anchor Bible Commentary (New York: Doubleday, 1970), 510–512.

8. *Pastoral Care* 1. 3; 2. 6.

9. These reforms, known as the "Carolingian Reforms," are well described by Eugen Ewig in "Part One: The Church Under Lay Domination," in H. Jedin and J. Dolan, eds., *Handbook of Church History*, vol. 3, *The Church in the Age of Feudalism* (New York: Herder and Herder, 1969), 1–193.

10. English translation from S. Z. Ehler and J. B. Morrall, *Church and State through the Centuries* (Westminster, MD: Newman Press, 1954), 43–44.

11. R. W. Dyson, *James of Viterbo: On Christian Government* (Woodbridge, UK: Boydell Press, 1995).

12. For a more nuanced reading of Torquemada's ecclesiology, see Thomas M. Izbicki, *Protector of the Faith: Cardinal Johannes de Turrecremata and the Defense of the Institutional Church* (Washington, DC: Catholic University of America Press, 1981).

13. For a thorough presentation of the conciliarist tradition, see F. Oakley, *The Conciliarist Tradition: Constitutionalism in the Catholic Church, 1300–1870* (Oxford: Oxford University Press, 2003).

14. See, for example, Luther's *Letter to the Christian Nobility of the German Nation* (1520).

15. *Letter on the Anabaptists* (1528), trans. P. Schaff, *History of the Christian Church*, vol. 7 (New York: Scribners, 1910), 530.

16. Martin Luther, *On the Bondage of the Will*, trans. P. Watson, *Luther's Works*, vol. 33 (Philadelphia, PA: Fortress, 1972), 71.

17. John Calvin, *Institutes of the Christian Religion*, trans. F. L. Battles (Philadelphia: Westminster, 1960), 1021.

18. Johann Adam Möhler, *Unity in the Church, or The Principle of Catholicism Presented in the Spirit of the Church Fathers of the First Three Centuries*, ed. and trans. P. C. Erb (Washington, DC: Catholic University of America Press, 1996).

19. Johann Adam Möhler, *Symbolism*, Milestones in Catholic Theology, trans. J. B. Robertson (New York: Crossroads, 1997).

20. For a brief but insightful summary of the dynamics of the Lamennais affair presented in light of the publication of the correspondence surrounding the case against Lamennais, see Joseph N. Moody, "The Condemnation of Lamennais: A New Dossier," *Theological Studies* 44 (1983): 123–130.

21. Excerpt translated by Norman Tanner, *The Decrees of the Ecumenical Councils*, 2 vols. (Washington, DC: Georgetown, 1990), 816.

22. For an excellent contemporary discussion of papal infallibility, see Francis A. Sullivan, *Creative Fidelity: Weighing and Interpreting Documents of the Magisterium* (Eugene, OR: Wipf and Stock, 2003), 80–92. For a history of the doctrine of papal infallibility, see Brian Tierney, *Origins of Papal Infallibility, 1150–1350: A Study of the Concepts of Infallibility, Sovereignty, and Tradition*, Second Edition (Leiden: Brill, 1988).

CHAPTER 4

The Second Vatican Council

For most students today, Catholic or otherwise, the Second Vatican Council probably seems about as relevant as the Council of Trent. Yet the Second Vatican Council stands out as a defining event in the history of the Church, and its deliberations, personalities, and documents have shaped its place in the world. As Joseph Komonchak, the eminent American authority on Vatican II, and other historians of the council are fond of saying, Vatican II was an event.[1] And that event became a turning point in Church history. While the documents of Vatican II play a central and decisive role in any interpretation, the council cannot be reduced to a set of texts. An authentic interpretation of the council must include an understanding of its origins, its implementation, and its reception. The personalities, discussions, disputations, and negotiations that took place at the council had a discernable and lasting impact on the universal Church, and it is only by recounting the basic contours of these exchanges that an adequate appreciation and interpretation may be realized.

THE CHURCH IN THE YEARS LEADING UP TO THE COUNCIL

The sixteenth century challenged and changed the face of Europe decisively, and the Catholic Church engaged those changes robustly and creatively. Nevertheless, in the wake of the upheavals of the sixteenth century, the Catholic Church also labored to keep up with the times. The Reformation eventually gave way to the Enlightenment, the rise of secularism (the neat division of the world into the public realm of the secular and the private realm of the religious), and the advent of industrialization. In the midst of these developments, the Church struggled to find its voice and to creatively engage the many changes that were beginning to define Western culture. It was not until the mid-nineteenth century that the Church took a more robust stance in response to these developments—a stance that was ultimately defensive. Elements within the Church, however, were exploring a more constructive and optimistic engagement with the developments of the modern world, and these elements helped to create the conditions that made the Second Vatican Council possible.

The Modernist Controversy

The panic that had taken hold of the Church in the nineteenth century amid the rise of secularism reached a fever pitch at the dawn of the twentieth century. During the pontificate of Pius X (pontificate 1903–1914), the social, political, and philosophical spirit of the nineteenth century was summarized by Rome under the term *modernism*. Although there was no official movement that labeled itself modernist, the pope, in essence, created a "heresy" out of a pastiche of the cultural and intellectual tendencies of the day that included the following:

- a critical view of Scripture based on history and comparative literature
- a rejection of scholasticism and its account of the harmony between faith and reason in favor of an emphasis on religious feeling or sentiment
- emphasis on the complete autonomy of the natural and human sciences
- a teleological view of history that privileges the revelatory character of an event in its consequences rather than in its origins

According to officials in Rome, the modernist movement had infiltrated the Church, and several prominent intellectuals were accused of sympathizing with and supporting the movement, including such luminaries as Alfred Loisy, George Tyrrell, and Friedrich von Hügel.[2]

Unlike the "heresies" of past centuries, no manifesto, no statement of heretical doctrine, and no individual could be easily identified with modernism. For Pius X, and many others, modernism was the outgrowth of the so-called Protestant heresy. The Reformation had morphed into the Enlightenment in the eighteenth century, and the Reformation's attack on church authority had given rise to two complementary movements: rationalism and secularism. These two movements combined to marginalize the voice of the Christian churches throughout the world. Of particular importance in the nineteenth century was the rise of thoroughly secular states in Europe and the Americas. In these states, the Church was disestablished and lost all influence and prestige. Throughout the nineteenth century and especially in the early twentieth century, Catholic leaders made a concerted effort to employ rhetoric and to pursue policies that would bring back the medieval ideal of "Christendom"—a vision of Europe united and directed by a single faith and a single shepherd. This rhetoric presupposed that civil society could not function unless the Church provided the foundation for that society.

As a new form of civil society emerged, one that had no explicit concern for the Catholic Church or religion in general, Church officials in Rome responded with what has been described as "catastrophic eschatology."[3] Joseph Komonchak suggests that the first encyclical letter from Pope Pius X, the archenemy of modernism, offers a perfect example of this catastrophic rhetoric. A portion of the encyclical provides a sufficient example:

> [T]here is good reason to fear that this great perversity may be as it were a foretaste and perhaps the beginning of the evils reserved for the last days and the "Son of Perdition" of whom the apostle speaks (2 Thessalonians 2:3) may already be in the world. Such, in truth, is the audacity and the wrath employed everywhere in persecuting religion, in combating dogmas of the faith, in brazen efforts to uproot and destroy all relations between human beings and the Divinity! While, on the other hand, and this according to the same apostle is the distinguishing mark of Antichrist, man has with infinite temerity put himself in the place of God, raising himself above all that is called God; in such wise that although he cannot utterly extinguish in himself all knowledge of God, he has contemned God's majesty and, as it were, made of the universe a temple wherein he himself is to be adored.

— *E SUPREMI*
[ON THE RESTORATION OF ALL THINGS IN CHRIST], NO. 5

Such rhetoric was used to galvanize the faithful in order to battle against the forces of evil, the forces of secularism. This battle was to be fought through the cultivation of a distinctive Roman Catholic subculture that would resist the powers of secularism and the encroaching power of the state.[4]

One important tool in the promotion of the Catholic subculture (really a counterculture) was a distinctively Catholic devotionalism. In particular, devotions to the Blessed Mother were popularized, given official sanction, and co-opted in what was viewed as the fight against the evils of the modern world, especially against communism. Although Marian devotions had a long history in the Church, late-nineteenth- and early-twentieth-century Catholicism gave birth to a new form of devotion, one that was anchored in the catastrophic rhetoric of Pius X's encyclical. Mary was interpreted as "the woman clothed with the sun" in Revelation 12 and as the enemy of Satan. Devotion to the Blessed Mother became a source of comfort for many Catholics even while she was the great champion against the forces of secularism and communism. Other devotions also had significant cultural and political dimensions, especially such ones as "Christ the King." Honoring Christ as "king" sent a powerful and unambiguous message to the secularists: Christ is the true king, and Catholics are devoted to this king and not to secular rulers. These devotions with their strong political overtones flourished among the faithful, particularly when they were joined to various fraternal and devotional associations.

Like many of the devotional practices just mentioned, Catholic associations usually started as grassroots organizations founded as support networks for Catholics in an increasingly hostile secular environment. These associations were often oriented to some form of activism — supporting those in need, advocating for justice, and providing fellowship. The hierarchy eventually used them as a means of advocating for the rights of the Catholic Church and promoting a distinctive Catholic identity and subculture.

As the governments of the new secular nation-states had become centralized and bureaucratized, so did the Church. Throughout the nineteenth and well through the twentieth century, the role of local and national ecclesial bodies began to be usurped by papal powers and interventions by nuncios (the pope's ambassador or representative in a particular country) or through the Vatican's bureaucracy, the Roman Curia. In some ways, the pope began to take on the role of chief executive

Pius IX and the Ordinary Magisterium of the Church

During the nineteenth century and into the twentieth century, the Vatican placed a growing emphasis on the power and authority of Rome in theological matters. The centralization of teaching authority was accompanied by stricter controls on the work of theologians. Part of this centralization can be seen in Pius IX's letter to German theologians concerning their debates about the obligatory nature of recent pronouncements that had come from Rome. Many theologians were insisting that they were only obligated to adhere to those things that were solemnly defined as infallible, but the pope insisted on their obligation to strictly adhere to all those things set forth by the "ordinary Magisterium" (noninfallible teachings included).

> We desire to reassure ourselves that they did not mean to limit the obligation, which strictly binds Catholic teachers and writers, to those things only which are proposed by the infallible judgment of the Church as dogmas of faith to be believed by everybody. In a like manner, we are convinced that it was not their intention to state that the perfect adherence to revealed truths (which they regard as absolutely necessary for true progress in science and for refuting errors) can be maintained, if the submission of faith is given only to those dogmas expressly defined by the Church. The reason for this is the following: even supposing that we are treating of that subjection which is to be made by an explicit act of divine faith, this must not be limited to those things which have been defined in the express decrees of the ecumenical councils or of the Roman Pontiffs of this See; but it must also be extended to those things which, through the ordinary [Magisterium] of the whole Church throughout the world, are proposed as divinely revealed and, as a result, by universal and constant consent of Catholic theologians are held to be matters of faith.

— *Tuas libenter* [Letter to the Archbishop of Munich Dec. 21, 1863][5]

The pope's concern is to safeguard the integrity of the faith. What Christians believe and are obliged to believe transcend merely those things that have been set forth infallibly by ecumenical councils or by the pope. The matters of faith that were solemnly defined at ecumenical councils were not merely pious opinions before their solemn definition by a council. A good example of this might be the canon of Scripture. Although it was not precisely defined until the Council of Trent in the sixteenth century, it would have been deeply problematic for someone in the Middle Ages to deny that the Gospel of John was holy and inspired by God, because by the Middle Ages there was a consensus on this matter.

of a worldwide organization, complete with its own infrastructure and its own laws, the *Codex iuris canonici* (Code of Canon Law).

The systematic codification of Church law at the turn of the twentieth century represented a major development. Previously, Canon Law had been, in some ways, a collection of ad hoc pronouncements. It was a legal tradition in which the canons (regulations or dogmas) of various synods and councils were placed alongside pontifical pronouncements as well as the pronouncements made by important bishops. Although these decrees had been collected and edited at various points in the history of the Church, most notably by the medieval monk Gratian (c. 1100s), it was not until the pontificate of Pius X (early 1900s) that the legal system of the Church was codified along the lines of the Napoleonic Code. The result was a set of clear laws for the government of the Church through a centralized bureaucracy and court system—powerful and efficient.

The theological scene in the late nineteenth and early twentieth centuries was hampered by the demise of Catholic theology through the eighteenth and into the early nineteenth century. The situation created a vacuum just when the Church needed powerful and creative theological resources with which to engage the social and cultural movements of the day. Instead, centralization was applied to theology, and the powers of the Vatican enforced greater conformity and uniformity.

The threat of modernism was seen by Rome as the synthesis of all heresies, against which the Church must fight, and it viewed its seminaries and universities as the places most in danger. It was to these educational settings that the officials in Rome turned their attention, for it was in them that some ferment was beginning. At this time, papal encyclicals became longer, more frequent, and more directive (even juridical) in tone. Officials in Rome, including the pope (particularly Pius X), encouraged bishops to become especially vigilant in monitoring intellectual activity in their dioceses.

In his 1907 encyclical *Pascendi dominici gregis* (On the Doctrines of the Modernists), Pius X helped to establish some of the most rigid controls on theological activity ever seen in Church history. Censorship, monitoring, and reporting of suspected modernists were encouraged and even demanded in the encyclical.[6] This encyclical was supplemented by *Sacrorum antistitum* (Oath against Modernism; 1910), an oath required of all clergy, religious, and seminary professors. The effect of these actions was to put a chokehold on the intellectual life of the Church.

Yet paranoia and punishment did not entirely rule the day. A renewed interest in the thought of the medieval theologian Thomas Aquinas (Leo XIII, *Aeterni Patris*, On the Restoration of Christian Philosophy; 1879) had given rise to a distinctively Christian philosophy. This in turn prompted an emerging theological renaissance. Though sponsored by Rome as a means of combating secularized education and secularized accounts of reason, this rebirth would also provide some of the most robust challenges to the centralized and combative spirit of the day.

Signs of the Impending Renewal

The seeds for renewal had been sprouting for more than a century by the time Vatican II was convened. In fact, a major resurgence in religious life occurred in the nineteenth century with the founding anew of several monasteries that had been abolished in the previous century. Of special importance was the revival of Benedictine monasticism in Europe, which sowed the seeds of liturgical renewal.[7]

The celebration of the liturgy had succumbed to destructive tendencies (inaudible celebrants, distracted and disconnected congregations, disorder in the liturgical calendar, the deterioration of the liturgical arts), and there was widespread appreciation of the resulting negative consequences. As early as the 1830s, there was a movement afoot in France, Belgium, and Germany to reestablish recently disbanded monastic communities. Of particular interest in this regard is the work of Prosper Guéranger (1805–1875), the Frenchman who founded the Benedictine monastery at Solesmes. He was a prolific writer who was fond of historical study in his efforts to reinstitute the liturgy and to recover ancient practices such as Gregorian chant. An interesting man with a strong ultramontane sensibility (he constantly looked to Rome for guidance), Guéranger, nonetheless, wanted to reform the liturgy, particularly by weeding out local customs that had been inserted into it in order to comply with the practices of the Church in Rome.

Subsequent efforts in Belgium and Germany helped to further the liturgical movement, and Pius X, by almost any standard a conservative pope, authored some important liturgical innovations in the first year of his pontificate. Of special note is a document that acknowledged the liturgical abuses and the need to bring about the full and active participation of the people. In the introduction to this document, the pope asserts the connection between a vital Church and full lay participation in the liturgy.

> Filled as We are with a most ardent desire to see the true Christian spirit flourish in every respect and be preserved by all the faithful, We deem it necessary to provide before anything else for the sanctity and dignity of the temple, in which the faithful assemble for no other object than that of acquiring this spirit from its foremost and indispensable font, which is the active participation in the most holy mysteries and in the public and solemn prayer of the Church.
>
> — INTER SOLLICITUDINES
> [INSTRUCTION ON SACRED MUSIC][8]

This emphasis on lay participation in the liturgy had far-reaching effects. In the United States, the Benedictine monk Virgil Michel (1890–1938), from the Benedictine Abbey of St. John's in Collegeville, a small town near St. Cloud, Minnesota, launched a socially conscious form of the liturgical movement. For Michel, four principles had to govern authentic liturgical reform:

- Full participation of the laity in the liturgy could build church communities through service and love.
- The liturgy must emerge out of the concrete lives of its participants, and it must enable people to return to their lives.
- Marginalized, suffering laity must receive hope for their lives in the liturgy.
- The liturgy must fully express the faith of the Church and, therefore, safeguard the dignity of the individual and the importance of the community.

As the liturgical movement matured, it emphasized the dignity of the laity and the necessity of their full and active participation in the liturgy. Through the work of Michel and others, the Church affirmed that the formation of the laity in the liturgy was crucial in order for the Church to live its mission in the world. The liturgical movement, therefore, became an important precursor to the developments in ecclesiology that would be enshrined in the documents of the Second Vatican Council.

While the importance of the liturgical renewal for ecclesiology cannot be overestimated, the renewal was accompanied by other important ecclesiological shifts that took place during the pontificate of an otherwise conservative figure, Pius XII (pontificate 1939–1958). The renewal of religious life and the liturgy, and the emphasis on the laity that was emerging throughout the Church in the Catholic Action movement,

The Emergence of Liturgical Scholarship

The liturgical movement was aided by the historical studies that emerged in the early decades of the twentieth century. Perhaps no figure was as important to the movement as the Austrian Jesuit, Joseph Jungmann (1889–1975). Jungmann wrote a masterful study of the liturgy titled *The Mass of the Roman Rite*, in which he set forth the history of the liturgy and helped to prepare the way for the liturgical reforms of the council. Additionally, the promotion of intensive congresses on liturgy and worship, called "liturgical weeks," gave rise to academic programs in the study of the liturgy, the most notable of which was the program at the University of Notre Dame that emerged shortly after World War II.

spurred an encyclical that signaled a significant change in ecclesiology.

The year 1943 saw the publication of two important encyclicals from Pius XII, encyclicals that might not appear, at first glance, to be related to one another: *Mystici corporis Christi* (The Mystical Body of Christ) and *Divino afflante spiritu* (Promoting Biblical Studies). The former discussed the nature of the Church, the latter the state of biblical studies. However, both encyclicals ushered in a more historically conscious—even arguably a more *incarnational*—approach to divine revelation and the work of God in history.

Divino afflante spiritu addressed the precarious state of Catholic biblical scholarship in the twentieth century, in which biblical scholars who took a historical approach to the Bible were often viewed with suspicion by Roman authorities and labeled as modernists. *Divino afflante spiritu* provided a significant endorsement of what were designated historical critical approaches to Scripture by calling on biblical

scholars to understand the historical and cultural context within which the human authors were operating when they composed the sacred books.

What is the literal sense of a passage is not always as obvious in the speeches and writings of the ancient authors of the East, as it is in the works of our own time. For what they wished to express is not to be determined by the rules of grammar and philology alone, nor solely by the context; the interpreter must, as it were, go back wholly in spirit to those remote centuries of the East and with the aid of history, archaeology, ethnology, and other sciences, accurately determine what modes of writing, so to speak, the authors of that ancient period would be likely to use, and in fact did use.

— *DIVINO AFFLANTE SPIRITU*, NO. 35

Such an admission of historically conditioned revelation was of great consequence because it helped to move revelation and the life of the Church into a more historical context—seeing God as active within human history and as such, justifying robust historical investigation and reflection and no longer viewing these as antithetical to Christian accounts of revelation. This move was to pave the way for much of the innovation accomplished at the Second Vatican Council and renewal of a more historical approach to the Church's self-understanding and its mission in the world.

In *Mystici corporis Christi*, Pius XII placed front and center the image of the Church as "the mystical Body of Christ." This image had been developed extensively by Johann Möhler in the nineteenth century and was also used by Leo XIII in his encyclicals: *Satis cognitum* (On the Unity of the Church; 1896) and *Divinum illud munus* (On Christian Education; 1897). While Pius XII did not abandon the Counter-Reformation emphasis on the visible structures of the Church, he did integrate these structures with a more holistic account of the Church, one that emphasized collaboration of the laity and the hierarchy.

> And so We desire that all who claim the Church as their mother, should seriously consider that not only the clergy and those who have consecrated themselves to God in the religious life, but the other members of the Mystical Body of Jesus Christ as well have, each in his degree, the obligation of working hard and constantly for the building up and increase of this Body. We wish this to be borne in mind especially by members of Catholic Action who assist the Bishops and the priests in their apostolic labors—and to their praise be it said, they do realize it—and also by those members of pious associations which work for the same end.
>
> — Mystici corporis Christi, no. 98

Such an emphasis on the union of hierarchy and laity was intrinsic to the image of the Mystical Body, and this image had the power to turn attention to the relationship of the Catholic Church to those who were beyond its visible boundaries. For example, the pope made special reference to those who were not part of the visible Church:

> We do not deny, rather from a heart filled with gratitude to God We admit, that even in our turbulent times there are many who, though outside the fold of Jesus Christ, look to the Church as the only haven of salvation.
>
> — Mystici corporis Christi, no. 3

While all of this has precedence in the long history of the Church, these two encyclicals, along with the work of the liturgical movement and other movements, helped to prepare the way for the council. These events provided the groundwork, yet nothing could have really prepared anyone for the announcement of the council itself—it was entirely unexpected and even traumatic for some.

EVENTS AT THE COUNCIL

Any account of the achievement of Vatican II has to include at least a brief narrative of the events that took place at the council. After all, as was stated above, Vatican II is not simply a set of documents. The documents produced by the council can only be properly understood when read against the backdrop of the discussions and controversies at the council sessions. The following brief overview of the sessions is provided so that the reader might better understand the significance of two of the major documents: *Lumen gentium* (The Dogmatic Constitution on the Church) and *Gaudium et spes* (The Pastoral Constitution of the Church in the Modern World). If the council was primarily about the Church, then the council sessions themselves give a sense of how at least some of the most important parts of the Church operated.[9]

Key Dates in Preparations for the Council (1959–1960)

* October 28, 1958—Giovanni Giuseppe Angelo Roncalli, Cardinal Archbishop of Venice, elected as Pope John XXIII
* January 25, 1959—Announcement of the Council (Basilica of Saint Paul Outside the Walls)
* February 5, 1959—Formation of the Pre-Preparatory Commission, made up entirely

of Roman officials and placed under the leadership of the Vatican Secretary of State, Cardinal Tardini

- June 5, 1960—Formation of the Central Preparatory Commission along with the ten commissions that would handle the different thematic issues identified by the Pre-Preparatory Commission
- December 25, 1961—Formal convocation of the Council (*Humanae salutis*)
- February 2, 1962—Closing of the formal preparatory phase and marking October 11, 1962, as the opening of the council

The Plan for Order at the Council

There was no real template for running a council. Consensus demanded that the procedures of Vatican I be used as a model, but over time and in the course of deliberations, this model would prove clumsy. A general outline of the council's working structure looked like this:

- **Plenary sessions** (Saint Peter's Basilica) would meet in the mornings; Mass would be celebrated, and the council fathers would discuss issues related to the work of the commissions.
- **Working groups** (off-site), or commissions, would draft documents to reflect the wishes of the council fathers as expressed in plenary sessions.
- **Solemn Sessions** (Saint Peter's Basilica) would be when votes were cast on the documents. Council fathers could vote *placet* (approve), *non placet* (reject), or *placet iuxta modum* (conditionally approve). To pass, documents required a two-thirds majority vote from the fathers.
- **Council of Presidents** (at first, ten cardinals and then later twelve), assisted by a general secretary, headed each of the commissions.

These were designated by the pope, who would then select eight bishops for the commission while the council fathers would elect the sixteen other members from among their numbers.

- *Periti*, or theological experts, were also selected to assist the commissions with their work. *Periti* (such as Joseph Ratzinger, Karl Rahner, Yves Congar, John Courtney Murray) could not vote, though they exerted considerable influence.
- **Observers** from Protestant and Orthodox churches were invited to witness the council proceedings, but their influence and participation in the deliberations were obvious if unofficial. Additionally, after the first session, several representatives of women's religious communities and laywomen attended the council as "auditors" and made significant contributions to the discussions. Only one layperson was ever allowed to address the assembly of bishops. Patrick Keegan addressed the bishops on the connection between the schema on the Church and the working document on the laity.

Key Developments in Preparations for the Council (1959–1960)

The announcement of the council was a total surprise to the Roman Curia as well as the rest of the world. So much was this the case that official journals managed to ignore the announcement for the better part of 1959. It was apparent that the need for a general or ecumenical council was not recognized by most of the Vatican bureaucracy.

The struggle for the council began almost immediately. Alfredo Cardinal Ottaviani headed the Holy Office (the office responsible for enforcing doctrine), and he vied with several others, especially Augustin Cardinal Bea of the newly formed Secretariat for the Promotion of Christian Unity, for influence in setting the agenda and outlook of the council. Ottaviani wanted a doctrinal council and prepared several texts that reflected this concern, including a new formula for the Profession of Faith, and documents on the deposit of faith, the moral order, the social order, the Blessed Mother, and on marriage, family, and virginity.

Secrecy during the preparatory proceedings had a negative impact on the preparations for the council. The famous French Dominican theologian Yves Congar, who was part of this work, would later remark that because the Roman theologians and bishops knew one another, they could freely speak about the preparatory work with one another, while those who were not part of the Vatican bureaucracy were left in a cloud of secrecy and silence. They could speak freely to no one, and the upshot was a "Roman" preparation for the council.

During this period, Pope John XXIII ensured that three features of the council began to materialize: (1) the council was to be ecumenical but was not to be dominated by the issue of Christian unity; (2) the council was to privilege a pastoral (rather than a dogmatic or doctrinal) approach to topics; (3) the council was to operate in freedom as a deliberative body (it was not to be dominated or controlled by the Roman Curia or the pope).

The First Session (Autumn 1962)

The preparatory period had been marked by attempts to control the council's agenda. The Doctrinal Commission, in particular, exercised a kind of hegemony over the other commissions, and its head, Alfredo Cardinal Ottaviani, the Prefect of the Holy Office, wielded enormous power. The documents prepared for the bishops reflected the Doctrinal Commission's concern to complete the agenda of Vatican I, that is, they wanted to offer an ecclesiology that would complement *Pastor aeternis* (Dogmatic Constitution on the Church of Christ). To the extent that the Doctrinal Commission was able, it subsumed the pope's concerns about addressing the modern world in a series of polemical documents that often reaffirmed the triumphalism and antagonism that was consistent with the modernist crisis. When the agenda had been crafted and presented to the council fathers, there was alarm, and a revolt began to unfold against the Doctrinal Commission and the Holy Office.

Pope John XXIII's opening remarks set the tone for the council's work in the first session.[10] As the pope stood in St. Peter's Basilica, surrounded by his closest advisors and by members of the Curia who had constructed the documents that the council fathers were preparing to discuss, he issued a dramatic rebuttal of the "prophets of doom." These prophets were those who held on tenaciously to the rhetoric of apocalyptic confrontation with the modern world. The pope's agenda of "updating," or *aggiornamento*, was under attack in the preparations for the council, and the pope was determined to ensure that the council would not simply renew the acrimonious relationship with the modern world enshrined in documents such as Pius X's *Pascendi dominici gregis* (Syllabus Condemning the Errors of Modernists). It was clear that the pope wanted the council to function as a deliberative—not merely consultative—body. His vision for the council was put to the test almost immediately.

At the council's first working session, on October 13, 1962, two days after its ceremonial opening, plans were made to take an immediate vote to establish the commissions that would work through the various documents the council would produce. However, Cardinal Frings (Germany) and Cardinal Liénart (France), two prominent members of the College of Cardinals, intervened in order to postpone the vote.[11] They believed that the bishops who gathered for the council had not had sufficient time to get to know one another and to discuss the issues at hand in order for the council to function as the pope seemed to have indicated. The vote to establish commissions at this point would have forced the majority of the bishops present simply to vote for those bishops who had been part of the various preparatory commissions. If that was to be the case, then what need was there for a council? The documents of the preparatory commissions would have remained largely intact. The intervention of Liénart and Frings was successful, and the eventual vote for the commission represented a blend of preparatory commission members and other council fathers.

As the council began, it became apparent that virtually none of the draft documents could serve as adequate bases for preliminary discussion and debate. The only exception was the document on the liturgy. The reform of the liturgy had been under way for a century, and all agreed that further reformation was needed.[12] The draft document was approved as the basis for further (contentious) discussion. As for the other documents, they had to be completely redrafted. Though there appeared to be general agreement on the inadequacy of the draft documents, there was no unanimity on what the council should say; and so the council truly became a deliberative body, with bishops and their theological advisors seeking to influence and cajole one another.

Although some council fathers had hoped that only one session would be needed, the events that took place in the autumn of 1962 indicated that new draft documents were required, and this work was undertaken that winter and in the spring of 1963. The discussions at the council became the basis for creating new draft documents, and these documents would then be circulated in preparation for the next session of the council, scheduled for October 1963. The work of these commissions was accompanied by the death of John XXIII and the election of his successor, Cardinal Montini of Milan, who took the name Paul VI.

Unlike his predecessor, the new pope had been a Vatican insider for years, having served in the Vatican diplomatic corps for a significant part of his career. He had been sent to Milan (he had fallen out of favor with Pius XII) but was now returning to the Roman Curia, which was now reeling from the events that had unfolded in the years leading up to the council and from the actions undertaken by the council itself.[13] Paul VI entered his pontificate with the expressed intention to see the council through to its conclusion, but his manner of dealing with the council would differ, in many ways, from that of his predecessor.

In the interim period, Paul VI undertook a reform of the council's administration. Under John XXIII, the procedures of the council were often chaotic and slow, and thus frustrating (until this time, bishops had been accustomed to acting merely as an advisory group rather than a deliberative body). The Curia tended to manage the operations of the council, and they were not prepared to move as swiftly as many in the majority had hoped. The majority of council fathers, for their part, were not unified or well organized. Paul VI tried to balance the needs of both the majority and the minority in an effort to create procedures that would facilitate debate and that would focus the work of the council. Generally his efforts were viewed as successful.

The Second Session (Autumn 1963)

The new draft document on the Church was the focal point of the council's work in the second session. The original draft of the document had been rejected at the first session due to its triumphalistic tone and overwhelming focus on church governance. The Theological Commission, which had been reformed in the course of the council, assigned Jesuit theologian Gérard

Philips to construct a new draft of the document on the Church, one that would reflect the concerns expressed by the council fathers at the first session.

Some of the main issues raised by the new document included papal authority and the collegiality of bishops. The emphasis on papal power and papal jurisdiction that had preoccupied the Church since the Middle Ages was also the focal point of the First Vatican Council. The new draft document, however, seemed to signal a modest retreat from this emphasis by stressing the role and authority of bishops in the Church.

A common assumption had animated a rather limited understanding of the role of bishops in the Church. For some, a bishop, in many ways, was simply a priest with a larger area of jurisdiction. A bishop received this jurisdiction from the pope and was essentially the pope's delegate, administering a diocese on behalf of the pope, who had the real power and authority. At the second session of the council, the fathers determined that bishops were really ordained, not simply appointed, and that they had their own charism or power as a result. Moreover, bishops formed part of a body, a college, comprised of all the bishops in the world. As part of this college, bishops were to teach and govern in union with their brother bishops, not simply follow orders from Rome. It was this emphasis on collegiality that alarmed many in the minority at the council, for they saw such an idea as a form of conciliarism, an attempt to circumscribe the power and authority of the papacy with that of the bishops.

The second session of the council dealt with other important issues. In particular, the order of topics to be covered in the document on the Church was revised. The discussion of the hierarchy was moved from the second to the third topic, after a discussion of the "People of God." Such a move signaled an important change in ecclesiology, a shift away from the emphasis placed on hierarchy and governance, to a more participatory understanding of the Church. Additionally, the second session saw the approval and promulgation of the *Sacrosanctum concilium* (Constitution of the Sacred Liturgy) that would rapidly lead to a complete overhaul of the Mass.

In all, the second session witnessed greater progress in the council's agenda. However, the continuation of the council into a third session was disappointing to many council fathers. The pace of the discussions was still slow, and the results of the council's work were seen as thin in comparison to the enthusiasm and energy the council seemed to generate. During the second interim period in the winter of 1963 and the spring of 1964, more revisions were made to the document on the Church as well as on a number of other documents. Additionally, more revisions were made to the working procedures for the council that seemed to speed the pace of the council's work, though nothing could have helped prepare the council fathers for the events of the third session.

The Third Session (Autumn 1964)

The third session opened with an overwhelming agenda. It was strongly hoped that this third session would be the council's last. However, discussions and deliberations on a number of contentious issues at the heart of the council's agenda remained. There were many successes during the third session, but these successes were accompanied by what some might regard as failures.

Among the most controversial topics was the question of the Church's relationship to the modern secular state. Since the time of Gregory XVI and his condemnation of the principles of modern liberal democracy in *Mirari vos*, 1832, the Church had taken a dim view of the so-called indifferentism of the state. Popes continued to insist that the state had an obligation to promote the Catholic faith and to secure the rights of the Church in the laws enacted by the state. The state could not simply remain indifferent to religious questions; it had an obligation under divine law to promote the truth and to destroy evil and error. Within this context, it had become axiomatic to declare, "error has no rights." It was possible, however, for Catholics to agree to a kind of separation of Church and state and to accept religious freedom if the Catholic Church was a small minority and the nation had no history of association with the faith. In this instance religious freedom would be the lesser evil in comparison to the alternative.

As a result of such thinking, many European bishops and theologians had difficulty with the question of religious freedom, and it was left to an American Jesuit to play the decisive role in revising Catholic teaching on religious freedom; his name was John Courtney Murray. Before the council, Murray had been censured by the Vatican for his writings on religious liberty and was kept away from the council by several prominent Church officials. Yet, Francis Cardinal Spellman of New York eventually had Murray appointed as his theologian advisor, a *peritus*, and it was in this capacity that Murray made some of the most important contributions to the council.

Murray's work on the question of religious liberty caused quite a stir at the council. His approach seemed like a complete reversal of Catholic teaching on the question—before the council, religious liberty was viewed as an evil, and after the council, it would be viewed as a good. How does one reconcile such an apparent reversal with the continuity of past teachings? The question seemed to be at the heart of so much of the controversy about religious liberty. However, this was not the only controversy unfolding during the third session.

The week of November 14–21 became known as the Black Week, because it witnessed three interventions that shaped the drama of the council in the minds of many participants and observers.[14] The first intervention came from the Theological Commission at the behest of the pope. The commission had inserted a note into the document on the Church that addressed the issue of episcopal collegiality. To some of the more conservative bishops, the notion of collegiality was dangerously reminiscent of the conciliarist position (revived as Gallicanism in France in the nineteenth century) from the later medieval and early modern periods. The note reinforced the primacy of the pope in relation to the bishops and circumscribed the collegiality of the bishops with the power of the pope. Although the concerns of the note were addressed in the third chapter in the document on the Church, the note was introduced on behalf of the minority in an effort to secure the widest possible approval of the document as it was presented to the council for a vote. The second intervention came from the Council of Presidents, a group of cardinals whose role had been sharply reduced at the council. They announced that the vote on the document on religious freedom was not going to take place, much to the dismay of the council fathers. The allegation was that recent revisions to the document were so substantial that the document had to be debated and discussed more. The third intervention that defined the Black Week came from the pope himself. He had made some twenty modifications to the document on ecumenism (the relationship between various Christian churches) without allowing time for discussion of the document.

This last week of the third session, the Black Week, epitomized the council in many ways. The council was a contentious meeting; there were battles, maneuverings, and procedural stunts, which is not uncommon. Church councils have always been lively and unwieldy events. Perhaps this is the reason they are held so seldom—participants do not necessarily know how they will all work out in the end. Although the third session was marked by significant controversy, it also heralded several important achievements, including the promulgation of the *Lumen gentium* and the *Unitatis redintegratio* (Decree on Ecumenism).

The Fourth Session (Autumn 1965)

The period before the fourth session saw the implementation of the initial reforms of the liturgy. Contrary to popular belief, many of the changes to the liturgy were not mandated by *Sacrosanctum concilium*; rather, the constitution had enumerated several principles for the reform of the liturgy, and the Consilium (a group of liturgical scholars gathered by the pope) was charged with the actual implementation of those principles in the reform of the liturgy. The Consilium had established March 7, 1965, as the date for the inauguration of the new rite for the celebration of the Mass, and for most of the faithful, this was

The Consilium and ICEL

Sacrosanctum concilium (The Constitution on the Sacred Liturgy) enumerated the principles of the liturgical reform demanded by the council; however, Pope Paul VI created a group of experts to actually implement those principles. This group of liturgical scholars was known as the Consilium, and it was their responsibility to devise the specific changes that needed to take place. It was the Consilium that rewrote the Sacramentary, the texts for various rituals, and the Lectionary. In doing so, the Consilium was much criticized. In fact, at one point, Paul VI reformulated the membership of the Consilium because of pressure from various constituencies who felt the group had gained too much power. This resulted in the creation of a new curial office (an office of the Vatican bureaucracy), the Congregation for Divine Worship.

One of the most controversial aspects of the Consilium's work was the translation of Latin texts into the vernacular. For the English-speaking world, this task fell to two transnational groups: the International Commission on English in the Liturgy (ICEL) and the International Consultation on English Texts (ICET). The former was established by the bishops' conferences of English-speaking countries in 1963, and the latter was an ecumenical working group established in 1969. It was in 1969 that the Vatican issued an instruction, *Comme le prévoit* (On Translation of Liturgical Texts), in which it called for "dynamic equivalence" as the standard that was to govern all translations. This document also called for the creation of new liturgical texts in the target language rather than confining the liturgical renewal of Vatican II to mere translation.

The liturgical renewal certainly caught many parishioners off-guard, and some people treated the innovations with suspicion. The work of ICEL also became the subject of controversy, with some people feeling threatened by the innovations of "new" liturgical prayers. In the decades following Vatican II, ICEL often found itself under attack from conservative groups who believed that the translations they offered distorted traditional Catholic theology, while others argued that ICEL was working in the spirit of the council and that those who were critical of its work really were seeking to turn back the council's reforms. For a history of the Consilium and other related developments, see P. Marini, *A Challenging Reform* (Collegeville, MN: Liturgical, 2007).

the most tangible sign of the council's work. The achievement of the council was beginning to hit home, with the implementation of the liturgical reforms in local parishes, even before the council itself had been concluded.

The interim period between the third and fourth sessions of the council also witnessed significant developments in the Church's relationship to the modern world. The positive attitude emphasized by John XXIII had carried great momentum at the council, yet many still feared the modern world and its implicit, and sometimes explicit, challenge to Church teaching and authority. As the draft of "Schema XIII" (the name given to the document that would later become *Gaudium et spes*) was being improved, questions related to the Church's teaching on religious freedom, ecumenism, and religious pluralism continued to cause a stir among council fathers. In the end, several important documents were being edited and voted upon as the final session of the council came to a close: *Dignitatis humanae* (Decree on Religious Liberty), *Nostra aetate* (Declaration on the Relation of the Church and Non-Christian Religions), *Dei verbum*, as well as *Gaudium et spes*.

The question of religious freedom was simmering between the third and fourth sessions (Nov. 1964–Sept. 1965), and this issue became increasingly bound with the issues of religious pluralism and the relationship between the Church and the modern world. At the fourth session, debates on the documents relating to these issues concluded amid much controversy. Many council fathers viewed the move to embrace religious freedom and a broad ecumenism as a repudiation of Church teaching. In fact, some of the so-called traditionalist Catholics (many of whom were followers of the Swiss Bishop Marcel Lefebvre) separated from the Catholic Church because they viewed this change as highly problematic at best and heretical at worst. Though by no means a majority at the council,

the traditionalists made the debates around the issues related to religious freedom and ecumenism extremely contentious. Additionally, the document on non-Christian religions remained controversial because it seemed to some council fathers that the missionary obligation of the Church was being attenuated.

Dei verbum also occasioned much debate because it sought to understand revelation in the context of human history, which struck many conservative council fathers as a tendency of modernism. Of particular significance in this document was its account of tradition and its development. The Catholic Church teaches that Sacred Tradition emerges over the course of history in conjunction with Scripture. Scripture and tradition do not form two separate "fonts" of revelation, as earlier drafts of the document suggested. Rather, divine revelation, accomplished definitively in Christ, unfolds in the course of human history through the intersection of the apostolic preaching, the witness of sacred Scripture, and the emerging sense of the faithful. Such an account of revelation is intimately tied with an understanding of the Catholic Church that is at once hierarchical, communal, and historical. This represented a significant departure from the approach to revelation that seemed to become enshrined at the First Vatican Council and in the theological manuals and textbooks throughout the nineteenth and early twentieth centuries.

The fourth session brought the council to a close on December 8, 1965, and it also brought a sigh of relief to its participants. The arduous work, the endless debates, the difficulties posed by bureaucracy, and the inexperience of the council fathers in deliberative situations helped to make the council much longer than anyone had anticipated. The conclusion of the council moved the debates out of Rome and into the world where the laity would be crucial to the real work of Church updating and reform.

Decrees, Declarations, and Constitutions

The Second Vatican Council produced sixteen documents: four constitutions, nine decrees, and three declarations. Some principles can help one distinguish among these types of documents:

1. Constitutions are usually regarded as those documents that set forth major principles related to some aspect of Church life.

2. Decrees tend to focus on the implementation of the major principles set forth in the constitutions.

3. Declarations are not as practical as decrees but also function to specify the principles that have been developed in one or more of the constitutions.

Yet, the council itself was fairly clear that the weight of its teaching is not determined by the category of the document. Rather, the import of a teaching is defined as follows:

> In view of conciliar practice and the pastoral purpose of the present council, this sacred synod defines matters of faith or morals as binding on the Church only when the synod itself openly declares so.
>
> Other matters that the sacred synod proposes as the doctrine of the supreme teaching authority of the Church, each and every member of the faithful is obliged to accept and embrace according to the mind of the sacred synod itself, which becomes known either from the subject matter or from the language employed, according to the norms of theological interpretation.
>
> — EXPLANATORY NOTE ATTACHED TO *LUMEN GENTIUM*

The council itself then, its debates, and its intentions, must be examined carefully in order to adequately interpret and implement its teaching.

THE CHURCH AT VATICAN II

Most scholars would agree that the Second Vatican Council was primarily concerned with formulating a better understanding of the Church, its relationship to God, and its place in the modern world. Following is a brief look at two of the most important documents from the council: *Lumen gentium* and *Gaudium et spes*. Each document treats the major questions at hand in the council itself while helping to map out a course for understanding the nature and mission of the Church. In doing so, each of the documents reorients the Church in its relationship to the world, a relationship that is now understood as less confrontational and more dialogical. Furthermore, the tone of the Church is far less triumphalistic than seen in the controversies surrounding the battles between the Church and secularism in the nineteenth and early twentieth centuries.

Lumen gentium (The Dogmatic Constitution on the Church)

Lumen gentium is perhaps the centerpiece of the council's theological achievements. Although many of the themes explored in this document have their roots in earlier papal pronouncements and in the works of theologians from both the distant and the more recent past, the document still stands as a sign of reform and renewal in ecclesiology. While a complete discussion of the text is impossible here, a few issues demand attention. These issues include the notion of the Church as "mystery," the document's focus on the Church as "the people of God," and the Church's hierarchical constitution.

Unlike the approaches to ecclesiology characteristic of the Counter-Reformation (Bellarmine) that focused on the visible structures of the Church, *Lumen gentium* begins with a reflection on the Church as "mystery." The Greek word *mystērion* is used in place of the Latin word *sacramentum* to refer to Eucharist and baptism. In Greek, the word carries with it the notion of something that is hidden and then made known. In the context of the Church, this revelation is uniquely connected to the work of Christ, and it involves the manner in which the very life of the triune God is revealed to the world in the life of the believing community.

> Christ, the one Mediator, established and continually sustains here on earth His holy Church, the community of faith, hope and charity, as an entity with visible delineation through which He communicated truth and grace to all. But, the society structured with hierarchical organs and the Mystical Body of Christ, are not to be considered as two realities, nor are the visible assembly and the spiritual community, nor the earthly Church and the Church enriched with heavenly things; rather they form one complex reality which coalesces from a divine and a human element. For this reason, by no weak analogy, it is compared to the mystery of the incarnate Word. As the assumed nature inseparably united to Him, serves the divine Word as a living organ of salvation, so, in a similar way, does the visible social structure

of the Church serve the Spirit of Christ, who vivifies it, in the building up of the body.

> — *LUMEN GENTIUM*, NO. 8

Thus, *Lumen gentium* signaled an important development in Catholic ecclesiology: a shift from an ecclesiology focused on the visible structures and hierarchies that constitute the Church to an understanding of the Church based on the analogy of the Incarnation itself, in which the sacramental encounter with God takes center stage (*Lumen gentium*, 7).

In the various revisions to the document before its final approval, no change was perhaps more important than the ordering of themes within the document itself. In the final draft of *Lumen gentium* the first chapter presents the Church as the mystery of humanity's encounter with the triune God, followed in chapter 2 with a presentation of the Church as "People of God." In making this move, the document emphasizes that in baptism, all members of the Church are united in faith and new life in Christ. Any hierarchical divisions within the Church are secondary in relation to this foundational commonality. Popes, bishops, priests, religious, and laity are all called by God and given a vocation as God's people by virtue of their baptism. In baptism, all are called to participate in the threefold office (*munus triplex*) of Christ as priest, prophet, and king, an idea that had been an important part of Calvin's theology.[15] Of particular interest is the notion of the "priesthood of all believers," a concept that was at the heart of Luther's ecclesiology.

> Christ the Lord, High Priest taken from among human beings, made the new people "a kingdom and priests to God the Father." The baptized, by regeneration and the anointing of the Holy Spirit, are consecrated as a spiritual house and a holy priesthood, in order that through all those works which are those of the Christian man they may offer spiritual sacrifices and proclaim the power

of Him who has called them out of darkness into His marvelous light. Therefore all the disciples of Christ, persevering in prayer and praising God (Acts 2:42–47), should present themselves as a living sacrifice, holy and pleasing to God. Everywhere on earth they must bear witness to Christ and give an answer to those who seek an account of that hope of eternal life which is in them.

— *Lumen gentium*, no. 10

Lumen gentium's emphasis on the common priesthood of believers stands as an important ecumenical development, but it also highlights the growing importance of the place that all believers have in the Church's ministry in the world. Later in this same chapter, *Lumen gentium* emphasizes the participation of all members of the Church in the prophetic office of Christ brings with it the powerful charism of infallibility.

> The holy people of God shares also in Christ's prophetic office; it spreads abroad a living witness to Him, especially by means of a life of faith and charity and by offering to God a sacrifice of praise, the tribute of lips which give praise to His name. The entire body of the faithful, anointed as they are by the Holy One cannot err in matters of belief. They manifest this special property by means of the whole peoples' supernatural discernment in matters of faith when "from the Bishops down to the last of the lay faithful" they show universal agreement in matters of faith and morals. That discernment in matters of faith is aroused and sustained by the Spirit of truth. It is exercised under the guidance of the sacred teaching authority, in faithful and respectful obedience to which the people of God accepts that which is not just the word of men but truly the word of God. Through it, the people of God adheres unwaveringly to the faith given once and for all to the saints, penetrates it more deeply

with right thinking, and applies it more fully in its life.

— *Lumen gentium*, no. 12

The presentation of the Church as "people of God" in the second chapter of *Lumen gentium* thus shifts Catholic ecclesiology, without repudiating the ecclesiologies of the past, to a more integrated account of the Church and its authority.

Of special significance in chapter 2 of *Lumen gentium* is the manner in which the Catholic Church is described in relation to "separated Christians" (Orthodox and Protestant Christians) and especially to those who do not share faith in Christ. In chapter 1, the text states that the unique Church of Christ (the Church established by Christ) is "constituted and organized in the world as a society, subsists in the Catholic Church." In his commentary on *Lumen gentium*, Aloys Grillmeier points to the discussion of the draft version of this text in which the fathers of the council (the bishops) rejected the strict identification of the Catholic Church as the Church established by Christ.[16] Rather, Grillmeier states that the document is only reinforcing the fundamental statement expressed later in this same section of *Lumen gentium*, namely that "outside the visible structures" of the Church, one finds "elements of sanctification and truth." In chapter 2 of *Lumen gentium*, this notion is spelled out more firmly in relation to the people of God. In sections 14 through 16, an account of the people of God encompasses not only those Christians who live beyond the visible boundaries of the Catholic Church but also those of different faiths and those with no faith at all. Of particular interest is section 16, which reads:

> Nor does Divine Providence deny the helps necessary for salvation to those who, without blame on their part, have not yet arrived at an explicit knowledge of God and with His grace strive to live a good life. Whatever good or truth is found amongst them is looked upon by the Church as a preparation

for the Gospel. She knows that it is given by Him who enlightens all men so that they may finally have life.

— *LUMEN GENTIUM*, NO. 16

The ecumenical vision of this section embraces interreligious connections; consequently, it represents a positive assessment of the religious pluralism that defines the experience of contemporary Christians. It was this experience that the council sought to constructively address from the outset and to which it turns consistently in its major documents.

Although the presentation of the Church as people of God captures the attention of the reader, chapter 3 of *Lumen gentium* also demands

Mary and the Church at Vatican II

Given the Catholic hierarchy's emphasis on Marian devotions in the nineteenth and twentieth centuries, it should come as no surprise that many of the council fathers were interested in composing a document that would treat the theological significance of Mary in the life of the Church. Yet, many council fathers who were more ecumenically inclined thought that such an emphasis on Mary would damage attempts to heal the division between Catholics and Protestants. Franz Cardinal König, the Archbishop of Vienna, spoke persuasively during the debates, and his desire to see the discussion of Mary contextualized within the constitution on the Church won the day.

For most mariologists (theologians devoted to the study of Mary's theological significance), the decision to contextualize Marian devotions and Marian doctrines with an account of the Church has borne considerable fruit. Although some have suggested that placing the chapter on Mary at the end of the document reduces her significance, others contend that the progression of the document suggests that chapter 7 (on the eschatological nature of the Church as "pilgrim") and chapter 8 really focus on the eschatological consummation of the Church. In other words, Mary is treated at the end of the document in order to signal her importance as the perfect model of the Church.

Perhaps no portion of the chapter on Mary deserves more attention than sections 60–63. In these sections, the document sets forth the proper relationship between Mary and Christ even as it extols the virtues of Mary as mediatrix of grace. Yet, the document is clear about the subordinate role Mary plays in the work of salvation:

For no creature could ever be counted as equal with the Incarnate Word and Redeemer. Just as the priesthood of Christ is shared in various ways both by the ministers and by the faithful, and as the one goodness of God is really communicated in different ways to His creatures, so also the unique mediation of the Redeemer does not exclude but rather gives rise to a manifold cooperation which is but a sharing in this one source.

The Church does not hesitate to profess this subordinate role of Mary. It knows it through unfailing experience of it and commends it to the hearts of the faithful, so that encouraged by this maternal help they may the more intimately adhere to the Mediator and Redeemer.

— *LUMEN GENTIUM*, No. 62

attention for the manner in which the Church's hierarchical structures are presented. As already noted, ecclesiology in the nineteenth and early twentieth century tended to focus on the power of the papacy and the manner in which the Catholic Church was an ordered society under the governance of the pope. All of this had the tendency to reduce the role of the local bishop to

Different Types of Communion Ecclesiology

The interpretation of the ecclesiology of Vatican II has been a point of contention in theological circles for more than forty years. Many different groups have emerged with their own visions of the Church that they claim to be rooted in the ecclesiology of the council. In particular, the theme of "communion" has emerged as a contentious issue. What vision of communion is faithful to the council's ecclesiology? In his study of Catholic communion ecclesiologies, Dennis M. Doyle (*Communion Ecclesiology* [New York: Orbis, 2000]) draws together six different ecclesiologies under the heading "communion ecclesiology." The diversity of these ecclesiologies stands as testimony to the power of the language of communion and the work of the council.

COMMUNION ECCLESIOLOGY

Type	Points of Emphasis
CDF (Vatican)	• priority of the Church universal (catholic) over the local church • importance of visible structures of the Church
Rahnerian	• sacramental obligation of the world • communion with God that exists within all humankind
Balthasarian	• uniqueness of Christian revelation • aesthetics
Liberation	• option for the poor • political and economic implications of communion
Contextual	• gender, ethnicity, social location as central for appreciating relational perspectives and communion
Reforming	• need for Roman Catholics to challenge their ecclesiological presuppositions in the interest of ecumenical progress

The communion ecclesiology of the council spawned several different versions that span the spectrum of theology and Church politics. Doyle suggests that these versions of communion ecclesiology need not be exclusive of one another. Instead, he advocates for a complementary interpretation of these approaches so that a more rich and powerful form of communion ecclesiology may emerge, faithful to the vision of the council itself.

that of a regional manager in a large corporation. In chapter 3 of *Lumen gentium*, the ministry of bishop is given great attention, and in particular, the dignity of the bishops as leaders of the local church and their dignity as a group or "college" become central.

> Individual bishops are the visible source and foundation for the unity in their own particular churches, which are modeled on the universal Church; it is in and from these that the one and unique Catholic Church exists. And for that reason each bishop represents his own church, whereas all of them together with the people represent the whole Church in a bond of peace, love, and unity.
>
> The individual bishops, who are placed in charge of particular churches, exercise their pastoral government over the portion of the People of God committed to their care, and not over other churches nor over the universal Church. But each of them, as a member of the episcopal college and legitimate successor of the apostles, is obliged by Christ's institution and command to be solicitous for the whole Church, and this solicitude, though it is not exercised by an act of jurisdiction, contributes greatly to the advantage of the universal Church.
>
> — *LUMEN GENTIUM*, NO. 23

Here one finds the seeds of a vision of the Church often identified as "communion ecclesiology," which has become a somewhat contentious topic in contemporary ecclesiology.

Communion ecclesiology emphasizes the place of the local or particular church and its relationship to, or its communion with, other local or particular churches and the universal (the catholic) Church. This communion has both vertical and horizontal dimensions. The communion, or fellowship, is primarily with Christ, and in Christ, particular churches have

fellowship or communion with one another. For many theologians and many council fathers, such a vision of the Church represented an important shift in the understanding of how the Church was to be governed and lived. Priority seemed to shift from the papacy to the local church and the local bishop, who, in communion with Rome, was the primary shepherd of the local community and not merely a representative of an all-powerful monarch.[17]

There are many more nuances to *Lumen gentium*, but three points mentioned above stand out as characteristic of the council's teaching on the Church. *Lumen gentium* stands as a monumental achievement to the courage and vision of the council fathers and their *periti*. The document manages, without directly repudiating past teachings, to incorporate significant changes in ecclesiology while articulating those changes within the broader context of continuity. It is with these developments that the Catholic Church began to reenvision its relationship to the modern world and to engage it constructively and critically.

Gaudium et spes (The Pastoral Constitution on the Church in the Modern World)

During the preparation period, it was assumed that the council would address the theology of the Church. The First Vatican Council had planned to do this but was unable to complete the task due to political events that forced the council's untimely close. The treatment of the Church itself, or the question of the Church considered "inwardly" (*ad intra*), needed to be complemented by an understanding of the Church in relation to the world, or the Church considered "outwardly" (*ad extra*). This was the point made by Léon Joseph Cardinal Suenens to Pope John XXIII in the months leading up to the council. It was at the first session that Suenens argued for a separate document on the Church and the modern world, and this document (in its draft form named Schema XIII) was to become one of the council's most debated documents.

Unlike the other documents produced at the council, the document that would become *Gaudium et spes* was composed entirely in a modern language—French—for a specific purpose. The document reflected the concerns and the theological methodology of many French-speaking theologians and bishops, particularly Marie-Dominique Chenu (1895–1990), a French Dominican theologian. Chenu had long argued for an inductive approach to a theology of the Church and of the human—one that began with concrete history. Through such an "incarnational approach," Chenu examined contemporary society for "toothing stones" (in French, *pierres d'attente*), or signs of spiritual hunger to which the Church could address their message about Christ. Chenu was adamant about this method of reading the "signs of the times" within modern culture—for this method afforded the Church the opportunity to engage the world within the context of dialogue and not simply through dogmatic prescriptions.[18]

While the inspiration for the document rested with Chenu, the French priest and sociologist Pierre Haubtmann accomplished the actual drafting of the text, and he took an approach that reflected a growing interest among theologians in the social sciences. However, this approach was not well received by many of the German-speaking theologians and bishops, who found the document oddly out of place at the council. Their criticisms of the document revolved around three issues:

1. The methodology of the document was not theological.
2. The document's assessment of the modern world was too positive.
3. The issues it treated were too specific for a conciliar document.

These issues made the debates around the documents heated, but in the end, the document won convincing support from the council fathers. This support, however, masks that the document was drafted and discussed almost entirely apart from the concerns that dominated the discussions of other documents, including *Lumen gentium*. This fact, in the eyes of many, marked the document as somewhat eccentric in relation to the other council documents, yet it was very much at the center of the council's defined purpose—to articulate anew the relationship between the Church and the modern world.[19]

Gaudium et spes opens with the recognition of the modern world's predicament and the mission of the Church within that world. The document strikes a note of solidarity and engagement even as it identifies sin at the root of the world's problems and Christ as the solution:

> The world which the council has in mind is the whole human family with the totality of realities among which it lives, the world as the theater of human history, marked by human labor, failures and triumphs, the world which Christians believe to have been established and sustained by the Creator's love, reduced to slavery and to sin, yet freed by the crucified and risen Christ who has broken the power of the Evil One so that it might be transformed according to God's plan and may reach perfection.
>
> — *GAUDIUM ET SPES*, NO. 2

The Church's mission is thus intimately bound with the world and its problems, and the council signals the Church's renewed attention to the plight of the world and the Church's mission to serve it rather than to despise it.

The body of the document is divided into two major sections: the first section sets forth a Christian anthropology, in which Christ is presented as the answer to modern humanity's hopes and aspirations, and the second section treats a range of issues from family life and culture to the nuclear arms race, war, and poverty. *Gaudium et spes* is by far the longest of the council's sixteen documents. Given the limitations of space, however, only a few portions of the document will be discussed here.

The opening chapters of *Gaudium et spes* give voice to the cares and concerns of modern humanity and offer Christ as the answer to these aspirations. The document develops the theme of human dignity as the nexus at which the concerns of the world and the concerns of the Church meet. It then moves on to read "the signs of the times" in an effort to understand the challenges the modern world faces regarding the dignity of the human. A few passages in the first section of the document demand our attention, for they help set up the presentation of the concrete issues treated in the second part of the document.

First, *Gaudium et spes* makes a clear statement on the common good, which is "the sum of those conditions of social life which allow social groups and their individual members relatively thorough and ready access to their own fulfillment" (*Gaudium et spes,* 26). The common good thus requires societies to respect and uphold the dignity of the human and to allow religious groups to freely live out their mission. This account of the human good grounds much of what *Gaudium et spes* will affirm in the second part of the document.

Second, in the last part of section 1, the document makes a careful transition to the second part of the document that treats specific and controversial issues confronting modern society, issues over which many of the council fathers themselves were divided.

> Christ, to be sure, gave His Church no proper mission in the political, economic or social order. The purpose which He set before her is a religious one. But out of this religious mission itself come a function, a light and an energy which can serve to structure and consolidate the human community according to the divine law. As a matter of fact, when circumstances of time and place produce the need, she can and indeed should initiate activities on behalf of all men, especially those designed for the needy, such as the works of mercy and similar undertakings.
>
> — *GAUDIUM ET SPES,* NO. 42

Gaudium et spes thus reflects the concern of many of the council fathers that there should be no endorsement of one particular social or political system over and against another. At the same time, it is clear from what follows that *Gaudium et spes* refuses to remain neutral in the face of the major political, social, and economic questions of the day. Although the Church stands indebted to the world for all that it has received (the advance in sciences, the growth of cultures, etc.), it also stands apart from the world to call it to its true vocation that the entire world might become more human and that all might come to know Christ (*Gaudium et spes*, no. 45).

Third, before addressing itself to the major issues that confront modern culture, the document makes a stunning and important, even if somewhat obvious, admission:

> Let the layman not imagine that his pastors are always such experts, that to every problem which arises, however complicated, they can readily give him a concrete solution, or even that such is their mission. Rather, enlightened by Christian wisdom and giving close attention to the teaching authority of the Church, let the layman take on his own distinctive role.
>
> — *GAUDIUM ET SPES,* NO. 43

The humility evident in this statement stands in sharp contrast to the confidence and surety of the previous century in which the pope, the Curia, and even the First Vatican Council spoke with great clarity and assurance. Additionally, it puts the pastors of the Church in a position of collaboration and dependence on experts (presumably this means laypeople) in various areas. The first part of *Gaudium et spes*, thus, establishes the Church's voice in relationship to the modern world while at the same time sets the Church in a position to listen to the modern world and to take advantage of its insights and expertise as it helps to discover, rather than dictate, the right course of action in the face of a wide range of problems confronting the modern world.

The second part of the document turns its attention to a range of issues confronting modern societies, from the most intimate issues (sexual practices and the place of the family within society) to issues of economic, cultural, and military significance. While the anthropology of the first part of *Gaudium et spes* is always at the fore, constantly reinforcing the dignity of the human and the obligations of governments to foster that dignity and the social bonds that come with it, the document is perhaps most remarkable for its underlying assumption about what it means to call the world *modern*. No longer is "the world" a given, an established and fixed reality. "The *modern* world," as it is set forth in *Gaudium et spes* 2, is a dynamic and changing reality; it is the product of responsible decision making on the part of individuals, groups, societies, and cultures. The world is a work in progress and it is reflective of the drive for human authenticity. Put succinctly, "we are witnessing the birth of a new humanism in which [a human being is] defined before all else by his responsibility for his brothers and before history" (*Gaudium et spes*, p. 55). Whatever else one might say about the manner in which the issues treated in the second part of the document are presented, the document issues

a clarion call to Christians to take responsibility for the world and how it is shaped. Such responsibility requires expertise, dialogue, and cooperation—virtues that were not always at the fore in the Church's engagement with the modern world in the decades or even centuries leading up to the council.

The Reception of the Council

Even as the council came to a close, many of its participants expressed concern about how the council was to be interpreted and how it would be received. Among the most interesting interpreters of the council was one of its most active participants, Joseph Ratzinger—later to become Pope Benedict XVI, who had attended as the theological advisor (a *peritus*) to Cardinal Frings, Archbishop of Köln. Ratzinger was at the center of several major debates at the council and played an active role in the formation of several documents. In the years following the council, however, he viewed with suspicion many of the developments that were taking place "in the spirit of the council" and began to adopt what many would regard as a more conservative stance. In his position as Archbishop of Munich and then as the head of the Vatican's Congregation for the Doctrine of the Faith, he led an effort to interpret the council and its achievements. When he became Pope Benedict XVI, his interpretation of Vatican II, though it remained unchanged, had even greater authority.

In an address titled "A Proper Hermeneutic for the Second Vatican Council," Benedict XVI poses the following question: why has the implementation of the council, in large parts of the Church, thus far been so difficult?[20] The answer he says rests in the fact that there are at least two competing hermeneutics (principles of interpretation) for the council: a hermeneutic of discontinuity or rupture, and a hermeneutic of reform. According to the pope, the hermeneutic of rupture plays to the mass media and popular cultural sensibilities by contrasting the preconciliar Church and the postconciliar Church, as if the Church had been radically transformed by the council and had repudiated its past. Such a move, the pope suggests, leads one to downplay or even to ignore the actual documents of the council and to instead appeal to the "spirit of the council." The pope sees many of the developments that have taken place subsequent to the council as having had little to do with the actual documents and teachings of the council, and the proponents of these reforms having done an injustice to the council by ignoring these documents and teachings.

Pope Benedict calls, instead, for a hermeneutic of reform. This hermeneutic embraces the fact that "things have changed" as a result of the council, but the emphasis here is on the continuity of the Church and its teaching amid these changes. He argues that the council recognized that the new situation in which the Church found itself (the modern world) demanded new formulations of the Church's teachings and new insights into its teachings that would allow the gospel to be lived in new ways.

In defense of this hermeneutic of reform, the pope examines the work of the council, particularly as it seemed to involve three areas of concern:

1. The relationship between faith and modern science

2. The relationship between the Church and the modern state

3. The question of religious tolerance

Each of these areas of concern was related in one way or another to the emergence of new sensibilities in the modern era, but these new sensibilities did not precipitate a change in the Church's basic teaching. Rather, there was only a reformulation of it; a reformulation that maintained the unchanging truth that is God's own

revelation. As an example, the Church's teaching on the relationship of the Church to the state underwent significant development at the council, in part because new sensibilities about the respective roles of Church and state had emerged and new sensitivity to religious pluralism had accompanied this development. In the course of the conflict between the divergent views over the years leading up to the council and during the council itself, the opposing sides began to gradually open to one another, and a new consensus emerged.

The pope embraces a hermeneutic of reform that envisions a dynamic fidelity to the truth of Christian faith. This truth is unchanging, but the historical circumstances in which it is understood and articulated are constantly changing. The primarily pastoral nature of the council also helps to contextualize its teachings by placing a premium on the new social and cultural context within which the Church now lives out its vocation to proclaim the gospel. Yet, not everyone is convinced by the pope's perspective on the council, and major fault lines have developed within the Church over how to rightly understand and implement the council.

Joseph Komonchak, perhaps the most prominent American expert on the council, has made note of the pope's remarks and has taken the opportunity to engage the discussion.[21] As noted in the introduction to this chapter, Komonchak and Giuseppe Alberigo have edited the definitive history of the council, characterizing the council as an "event." Komonchak has worked to underscore the real changes that took place as a result of the council. He is always conscious, however, of contextualizing those changes in terms of developments over the course of time—the changes that occurred at the council reflect developments in the tradition while at the same time representing something new. For Komonchak, the council cannot be reduced to its documents, but it must be interpreted in light of the debates and discussions of the council fathers and interpreted in light of its reception in the years following the official close of the council.

A small but influential group of Roman officials, including Camillo Cardinal Ruini, the president of the Italian bishops' conference and the pope's vicar for the Diocese of Rome, anticipated a backlash against the interpretation of the council offered by Komonchak and Alberigo.[22] They expected the pope to repudiate Komonchak's approach to the council. Yet, as Komonchak reads the pope's subsequent remarks, it appears as though he and the pope share some important common ground. First, the pope offers two ideal types in the dichotomy of "rupture" and "reform." As is the case with all such dichotomies, no individual or writing could actually be reduced to one position or the other. Instead, "rupture" and "reform" represent two ends of the interpretive spectrum, two ideal types. Second, Komonchak is fully supportive of the pope's criticism of those who would emphasize a vague "spirit of the council" over and against the actual documents produced by the council. An emphasis on such a vague concept is often used to legitimatize the worst theological and pastoral experiments.

Nevertheless Komonchak reiterates his emphasis on a fully contextualized appreciation of the council's proceedings and interpretations since. He is critical of the pope's remarks that seemed to suggest that discontinuity was only "apparent" in the Church's teaching on matters pertaining to its engagement with the world. Komonchak argues that the conciliar debates the pope mentions in his address were of considerable doctrinal as well as pastoral importance.

Once again, Komonchak (and many others) see Vatican II as an "event." While not wishing to highlight the extreme notion of rupture, Komonchak is, nonetheless, committed to the interpretation of the council that emphasizes significant discontinuity, a discontinuity that is at the heart of any notion of reform. While

this discussion may seem somewhat academic, it has immense significance for implementing the council's documents, and it becomes even more important as the Church moves forward and comes to better understand itself as part of history and not above it or outside it.

CONCLUSION

The brief overview of the council presented in this chapter highlights the significant turn in the Church's self-understanding and its relationship to the world. This shift is controversial, but the Second Vatican Council, particularly through the vision articulated in *Gaudium et spes*, put to rest the facile assumptions about the nature and role of the Christian faith in relation to the world—assumptions that focused on the interior alienation of the individual from modern society. Instead, the council placed front and center the contention that the Church has no other mission than to foster redemptive recovery in history. Through a constructive engagement with modern culture and with a better understanding of both the theological and critical value of history, the Church has positioned itself to initiate and participate in a broad and transformative ministry in the world. However, the council's achievement does not rest in the past, but in the contemporary appropriation of the council as an event along with robust commitment to the sound interpretation of the documents produced at the council as a work in progress.

In chapter 5, some of the issues involved in contemporary attempts to wrestle with the council and the Church's new sense of mission will be discussed. As always, amid these conversations, echoes of the debates that were ongoing in the nineteenth and twentieth centuries are still heard, and the history of the council is still being rewritten.

Questions for Understanding

1. What is modernism? What are some of its main characteristics?

2. Describe the rhetoric used to combat the growth of secularism and modern thinking in the nineteenth and early twentieth centuries.

3. What were some of the signs of renewal that emerged in the nineteenth and early twentieth centuries?

4. Describe the events at the first session of the Second Vatican Council. What were the most contentious issues?

5. Describe three major contributions to ecclesiology made in *Lumen gentium*.

6. Why were many German-speaking theologians unhappy with *Gaudium et spes*?

7. Describe the two hermeneutical perspectives on the council offered by Pope Benedict XVI. How does Joseph Komonchak respond to these alternatives offered by the pope?

Questions for Reflection

1. The opening sections of this chapter discussed the modernist controversy and the way Church officials used catastrophic and even apocalyptic imagery to define and condemn those forces aligned with modernism. The use of such rhetoric against an enemy is not unusual. In fact, it is used frequently in political discourse. How might such imagery and such language be destructive? Is the use of such a tactic ever appropriate? Explain.

2. The Second Vatican Council was a complex event. Tough political maneuverings, harsh words (and not always spoken by the conservative minority), and many hard feelings carried beyond the council itself. How did the debates, interactions, and appeasements of various factions affect the final documents of Vatican II? Explain.

3. The Second Vatican Council is often seen as something of a Rorschach test—how people interpret the council often discloses more about the person doing the interpreting than about the council itself. Ask three people (make sure at least two of them are Roman Catholic) about the importance of the Second Vatican Council, and be sure to pick one person from each of the following age groups: 18–35, 35–55, and over 55. What do their responses tell you, if anything, about how different generations understand the council?

Suggestions for Further Study

Alberigo, Giuseppe. *A Brief History of Vatican II*. New York: Orbis, 2006.

This is the abridged version of the definitive five-volume history of the council edited by Alberigo and Joseph Komonchak.

Alberigo, Giuseppe, Jean-Pierre Jossua, and Joseph Komonchak, editors. *The Reception of Vatican II*. New York: Paulist Press, 1987.

This is a collection of essays by international scholars reflecting on the twentieth anniversary of the close of the council.

Lamb, Matthew, and Matthew Levering, editors. *Vatican II: Renewal within the Tradition*. Oxford: Oxford University Press, 2008.

Lamb and Levering open this collection of essays with Benedict XVI's admonition regarding the interpretation of the council, and they follow up with a series of essays that reflect a more conservative interpretation of the council.

Madges, William, editor. *Vatican II: Forty Years Later*, Annual Publication of the College Theology Society. Vol. 51. Maryknoll, NY: Orbis, 2006.

This collection of essays addresses issues raised at the council as well as developments the council did not foresee.

O'Connell, Marvin R. *Critics on Trial: An Introduction to the Modernist Controversy*. Washington, DC: Catholic University of America Press, 1994.

This book provides the most comprehensive overview of the complexities of the modernist crisis.

Endnotes

1. Joseph Komonchak, "Vatican II as an 'Event,'" *Theology Digest* 46 (1999): 337–352.

2. For the definitive account of the modernist crisis in English, see Marvin R. O'Connell, *Critics on Trial: An Introduction to the Catholic Modernist Crisis* (Washington, DC: Catholic University of America Press, 1994).

3. E. Poulat, "L'Eglise, c'est une monde," in *L'Ecclésiosphere* (Paris, 1986), 254–258, cited in J. Komonchak, "Modernity and the Construction of Modern Roman Catholicism," *Cristianesimo nella storia* 18 (1997): 353–385, 360.

4. See Komonchak, "Modernity and the Construction of Modern Roman Catholicism," for most of what follows in this section.

5. The translation is from John P. Boyle, "The Ordinary Magesterium: Towards a History of the Concept," *Heythrop Journal* 20 (1979): 380–398, at 397.

6. *Pascendi dominici gregis*, 50–58.

7. For an overview of the liturgical reform, see James F. White, *Roman Catholic Worship: Trent to Today* (Collegeville, MN: Liturgical Press, 2003).

8. Quoted in Jozef Lamberts, *"Ars Celebrandi,"* The Art to Celebrate Liturgy, 'L'Art de Célébrer la Liturgie,' Studies in Liturgy 17 (Leuven: Peeters, 2002), 8.

9. For most of what follows, see Giuseppe Alberigo, *A Brief History of Vatican II*, trans. M. Sherry (Maryknoll, NY: Orbis, 2006). This is a highly abridged version of Giuseppe Alberigo and Joseph A. Komonchak, eds., *History of Vatican II*, 5 vols. (Leuven: Peeters/Maryknoll, NY: Orbis, 1995–2006).

10 Ibid., 21–23.

11. Ibid., 24.

12. Ibid., 25.

13. Ibid., 5.

14. For a complete description of the events of the Black Week, see Luis Antonio G. Tangle, "The 'Black Week' of Vatican II (November 14–21, 1964)," in *History of Vatican II*, vol. 4, 387–452.

15. *Institutes of the Christian Religion*, vol. 2, 15.

16. Aloys Grillmeier, "The Mystery of the Church," in H. Vorgrimler, *Commentary on the Documents of Vatican II*, vol. 1 (New York: Herder, 1967): 149–150.

17. On communion as a theme at the council, see Susan K. Wood, "The Church as Communion," in *The Gift of the Church*, 159–176; Joseph Komonchak, "The Local Church and the Church Catholic: The Contemporary Theological Problematic," *The Jurist* 52 (1992): 416–447; Jean-Marie Tillard, *Church of Churches: The Ecclesiology of Communion* (Collegeville, MN: Liturgical Press, 1992).

18. For a discussion of the significance of Chenu's positive assessment of modern culture, see Christophe Potworowski, *Contemplation and Incarnation: The Theology of Marie-Dominique Chenu* (Montreal: McGill-Queens University Press, 2002).

19. See Giovanni Turbanti, "Toward the Fourth Period," in *History of Vatican II*, vol. 5, 39–44.

20. "Ad Romanam Curiam ob omnia natalicia," *Acta Apostolica Sedis* 98 (January 6, 2006): 40–53.

21. Joseph Komonchak, "Benedict XVI and the Interpretation of Vatican II," *Cristianesimo nella storia* 28 (2007): 323–337.

22. See Joseph O'Malley, "Vatican II: Did Anything Happen?" *Theological Studies* 67 (2006): 3–33.

The Church in a Culture of Disbelief

The world that the bishops sought to engage at the Second Vatican Council no longer exists. Yet, recognizing this state of affairs is the easy part; articulating precisely how that world has changed is far more difficult. One example that might help shed light on these changes involves the strange place the papacy occupies in contemporary popular culture.

Pope Benedict XVI, in the tradition established by his predecessor, John Paul II, had landed in a troubled yet hopeful nation in sub-Saharan Africa on March 17, 2009. Accompanied by an enormous press entourage, he was received with appropriate pomp and ceremony at the airport by the country's president and a host of dignitaries. In subsequent press coverage, the mostly European press entourage immediately focused on the pope's deep-seated theological positions on the HIV-AIDS crisis in Africa. The press decried the pope's intransigence on issues such as contraception and blamed him for contributing to the proliferation of AIDS in Africa.[1] The press routinely shows this ambivalence regarding the pope: they can't get enough of him in still photos and video clips, but let his message veer from "mainstream" sensibilities, and they turn immediately and sharply negative. For the media, the pope's pilgrimage is a great celebrity photo-op, but the moral vision articulated by the pope is considered dangerous, narrow-minded, and antiquated.

What accounts for this bifurcated phenomenon of fascination and revilement? The situation described is a far cry from the nearly universal adulation John XXIII received when he became the first pope in modern times to visit a prison (Regina Coeli Prison in Rome). Today, scenes such as a papal pilgrimage are far more customary, yet Western attitudes toward the papacy and the Church have shifted dramatically. The work of the Second Vatican Council, which Catholics are still struggling to understand and implement, seems to presuppose a culture that is comfortable and confident in identifying the place of the Church in the modern world. As has become apparent in the decades since the council (though theologians such as Chenu and others argued that it was a reality before the council), the world has become distinctly "post-Christian" to the extent that the model of dialogue and engagement offered by the council seems outdated and even quaint. Within the present context, frustration and even despair over present difficulties have characterized the response of some of the faithful. Yet others have pursued robust efforts to establish a new model for engagement with the "post-Christian" world. One would do well to take note of these efforts and to judge them against the soteriological backdrop presented in chapter 2. In other words, given the changes within contemporary culture, the Church must not only develop new ways of engaging the world but also must do so intelligently and with a clear understanding of its redemptive mission.

NEW ATTITUDES AND OUTLOOKS IN THE WAKE OF THE COUNCIL

As described in chapter 3, the construction of a Catholic subculture emerged as a response to the secularism of the modern age, particularly in the wake of the French Revolution and the Napoleonic wars. The tactic was deliberate: the world is dangerous, it belongs to the Evil One and can be redeemed only through battle, or so the thinking went. While such a siege mentality poses obvious dangers, it also helped to inspire revival and renewal in Catholic life. The liturgical movement, the revival of Thomism, and the proliferation of devotional life were the products of this emerging subculture (these developments also helped pave the way for reform that would eventually subvert the subculture itself).

The Church's new social context in the nineteenth and early twentieth century was complicated because Church members were part of a rapidly changing, industrialized world that had little room for religion. Providential moves by churchmen such as James Cardinal Gibbons of Baltimore helped to open the way for a positive and constructive engagement with the world's economic and social problems, thus yielding a rich tradition of Catholic social teaching. While figures such as Gibbons seemed to be the exception, the reality was that the modern wall constructed to separate the world from the Catholic "ghetto" (as some called it) was never really that high or that thick. Thus, the demise of the subculture, from the long view of history, represents an important shift in the life of the Church, but the subculture itself was really an aberration, a stopgap measure.

The work of constructing a new relationship with the world and with history remains the work of the Church. Yet a decisive element for constructing this relationship involves how one construes one's identity in relation to the Church amid the breakdown of the subculture, and this task has proved difficult and elusive in recent decades. Reasons for this difficulty and attempts to overcome it are numerous, but the present chapter offers a brief survey of some of the most important developments in the ongoing attempt to constructively and redemptively engage contemporary culture.

The Marketplace of Religion

The rapid demise of the Catholic subculture and the rise of a technologically empowered global-market economy have placed the Catholic faith, and religion in general, within a vast and high-speed marketplace. There is perhaps no better analysis of the impact of this phenomenon on religious practice than Vince Miller's insightful book *Consuming Religion*.[2] Miller offers a penetrating examination of the most complex and troubling developments confronting contemporary academic and pastoral theology in America—the intersection of religion and the marketplace. In a market-driven society—a society in which everything can be bought and sold—religious practices are marketable; they are just commodities like all others. The consumerism that is so often identified as the heart of contemporary Western societies, in particular, is not a set of beliefs that can be neatly contrasted with Christian beliefs. Rather, consumerism identifies a societal and cultural infrastructure that perpetuates and makes acceptable the set of beliefs people already hold. In other words, belief systems, whether Buddhist, Moslem, Christian, or Taoist, are made available through and appropriated within the marketplace—people have become consumers of various belief systems. This phenomenon is evident in the way in which marketing strategies become identified as a means of evangelization. However, such evangelization is often subservient to an exclusively individualistic account of salvation.

Charles Taylor, the eminent philosopher and social commentator, has provocatively identified the present age as "the age of authenticity."[3] According to Taylor, religious association (being part of a church community) was the primary vehicle for social engagement and social change throughout the nineteenth century (abolition, workers' rights, temperance, etc.). Today, however, religious association has become simply a matter of personal choice, and families are often defined by religious heterogeneity rather than religious homogeneity. Given this cultural shift, many Christian churches have tried to accommodate the rise of individuality by distancing themselves from their denominational affiliations and their institutional identities in an effort to identify with those younger generations who would describe themselves as "spiritual but not religious."[4]

The shift from "religion" to "spirituality" involves complex psychological and sociological issues that are beyond the scope of this text, but this shift has precipitated the rise of a very different set of ideals within our culture. Perhaps one of the most remarkable examples of these new ideals is the emergence of the religious "seeker" as an ideal type within early twenty-first–century Western culture. "Seekers" are able to move effortlessly between various religious experiences utterly detached from tradition, community, and institutions. Seekers create a pastiche of symbols, narratives, and rituals that reflect their desires and experiences.[5] As Miller notes, "people are not necessarily shallow and narcissistic. . . . Rather, they encounter religion in a commodified form."[6] In such a setting, the consumer is not only invited to pick and choose, but he or she is almost compelled to synthesize and juxtapose a variety of (often historically incompatible) religious elements into a convenient and personalized belief system. The creativity and the personal investment may be laudatory, but this development also poses some important questions about the agency of the individual and the manipulative nature of the marketplace.[7]

Commitments to advertising have gradually placed religion within an increasingly fluid and permeable marketplace. Within our culture, brands co-opt values. Take for example the kinds of values you would associate with a particular carmaker or line of shoes. Each product represents a brand, but perhaps more importantly,

A Fetish for Commodities

Karl Marx, the great nineteenth-century philosopher and political revolutionary, articulated a keen insight on the nature of the market system when he discussed the connection between a commodity and a fetish. Today the word *fetish* typically suggests sexual dysfunction. But the concept of the fetish originated in the study of anthropology, in which a fetish is a religious object that becomes invested with meaning to the point that what it represents or symbolizes is no longer relevant, rather the thing itself becomes the object of desire and attention.

The key insight for Marx, however, revolved around the commodity, and for us, it revolves around the extent to which religious traditions have become commodities. A commodity is anything that can be placed on a shelf, as it were, alongside other items for sale. One's grandfather could have made the same object, but then it would not be a commodity; it would be an heirloom, made by a grandfather for a grandchild. Like the commodity, the object grandfather made may serve a purpose, it may or may not be beautiful or expertly crafted, but because grandfather expressed himself in this work and shared it with his grandchild, it is not a commodity.

The commodity is an object that has been removed from any interpersonal context. The object on the store shelf has no provenance (except perhaps a "Made in Indonesia" label). The buyer is not at all concerned with the person who stands behind this object. Rather, the object sits on a shelf and beckons, tantalizing potential buyers. For those who love to shop, they will say that the purchase is exciting, but when they return home with their purchase, the thrill is marginal compared to the stimulation of shopping. The thrill of seeing the object, of desiring it, thinking about it, planning to acquire it—these are the real thrills of shopping. Similarly, when religion is marketed, particularly when churches become commodities, they become detached from their true meaning and value. They may be initially interesting and provocative, but the long-term commitment to a church proves unappealing. Marx understood that the market system cultivates, manipulates, and distorts one's desires in order to perpetuate itself. All people and all churches can become servants of the market, while the market gives nothing in return.

While Marx might be overly dismissive of markets, he identifies some of their problematic aspects, and his insights become even more disconcerting when one sees the Church as a participant in the marketplace. Religious traditions become disconnected from their communities (one can discover Buddhism or "Catholicism for Dummies" at the local bookstore). Moreover, Church marketing and advertising strategies are often portrayed as a benign use of modern systems of communication, but might such maneuvers taint the Church by the power of the market? Does the Church simply package itself for the market, in order to be attractive to consumers? Does the market now dictate how the Church understands and presents itself? Is the "success" of the Church measured by the numbers of new members?

each brand represents certain values. The consumer associates his or her own values with the brands he or she buys. Similarly, church leaders now tend to brand and market their message as they seek to evangelize more effectively, and they do so by distancing themselves from the "established brands" of mainstream religion, or what we would call denominations.[8] Saddleback Church in Southern California (home of Rick Warren and *The Purpose Driven* series of books) deliberately distanced itself from its Southern Baptist identity in order to establish its position within the market. Countless other churches are involved in similar moves in order to promote more effective evangelization, and many of these churches are doing a variety of wonderful work. Such an approach to evangelization, however, is questionable in part because of its tendency to detach the religious faith from history and make it more consumer-friendly. Within the religious marketplace of salvation, the unseen hand of the market has usurped the mediating role of the religious institution. What used to require institutional validation now requires validation in the marketplace—if it's good, it sells.

Compounding the destructive role of the market is the individualism that permeates modern religious sensibilities. Individualism underpins the fragmentation of contemporary Western Christianity by refusing to acknowledge the social (the ecclesial) mediation of the self and, therefore, the ecclesial mediation of salvation; what matters is my personal (understood as individual) relationship with God. Churchgoers increasingly identify with the congregation in which they worship rather than with a particular religious tradition: "I go to First Presbyterian," rather than, "I am Presbyterian." This subtle, but significant, change signals and contributes to a greater distance between the person and that person's congregation, and the tradition within which that congregation stands. Further, the individual evaluates religious affiliation and experience by the same criteria as any product in the marketplace, asking, what am I getting out of this?

These developments are not all bad. As previously mentioned, the empowerment of the individual in contemporary culture is something of a double-edged sword. On the one hand, it places greater emphasis on personal creativity, personal investment, and personal agency in the Church. On the other hand, this individualism tends to derive its power from market-based values that stand in some tension with Christian convictions about the role of the community of believers (the Church) in the work of salvation.

The Church is thus confronted with a social order that is no longer modern, but rather beyond modern (I'm deliberately avoiding the term *postmodern*). Consumerism (the ideological and conceptual infrastructure that makes contemporary culture possible) has been transforming Western culture for more than a century, and it has been radically and rapidly transforming the global situation for at least fifty years. The acceleration of global markets and the rapid development of the technologies that make these markets possible have put the Church and the world it serves into a strange and complex relationship. On the face of it, this interaction has not been beneficial for the Church; however, the damage that has been done is difficult to understand precisely. Sociological studies have identified some of the concerns raised by young people. For example, William Dinges and others at the Life Cycle Institute at the Catholic University of America have concluded that the political-cultural labels *liberal* and *conservative* more regularly predict values and behaviors than any denominational affiliation.[9] Not surprisingly, many younger people gravitate to religious communities and situations that promote values they already possess and affirm—whether conservative or liberal. In other words, competition validates religious communities and practices, and this feature of contemporary culture tends to disassemble religious traditions to suit the needs or even the tastes of individual consumers. In the face of this phenomenon, many young Roman Catholics have moved into a more distinctive form of Roman Catholicism in an effort to combat the individualism and consumerism of the culture.

Evangelical Catholics

Among Roman Catholics under thirty, there has been a movement toward a more conservative expression of Catholic identity in the face of the forces of contemporary society described previously. Although the designation *conservative* is, in many ways, a legitimate moniker for these young Catholics, the phenomenon is far more complex than that term might imply. Several years ago, William Portier published a provocative essay titled "Here Come the Evangelical Catholics," in which he sought to provide a hopeful interpretation of the so-called conservative trend among many younger Catholics.[10] In that essay, he argued that these younger Catholics were not truly "conservative"; rather, they were evangelical, and their evangelism stood as a hopeful sign for the future of the Church.

Portier insists that these Catholics cannot be dismissed simply as ideological conservatives, because such a designation ignores what they really embrace and why they embrace it. First, they do not repudiate the teachings of the Second Vatican Council. Rather, they are seeking a renewal of Church life and ministry in the wake of the demise of the Catholic subculture, and they often do so out of an enthusiastic reading of the council. Second, these Catholics are thoroughly postmodern in their approach to Catholic identity. They are busily wrestling with various elements of contemporary culture and tradition in order to better construct, articulate, and make known a distinctively Catholic identity. As such, they are regularly drawn to the most distinctive elements of Catholic culture: the pope, devotion to the Blessed Mother, and the Eucharist.[11] Third, they generally reject the preoccupations of older generations of Catholics, namely protests against Church authorities and calls for more openness to dissent. Many Catholics, especially older Catholics, find this feature of evangelical Catholics particularly frustrating, because many

of their interactions with the Church (and with the wider culture for that matter) have been defined by struggles against structures of power: the hierarchy, the government, and the military. To them, evangelical Catholics look conservative and appear to be part of the problem rather than part of the solution.

Although evangelical Catholics represent perhaps only 30 percent of the Catholic population under forty, many older Catholics and others are alarmed by the way many younger Catholics embrace distinctively Catholic teachings and practices.[12] They fear that the evangelical Catholics' confidence in the tradition and in the Church, their enthusiasm for Catholic apologetics, and their lack of a critical and self-critical eye leave them susceptible to the triumphalism characteristic of the early twentieth century. Against the alarmists, Portier insists that the emergence of this more evangelical form of Catholicism should be a cause for celebration, not fear, within the Church.

Evangelical Catholics signal a new mission-oriented outlook, one that is better equipped to deal with the culture as it stands and is not wedded to the old worldview. Although the movement is not without its trouble spots (individualism, spiritual self-absorption, unidirectional political leanings), there is potential for it to renew the Church and prepare the Church to reengage the world, provided the movement connects with older Catholics and with the broader Church. According to Portier, some of the new lay ecclesial movements may be attractive and appropriate places for evangelical Catholics to connect to the Church in a substantive way that is in keeping with the outlook of the council.[13]

New Lay Ecclesial Movements

The Second Vatican Council boldly affirmed the rights of the laity as well as the laity's unique mission in the evangelization of the world. In keeping with this vision, the new Code of Canon

Law (1983) affirms the right of the laity to create and join movements without the prior approval of the clergy, because this right is intrinsic to the dignity of the human person and is correlative to the baptismal vocation of every Christian.[14] Such movements are meant to help the faithful progress in holiness and to proclaim the Gospel within those contexts that are particular to the laity. Of all the movements to emerge and flourish in the wake of the council, the following three will serve as examples of the power and mission of the many lay ecclesial movements operating today: the Catholic Charismatic Renewal, Communion and Liberation, and the Community of Sant'Egidio.

The Catholic Charismatic Renewal is an outgrowth of the proliferation of Pentecostal movements that began in the late 1960s. Although Pentecostalism grew and thrived in the early part of the twentieth century, its recent surge in growth has been accompanied by an ecumenical response. Within Roman Catholic circles, the movement has its roots in a series of retreats and workshops hosted by students and faculty at Duquesne University in the late 1960s. Those who participated in the retreats reported a common experience of empowerment, a powerful sense of God's presence. They came to identify that experience as "baptism in the Spirit," a deepening of the call of sacramental baptism.[15] Accompanying this experience was the bestowal of certain gifts common to the Pentecostal forms of Christianity, including speaking in tongues, prophecy, and healing. The movement caught fire and spread to universities such as Notre Dame and Michigan State. In the 1970s, the National Service Committee of the Catholic Charismatic Renewal found a home at the Franciscan University at Steubenville, Ohio, and the summer workshops and retreats held there helped to create a network of smaller charismatic communities that were focused on a deepening of faith, a cultivation of fellowship, and a commitment to evangelization in the world.

The relationship between the larger Church and members of the renewal has not always been cordial. In fact, the doctrinal committee of American bishops investigated the movement shortly after it emerged in the late 1960s. Although the bishops concluded that the movement was a legitimate expression of Christian faith and a valuable resource for the Church, such scrutiny nonetheless highlights the anomalous character of the movement within Catholic circles. Luminaries of the council were quick to encourage and praise the movement (Yves Congar and Cardinal Suenens were among the early supporters of the Charismatic Renewal), and Pope John Paul II was an enthusiastic supporter of the movement's ecumenical and evangelizing mission. The American bishops have tried to place the renewal within the broader context of the life of the Church in an effort to do two things: (1) to make the movement less threatening to outsiders and (2) to keep the charisms exercised within the movement ordered to the good of the Church under its visible structures. The bishops wrote:

> As experienced in the Catholic Charismatic Renewal, baptism in the Holy Spirit makes Jesus Christ known and loved as Lord and Savior, establishes or reestablishes an immediacy of relationship with all those persons of the Trinity, and through inner transformation affects the whole of the Christian's life. There is new life and a new conscious awareness of God's power and presence. It is a grace experience which touches every dimension of the Church's life: worship, preaching, teaching, ministry, evangelism, prayer and spirituality, service and community. Because of this, it is our conviction that baptism in the Holy Spirit, understood as the reawakening in Christian experience of the presence and action of the Holy Spirit given in Christian initiation, and manifested in a broad range of charisms, including

those closely associated with the Catholic Charismatic Renewal, is part of the normal Christian life.

— NCCB Ad-Hoc Committee
for Catholic Charismatic
Renewal, *Grace for the
New Springtime*

The Charismatic Renewal remains an important part of church life throughout North America and the rest of the world. However, as powerful and prolific as the movement is, many Catholics are still uneasy about the Charismatic Renewal and gravitate to other movements.

Communion and Liberation (CL) is one of the largest lay ecclesial movements in the world.[16] CL was founded in Milan in 1954 as part of a high school outreach program. In 1969, the movement matured and began to identify the importance of lived fellowship for promoting the liberation of humanity. It was out of this insight that the movement adopted the name Community and Liberation. Under the leadership of a Catholic priest, Luigi Giussani, CL developed as a movement of young people dedicated to weekly catechesis through which they would become formed in the life of Christ and develop communion with one another. It particularly emphasized the importance of social outreach.

CL focuses on education and cultural development, particularly through its "school of community." These "schools" help members, through reading and discussion of texts selected by the central committee of CL, to develop a clearer understanding of how the central convictions of the gospel ought to impact daily life. Particularly members consider how the theme of Incarnation, the central Christian conviction that in Christ, God became human, ought to change everything. An outgrowth of this conviction is an emphasis on the idea of communion: in Christ God has radical communion with humanity, so too in the Church, human beings are called into communion with one another in Christ. These convictions have concrete implications for how one ought to understand and pursue things like social action, politics, and the formation of culture.

The various schools of community established by CL are the principal means by which the movement carries out its mission. CL's charitable actions are an outgrowth of the belief in the Incarnation and the cultivation of a sense of communion. These charitable actions are not simply philanthropic deeds; rather, they are connected to the educative mission of CL and the conviction that through faithfully enacting charity (love), the ultimate ground of human existence (communion with God) is disclosed. Members of CL work together with nonmembers in a variety of associations designed to address systemic problems such as poverty, hunger, and disease.

The Community of Sant'Egidio (CSE) represents the third example of a lay ecclesial movement here. Inaugurated in Rome in 1968, in the period following the Second Vatican Council,[17] CSE is a lay movement consisting of more than fifty thousand members, dedicated to communal prayer, evangelization, ecumenical dialogue, and solidarity with poor people. CSE is located in seventy countries around the world, though it is most powerfully present in Italy, Spain, and Spanish-speaking countries of Central and South America. CSE has been a major player in promoting various peace accords throughout the world. Of particular import was its intervention in Mozambique, where the group helped broker a peace accord in 1992 that ended twenty-five years of civil war in that country. Additionally, the CSE helped to negotiate a peace treaty to end Uganda's civil war. That treaty, signed by both parties in the conflict (the Ugandan government and the rebels), required the rebel leader, Joseph Kony, to leave the jungle and to agree to be tried by a regional court. While the deal ultimately broke down, with Kony eluding capture, this treaty itself was an impressive development, one which the CSE attributes to its moral authority, prayer, and commitment to peace and nonviolence. To many of their admirers, the CSE stands as a remarkable example of the lay apostolate in which the world is engaged and evangelized by the peaceful and prayerful witness of a believing community.

Each of the movements mentioned above has its problems. Each has been racked with scandals, questions about recruiting tactics, and allegations of authoritarianism, and some in the media have taken aim at these movements with investigative reports and sensational exposés.[18] These movements are not presented here as models or ideals, but as representative attempts by some lay Catholics to engage modern culture in a new way, with the recognition that the life of the average parish is just not enough. Each of the movements discussed has its roots in the work of the Second Vatican Council, and each represents what many would call conservative ways of "doing church." These approaches, however, sometimes strike outsiders as elitist, secretive, and cliquish, and some allege that they actually subvert the council's emphasis on healthy and constructive engagement with culture. Given these suspicions, some question whether the Church can find a form or embrace a movement that helps it to remain true to its prophetic and redemptive mission while being faithful to the council's call for constructive engagement with the modern world.

The Emerging Church Movement

Among Protestant Christians, and evangelicals in particular, a movement exists that mirrors (in some ways) the lay ecclesial movements within Roman Catholic circles. Loosely defined as "the emerging church," this movement is distinct from the nondenominational movement associated with the large mega-church denominations (Calvary Chapel, Willow Creek, Saddleback, etc.). The emerging church seeks to distance itself from the sectarian and parochial denominationalism that defines much of contemporary American Christianity and has sought to reengage the universal or "catholic" tradition. Within the emerging church movement there is a new kind of ecumenism, one based on the recovery of a common tradition—a recovery that looks to the present and to the future in an effort to construct a vision of the Church that is faithful to the tradition and adequate to the Church's mission within a decidedly post-Christian culture. The emerging church focuses as well on social action, or living out the gospel, in ways that make concrete differences within the local community. Some emerging church movements have cultivated a new monasticism in which the ideals of asceticism, communal living, prayer, and stability anchor a small church community in the midst of a neighborhood in need. The new monasticism hopes to cultivate a redemptive presence within that community by forming relationships and promoting economic and social recovery. Key figures in this movement include Brian McLaren, Scott McKnight, and Ian Mobsby. To learn more about the new monasticism see Rutba House, ed., *School(s) of Conversion: 12 Marks of a New Monasticism* (Eugene, OR: Wipf and Stock, 2005), and on the emerging church, see Eddie Gibbs and Ryan Bolger, *Emerging Churches: Creating Christian Community in Postmodern Cultures* (Waco, TX: Baker, 2005).

Basic Ecclesial Communities

Each of the movements mentioned thus far has its genesis, at some level, in dissatisfaction with traditional parish life and a suspicion of the status quo. These dissatisfactions have been an indictment of most parishes' ability to (1) clearly bear witness to the gospel, (2) be responsive to the visions and longings of their parishioners, and (3) constructively and critically engage the demands of modern culture. While these shortcomings are fairly universal, they more acutely reflect the situation faced by the vast majority of Catholic Christians in the Southern Hemisphere who struggle with adverse economic and political conditions and for whom the parish system has proven largely unreliable and often irrelevant.[19]

The growing shortage of priests and religious over the past fifty years has hit rural Catholics the hardest. Even before the council, when seminaries and convents appeared to be full, priestless parishes had been a fact of life for many decades throughout Central and South America, and it was in response to this situation that an important lay ecclesial movement emerged. Small groups of people marginalized or impoverished by circumstance began to organize. Laypeople subsequently led these groups—often initiated by priests or religious who had care of the region. These groups began with dialogue, listening to one another's stories about the struggle to deal with systemic poverty, corrupt political practices, and the daily difficulties common among humans of every segment of society. Eventually they combined Bible study, liturgy of the hours, and basic fellowship with political action and mutual aid. These groups became known as Basic Ecclesial Communities (BEC), and they proliferated throughout Latin America, but particularly in Brazil where there are some eighty thousand BECs today.

BECs are not alternative parishes; they are more like small groups within a parish structure.

They afford the faithful an opportunity to build strong community and to create a deeper sense of fellowship with one another. BECs also help provide a ready-made context for projects and other endeavors to meet the immediate needs of the community. In places where large and sprawling parishes of twenty thousand people are more common, the need for such small groups is apparent. BECs have become the cornerstone of pastoral work within both Protestant and Catholic churches throughout Central and South America as well as in Africa and in parts of Asia. The popularity of various lay ecclesial movements within North America and Europe is an echo of the BEC movement in Latin America. Fundamentally, BECs and other ecclesial movements are concerned with the empowerment of the laity over and against hierarchical structures that are often unresponsive and unavailable. Within the present social and political context, all of these movements raise difficult questions about the hierarchical constitution of the Church and how hierarchical ministries need to be rethought in light of the Church's redemptive mission.

THE CALL TO ENGAGEMENT

The movements discussed in this chapter highlight a growing dissatisfaction with traditional parish structures and the inability of the Church to address the complexities of the post-Christian world. The emerging church movement provides a Protestant echo of both the BEC movement and the new ecclesial movements within Roman Catholic circles. These expressions of Church stand out as creative ways of promoting the Church's mission to proclaim the gospel to all nations while at the same time challenging and supplementing traditional parish structures. The prophetic and dynamic nature of these movements, however, may also raise questions about how they play out from a soteriological perspective. As one considers and assesses these movements, some points made in chapter 2 have particular relevance. In what follows, the soteriological principles mentioned toward the end of chapter 2 (Lonergan and the Law of the Cross) will be revisited in an effort to flesh out a framework for understanding how the Church might engage the world. Of primary importance is setting forth an account of history that does justice to both the seemingly determined or fixed aspects of history and those aspects that are open to the influence of human decision making. Within this context, one can then understand the social and cultural dimensions of sin and from there begin to construct a concrete understanding of the Church's mission in the world.

History as a System (Emergent Probability)

Many people are burdened with an overly deterministic worldview and, therefore, an overly deterministic account of history. Maxims such as "God has a plan, and everything happens for a reason" proliferate without ever being scrutinized. The sentiment expressed in the foregoing maxim reflects some truth about history and thus deserves serious attention, but it fails to capture either the structure of human history or the randomness that is also part of that history.

Consider the randomness of some of the events in your life. For example, say you left the house at 7:31 this morning rather than 7:26 because the toaster was not plugged in when you first tried it. That five-minute delay put you in heavier traffic, and you were caught behind a broken-down city bus. This made you late for an important class. The relationship between you and the professor is so strained at this point in the semester that you are now in a panic about your grade in the class. So you decided to stay home this weekend so that you could study more

and this caused you to forego the party that everyone had been anticipating for weeks. At the party, your best friend was looking for you to introduce you to the cousin of a friend from out of town who is probably a perfect match for you, but you weren't there . . . all because of the toaster! "Well, it wasn't meant to be."

Perhaps, but the series of events just described are common enough to give one pause about ascribing the course of life to some vague sense of destiny or to a mechanical notion of divine providence. The series of events that unfolded beginning with the toaster did not *determine* the outcome—missing the party and the opportunity to meet that special someone was the result of a whole range of factors. The randomness of such events, the contingencies that unfold in life every day, is part of each person's story, each person's history. Random occurrences affect all of us constantly; however, life is not all randomness—one does exercise a certain agency within history. We do have some choices in life. One's choices, however, do not necessarily *determine* all events, but they do set in motion a series of other occurrences and these events can be studied and understood.

History, whether it is one's own personal history or the history of a nation, is not simply a narrative; it is an intelligible system that is open to randomness and contingency. Events lead to other events, but not out of necessity. Rather, they happen as a result of other events, and the connection between various events yields a pattern. Once a pattern emerges, there is a far greater chance that the pattern will repeat itself. One should be careful, however, of thinking of events simply as a series of links in a chain because such a linear account of the interconnectedness of events belies the fact that there are a wide range of effects stemming from one event and each of those effects has the potential to initiate another set of effects. One should think of events, rather, as part of a circle or cycle, and these cycles have a propensity to entrench themselves as recurring

Emergent Probability (EP) and Schemes of Recurrence

Christians have long wrestled with the issue of free will and contingency (as opposed to necessity), or even randomness, in the workings of the universe. At the popular level, many Christians feel the need to emphasize God's sovereignty over creation, making statements such as "God is in control," and "God's will cannot be thwarted." Such statements often suggest or lead to explicitly ascribing all events to the will of God—even evil and the most barbaric events in history.

EP does not challenge the sovereignty of God and the power of God's will. It begins with the premise that God's will is irresistible, and goes on to affirm that if God wills contingency in the universe, then the universe that God has created will be characterized by contingency. Everything has a certain structure. Events unfold in a certain manner, but they do not "have to happen." Within EP, there is a certain probability that when A happens, B will happen (then C, D, etc.). However, the pattern is not a linear chain of events.

$A \rightarrow B \rightarrow C \rightarrow D \rightarrow E$, etc.

Rather, A, B, C, etc. are part of a pattern that emerges and perpetuates itself. Now, the pattern is not necessary (it does not have to happen this way), but once the pattern emerges, it is more likely to repeat and thereby sustain itself as long as there is no interference. Any given pattern or scheme of recurrence is not simply isolated as a system. One pattern or scheme can figure into another pattern or scheme. For example, A may cause B, and B may not only cause C within one pattern, but also B^2 within another scheme of recurring events (scheme of recurrence).

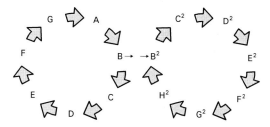

One can see how any single scheme of recurrence can be dependent upon another scheme or pattern and another and another. Environmental scientists often try to make this case about the way ecosystems are structured. The disappearance of a single species could have an impact on the environment in a variety of ways. Economies also unfold as systems that are interconnected. In the end, the major question involves the impact of human decision making in shaping various systems that structure societies and cultures. Patterns of thinking and behaving are part of the schemes of recurrence that make up human history. When those ways of thinking are twisted by short-term values and parochialism, destructive patterns emerge and repeat themselves. From afar, these patterns may appear to be easily identified and remedied, but as individuals, groups, and entire cultures become conditioned by these destructive schemes of recurrence, there emerge entrenched structures of sin and destruction.

cycles or patterns. These recurring patterns of events, or schemes of recurrence, arise and endure in history. Many of these patterns are natural, or random, and other patterns emerge as a result of human freedom. History, therefore, should be viewed as an intelligible system in which one attempts to identify and predict patterns or schemes of recurrence.[20]

The preceding paragraph sets forth a notion of history that Bernard Lonergan called Emergent Probability (EP). For Lonergan, the world is defined as emergently probable. In other words, the world is not simply random, nor is it determined. It emerges with a certain degree of probability. There are some classical laws that express and define what is determined (gravity is a classical law), and there are statistical laws that complement classical laws by giving expression to the manner in which events unfold according to statistical patterns (the Krebs cycle in biology, or even the evolutionary theory). Schemes of recurrence can be understood through statistical methods, but this does not necessarily yield a prediction of the future. There is no guarantee that any scheme will occur, or once it occurs, there is no guarantee that it will endure or recur. There is, however, a specific probability of its emergence and a higher probability of its survival once it has emerged. Schemes of recurrence make seemingly random events intelligible and place those events within a broader explanatory context.

Science, Darwin, and Emergent Probability (EP)

Christians are often troubled by the conflict between theories of biological evolution and the biblical accounts of creation, pitting one against the other as if they were mutually exclusive. Once the creation stories are placed into their appropriate historical contexts and interpreted theologically, however, the problem tends to diminish. However, many Christians are still troubled by evolution because it seems to ignore or radically downplay any intelligence or design behind the creation of the universe.

EP, however, takes the scientific insight about the fragility of the cosmic order into account by pointing to randomness, contingency, and chance as playing active roles in the unfolding of the universe, but the universe, nonetheless, remains intelligible even while it is open. Genetic mutations, the vagaries of climate, the probabilities of molecular structures and combinations are part of probable patterns that have emerged over the course of time to give us the world in which we live—a world that is fraught with contingency, but a world in which God is still nonetheless present, active, and discernable. The limitations of existence, one's very finitude, are part of one's humanity, so that disease, natural disasters, and tragic accidents are not attributable to the divine will (or a malevolent will for that matter); they are the product of an open universe into which God allows human freedom and responsibility. Humans may never be able to overcome being subject to disease and disaster. However, humanity is often called upon to use its intelligence, its moral judgment, to create its world, and this is precisely where the Church is called to be active.

Humans constantly attempt to discern why things are the way they are, and they always seek higher systems of understanding. That is, humans are interested in not only discrete facts, but also in causal relationships. Humans try to understand these relationships as components within larger systems so that they might comprehend and then judge these systems and ascertain where there is decline and decay and where there is progress and recovery. The human condition, to use an overwrought phrase, entails the creation of the self, the creation of environment, and the creation of history. The theological punch line is that the fabric of the universe, from the first moments of the universe through the evolution of life, is structured around contingency, such that far from making human decisions anomalous or illusory, the universe itself is fundamentally ordered to human freedom.

The worlds that humans create are not the achievements of heroic individuals, though some individuals do exert greater influence than others in the course of history; instead, these worlds are created by and for communities of people and by large societies. These communities and societies (a small parish is a community, and the United States is a society) establish family systems, schools, neighborhood associations, economic systems, and political arrangements that are all part of various schemes of recurrence (patterns of operation that produce the worlds in which humans live). These schemes themselves are subject to a wide range of statistical probabilities.

As an example of these schemes of recurrence, consider the relationship between weather-climate and the range of economic resources available in any particular community. For instance, farmers who live west of the Missouri River in North Dakota cannot grow sugar beets like farmers in the Red River Valley in the eastern part of the state, near Fargo. The land in the western part of the state can only support large ranching operations. As one might guess, the social and political situation in the Red River Valley is, therefore, distinct from the social and political situation in Mandan or Dickinson (cities west of the Missouri). For example, in the western part of the state there are fewer people

and larger ranches. In the east, migrant workers, many from Mexico, have made their way to the Fargo area for years because of sugar-beet production. These arrangements were not inevitable, but certain decisions were made over the course of years in response to climate and weather that yielded a distinctive communal and social structure in the Red River Valley in eastern North Dakota.

Climate was not the only factor in these decisions, but it has played a significant role in establishing a certain pattern. Of course, questions arise: Were these the best decisions? Should different decisions be made now? What are the limits of the decisions made in the past? Do changes in technology affect the options available? These questions presuppose some knowledge of the schemes of recurrence with which humans are dealing and some account of what constitutes progress and decline. In other words, dealing with the world and making appropriate decisions depends on an account of decline and an account of progress or recovery. The decisions and values articulated and embraced by individuals, groups, and entire cultures will play a decisive role in the emergence of one particular scheme of recurrence or another.

Sin in History

As the Church seeks to understand and engage the world redemptively, and as it explores alternative forms and movements, it must take into account the structure of sin in history. In the example given, the social and cultural situation of North Dakota or any other location is not solely the product of climate and natural resources; rather, people made decisions based on values, and these values contribute to the structure of life at any given place and in any given time. People in North Dakota (or New York or California or Pennsylvania, for that matter) have not always made good decisions, nor have they always chosen good over evil, but these choices are not simply "bad choices" made on any single occasion; rather, these choices and the values they express are part of the schemes of recurrence that make up human history. Within the Christian tradition, "the reign of sin," as it is often called, is a scheme of recurrence.

Lonergan, as discussed in chapter 2, determined that sin was a distortion of human knowing and human valuing. Working from the empirical methods used in the natural sciences, Lonergan observed that the human mind achieves knowledge by first experiencing data, then formulating an insight regarding the data, and finally, verifying the data in judgments of fact (answering the question, "Is it so?"). Lonergan offered a series of imperatives to which humans respond: be attentive to the data (even the data of experience), be intelligent (in one's interpretation of the data), be reasonable (in one's assessment of whether the interpretation is in fact true), and be responsible (as one acts in accordance with the truth discerned). Sin results as humans short-circuit, or arrest, the process by refusing to remain attentive to questioning and by becoming accustomed to accepting very limited answers to those questions.

Levels of Conscious Intentionality

Lonergan makes good use of the famous line from the opening of Augustine's *Confessions* in which the Bishop of Hippo writes: "You have made us for yourself Lord, and our hearts are restless until they rest in Thee." This fundamental insight suggests that the very structure of our minds, our intellect and will, is oriented to God. Lonergan spells this out in terms of the invariant structure of human interiority. In other words, how we come to know and value unfolds through four interrelated levels, moving from the most basic (experiencing) to the most advanced (deciding) levels.

4. Deciding ↑	Be Responsible! (Bring knowledge into concrete action; ask the question, "What should I do?")
3. Judging ↑	Be Reasonable! (Confirm the interpretation or reformulate the interpretation; judge whether the interpretation conforms to reality; ask the question, "Is it so?")
2. Understanding ↑	Be Intelligent! (Interpret the data of experience; ask the question, "What is it?")
1. Experiencing ↑	Be Attentive! (Pay attention to the data of experience; ask the question, "Am I open to this?")

As humans move from being attentive to the data of experience (often this means sense experience, but it can also refer to experiences beyond the senses), they construct interpretations of experiences, giving the data meaning. Yet, not content with mere interpretation, humans are driven to know whether their interpretation of the data is true; they want to know what is real. And humans work to determine criteria or questions the answers to which will help them determine if interpretation "X" is true. Having established the truth of the matter, the facts, they are compelled to ask the further question about how or why the truth is important; they are impelled to make decisions about how this truth matters and how they should act upon it.

For Lonergan, the human drive to know (third level of conscious intentionality) and to love (fourth level of conscious intentionality) opens humans up to the transcendent. In the acts of knowing and valuing, humans come to grasp and affirm a world beyond themselves. But ultimate self-transcendence cannot be obtained through the powers of human interiority. These powers open humans to the transcendent, to God.

The natural powers of human nature are fulfilled or perfected by grace (Aquinas' famous maxim: "grace perfects nature"). Through grace, God's knowledge and love flood humans' hearts and minds so that their drive to self-transcendence is gifted with fulfillment (Romans 5:5). In a world without sin this would be straightforward, but in a world of sin (bias), human drive to self-transcendence is skewed and distorted. Humans are inattentive, unintelligent, unreasonable, and irresponsible. As such, they cut themselves off from fulfillment, unless they are prepared to be healed and fulfilled by the gift of grace.

The Danger of Common Sense

Lonergan described the distortions of conscious intentionality in terms of bias. The biases revolved around preoccupations with the individual and the groups to which individuals belong. In these instances, one's knowing and valuing center on what might benefit the individual or the group to which the individual belongs. These distortions are often relatively easily identified, though they are often difficult to remedy. More insidious, however, is what Lonergan calls "the general bias of common sense." For Lonergan, common sense refers to knowledge that is "gained through the senses and is limited to the senses," and for the most part, this knowledge is a good thing. Common sense keeps humans safe when crossing the street, it helps them understand how to grow crops, nurse an injury, and do all sorts of practical things that are the bedrock of day-to-day survival.

The problem with common sense is that it has the tendency to assert its hegemony over the entire range of human cognition so that what is true and what is good become reduced to what is practical, tangible, and profitable. In brief, this is an inversion of many popular theological approaches to Satan and sinfulness. Many understand Satan as a prideful rebel rejecting divine authority by seeking to place himself above God.

However, for Lonergan, sin is rather an abandonment of transcendence in favor of something less; it is an "underreaching" in one's valuing. It is often compared to an addiction, the "infinite desire for a finite object."[21] Such an addiction is devastating for individuals and those around them, but what happens when the addiction is written into the social and cultural dimensions of human life?

The social dimensions of sin are manifested within the systems humans construct to promote living together. Put quite simply, humans live in community, in part, to promote a common welfare. When various forms of bias skew a person's thinking or valuing, however, that thinking or valuing is expressed and entrenched within social systems. The ordering of society reflects this. Consider for example the social situation, broadly speaking, in Central America, where the vast majority of the population is indigenous or a mixture of Spanish and indigenous ancestry (*mestizo* or *ladino*). The economic infrastructure of many of these countries, until very recently, was controlled by a small number of families, almost all of them descendents of Spanish colonizers. Land had been granted to these families by the Spanish government as a reward and as an obligation. Spanish colonizers were to work the land (and use the indigenous people as workers or slaves) in order to harvest natural resources (gold and other minerals) or to produce goods (sugar cane, cocoa, coffee, fruit) for sale and trade.

Notice the thinking of the Spanish colonizers that went into this enterprise: (a) the land belongs to us because we have the power and therefore the right to take it; (b) the land and its resources are to be harvested for the benefit of the Spanish and not for the indigenous people of the land; (c) the indigenous people of the land are here for our benefit and can be used as we see fit. In this pattern of thinking certain values emerge, values that reflect group bias and the general bias of common sense. The question of what is truly good is distorted and replaced with questions

The Biases

For Lonergan, sin is experienced as a distortion of human interiority. The drive to know what is real and value what is truly good opens the human person up to ultimate self-transcendence. Yet, because of sin, this process is distorted. That distortion takes on three dominant forms that Lonergan calls "bias."

INDIVIDUAL BIAS

Individual bias makes people focus on themselves. They fail to ask, "What is true?" and "What is good?" Instead, they are stuck in the rut of asking, "What is good for me?" and "What is true for me?"

GROUP BIAS

Group bias is individual bias that is enacted within a group. The questions of value (what is good) and fact (what is true) are asked and answered from the perspective of the group. Nationalism is one of the most obvious examples of group bias—national policy is defined as what benefits the nation, and what is true is defined as that which affirms that nation's values and identity.

GENERAL BIAS

The general bias of common sense sounds like a good thing—wouldn't it be great if everyone would use some "common sense"? However, Lonergan argues that humans are often given over to the tyranny of "what works" and "what I can see." Common sense is not a bad thing, but when it is celebrated as a pervasive assumption about reality, it wreaks havoc in history. When humans subscribe to the general bias of common sense (like with all the biases, one does not usually consciously embrace it), they ignore the human vocation to transcend themselves, their group, and what can be sensed—what is truly real and truly good in the universe is beyond themselves and their interests.

that revolve around limited goods: "what is good" means "what is good for us," and "what is good" is "what is practical and profitable."

These biases reflect the thinking of only a few people; however, they have been written into the social order. Sin is evident in the history of social relationships in these countries along the lines just described. A small percentage of the population controls the vast majority of the land and resources of the country. If one were to question this state of affairs, then one would be labeled a revolutionary or a subversive. Such labels then attempt to mark any challenge to the societal status quo as illegal,

and often those who pose such challenging questions are executed for their efforts (e.g., the Jesuit martyrs in El Salvador). The cultural dimension of sin, however, compounds and entrenches the social structure of sin.

The distortions of social systems are often reinforced by tradition. Societies develop systems of meaning and value (cultural norms) that often protect destructive patterns from criticism. The cultural dimension of sin is manifested in the signs, symbols, stories, and discourses that define and disseminate the meanings and values of a society. In the scenario depicted in the preceding paragraph, the privilege of the Spanish colonizers, the "inferiority" of the indigenous peoples, and the unquestioned propriety of imperialism are reinforced by the narrative world of the Spanish conquerors. It is a narrative that, until recently, was often unquestioned. Unfortunately, in the history of the Spanish conquest, the Catholic Church was often complicit in the construction of a society and a culture that revolved around exploitation of indigenous peoples. Consider the manner in which the hierarchy of the Church was established and supported by the Spanish government and how that relationship forced the Church, with only the rarest exception, to become complicit in the enslavement and exploitation of natural resources and indigenous peoples. Even the liturgy and the images around the liturgy helped to reinforce the superiority and dominance of the Spaniards. Rulers in the Church (bishops) and the secular government (governors) were always Spaniards or of Spanish descent. Democratic rule was not to be tolerated, even after the demise of the Spanish colonial system in the nineteenth century. Democratic rule, after all, would enshrine the will of the majority, the indigenous and *mestizo* citizens, and the idea of an indigenous leader had been made unfathomable for many. Indeed, military juntas and military presidents dominated most nations in Central and South America for more than a century, often propped up to support the interests of foreign governments (usually the United States) or foreign corporations (such as the United Fruit Company).

The examples used here to illustrate the social and cultural dimensions of sin are broad and sweeping, but they highlight the nature of the problem of sin. If the love of God is poured out in the life, death, and Resurrection of Jesus and continuously mediated through the ministry of the Church, then it makes good sense to have as robust an account of sin as possible. Purely spiritual or personal accounts of sin actually distort the

problem by neglecting the manner in which Christ and the ministry of the Church offer God's solution to that problem. Racism, sexism, materialism, violence, intolerance, environmental callousness, and greed pervade our culture and help to structure society. Addressing these problems requires an appropriate account of how grace operates in the world: the grace of God poured forth in the life, ministry, death, and Resurrection of Jesus and mediated in history by the Church, which according to the faith of the Christian Church, provides the solution to the problem of sin.

The Church, Grace, and History

Emergent Probability (EP) defines the world, and structures of sin emerge and are understandable as an expression of it. However, the world is also defined by grace, which is intelligible as an expression of EP. Just as sin does not remove the freedom of the human actor, so too grace allows for the exercise of freedom and, in fact, demands intelligence and ingenuity. In chapter 2, a soteriology that was inspired by the work of Bernard Lonergan and expanded by his interpreters (William Loewe and Joseph Komonchak) was discussed. In that soteriology, the symbolic language of Scripture, language that tended to privilege cultic images for understanding Christ's saving work, was transposed. What Lonergan calls "The Law of the Cross" was set forth as a principle of transformation, of religious conversion, which was the solution to the problem of sin manifested as bias, or the distortion of personal knowing and valuing. Lonergan describes the process by which bias is overcome as "conversion." A dramatic leap beyond the horizon of meaning and value is what defines a person and the world in which that person is located. One's intellection (to use a more classical term) may undergo conversion (what Lonergan termed "intellectual conversion"). When this conversion takes place, the human being moves from believing that reality is simply a matter of what can be seen and touched to recognizing that reality is much more than what one's senses can perceive. One's valuing can also undergo conversion ("moral conversion") so that one no longer believes simply that what benefits me or what benefits us is really good; rather, one comes to recognize that what is really good may work against one's own interest in the short run. Finally, in religious conversion, one can come to experience and understand that God loves humans beyond all reason and that they are called to total self-transcendence and union with God (in love). This religious conversion is expressed by Lonergan as "being in love in an unrestricted fashion." Working on the analogy of "falling in love" with an individual, Lonergan contends that religious conversion is not falling in love with "someone" (in which case, I become enraptured with person "X"—a limited, incomplete, and imperfect creature), but it is falling in love with love itself. Religious conversion, therefore, has the power to utterly transform one's life and one's outlook on the world. These conversions can happen in any order, but they tend to have an impact on one another.

In chapter 2, Lonergan's understanding of soteriology under the title "the Law of the Cross" was presented. This approach to soteriology transposed the customary presentation of the saving significance of Jesus' life, death, and Resurrection by seeking to understand these events as embodying and making available the possibility of human transformation, or religious conversion. In other words, instead of considering Jesus' death a necessary event whereby the punishment due for sin was visited upon Jesus instead of humanity, one is able to understand these events as the manner in which God freely chose to transform evil into good. That transformation entails confronting the evil of sin with the power of God's love. Such a confrontation will result in the cross—transformative "dying." What Christ accomplishes on the cross is made

available to humanity, is accomplished in humans both individually and collectively, to the extent that the power of God's love is allowed to take hold of and transform the human person so that her thinking and her valuing become God's own. Perhaps put more strongly, God's thinking and valuing occur through those who have experienced religious conversion.

The Church's mission is to promote such conversion, which is the work of God's self gift (grace), in order to bring about the salvation of the world. Human salvation does not occur but through conversion, and, as noted previously, conversion is not just a matter of the transformation of individuals. Societies and cultures stand in need of redemption as well. The Church's call, its mission, is to promote, make available, and prod the world at large so that it might experience the love of God in a manner that is intelligent and transformative. The history of the Church, as it was briefly related in chapter 3, provides ample evidence that the Church was indeed self-conscious of its encompassing mission—not just to change the hearts of individuals, but to confront and to conform society and culture to the demands of the gospel. The history of the Church demonstrates both great successes in this regard and great failures. As the Church finds itself in an increasingly post-Christian culture and society, it must consider how to be faithful to its mission. Can it change the lives of individuals while also influencing social and cultural development?

CONCLUSION

As the Church discovers its new situation in the twenty-first century, it has struggled with its understanding of the world and with its place in the world. The new ecclesial movements both within as well as without the Roman Catholic Church have provided rich resources for reconsidering the form the Church must take within the present cultural and social context. However, one must also be cautious about such movements and their capacity to vilify the world or even the larger Church community. The current cultural situation, with its globalized market and its post-Christian sensibilities, is not easily influenced by pronouncements from the Vatican or the bishops, or by the fellowship of small-group communities. Traditional parish structures seem to stand in need of the revitalizing efforts of the new ecclesial movements, for through the powerful witness of radical groups such as the CSE, the Charismatic Renewal, and the BECs of Latin America, the distortions of cultures are more readily confronted. However, the integration of these communities within traditional parish structures and the larger Church is not often accomplished. For better and for worse, the new ecclesial movements stay on the periphery even while their impact on Church life is substantial and their promotion of patterns of redemption for their members and for the world around them is undeniable.

In chapters 6 and 7, two basic dimensions of the Church's redemptive mission will be set forth: calling and sending. The Church calls humanity to a transformative encounter with the love of God. This encounter is made available, in a special way, through the liturgical life of the Church, through worship. In turn, Christians are sent. In the process of being transformed, Christians are sent into the world to proclaim the love of God in Jesus Christ. Certainly, this is an evangelizing mission, but this evangelization cannot be reduced to the promotion of Church membership. Evangelization is most authentic when it promotes redemptive transformation of the world, as evidenced by pertinent social teaching and effective social practices.

Questions for Understanding

1. What is a "commodity"? In what ways has religion become a commodity?
2. What are the "Evangelical Catholics," and why are some people concerned about them? What does Portier think of them?
3. Describe the origins of the Catholic Charismatic Renewal. How has the renewal been received in the Church?
4. What are the origins of Base Ecclesial Communities (BECs), and what do they do?
5. What is Emergent Probability (EP), and what is its connection to history?
6. Compare and contrast the social and the cultural dimensions of sin.

Questions for Reflection

1. When, if ever, have you heard an official Church pronouncement on a given topic or issue, and how did you respond? (For Roman Catholics, this might be a papal pronouncement or a pronouncement from the bishops' conference, and for Protestant Christians or students of other faith traditions, this might be a statement from the Church conference or some other body). Did you receive word of these pronouncements through the news, the Internet, or through your home church? Did these pronouncements make a difference in how you think about an issue or topic? Explain.

2. Reflect on the life of your home church, parish, or religious community, if you belong to one, and describe features of that community that make it appealing and helpful. Do some aspects of life in that community make it unattractive or unappealing? What sorts of changes would help to make your religious community a more vibrant part of your life and the life of the larger society?

3. Locate a nontraditional ecclesial group in or around your area (a Catholic Worker House, a new monasticism group, a CL group, a charismatic group, etc.) and ask if you could observe or participate in worship or some other activity with them. What did you observe? Were you warmly welcomed, or were you treated as an outsider? What impressions did you get from the group?

Suggestions for Further Study

Hanna, Tony. *New Ecclesial Movements: Communion and Liberation, Neo-Catechumenal Way, Charismatic Renewal.* New York: Alba House, 2006.

Hanna presents a sympathetic overview of some of the most popular lay ecclesial movements in the Catholic Church.

Komonchak, Joseph A. *Foundations in Ecclesiology*, Lonergan Workshop. Boston: Boston College Press, 1995.

This collection of essays systematically sets forth the groundwork for an ecclesiology born of the thought of Bernard Lonergan. The book can be difficult to acquire, but it is invaluable for considering the redemptive mission of the Church in the world.

Melchin, Kenneth R. *History, Ethics, and Emergent Probability: Ethics, Society, and History in the Work of Bernard Lonergan.* Lanham, MD: University Press of America, 1987.

Melchin's book is not an easy read, but it offers one of the best overviews of emergent probability and ethics from the perspective of Bernard Lonergan.

Rutba House, *School(s) for Conversion: 12 Marks of a New Monasticism.* Eugene, OR: Cascade, 2005.

This collection of essays is from an intentional community in Durham, NC. The essays reflect the spirit of the emerging church movement and the new monasticism within Protestant communities, though at least one of the contributors is Roman Catholic.

Endnotes

1. See John Allen, "Benedict in Cameroon: A Tale of Two Trips," *National Catholic Reporter*, March 20, 2009, (http://ncronline.org/blogs/all-things-catholic/benedict-cameroon-tale-two-trips).

2. Vincent J. Miller, *Consuming Religion: Christian Faith and Practice in a Consumer Culture* (New York: Continuum, 2003).

3. Charles Taylor, *A Secular Age* (Cambridge, MA: Harvard, 2007), 486–492.

4. There are many interesting counterexamples of churches rediscovering their histories and, indeed,

recovering the longer history of the church catholic (e.g., the resurgence of Calvinist studies among many Reformed Christians, or the recovery of the broader catholic tradition in Baptist circles evidenced in the series, Studies in Baptist History and Thought, from Paternoster Press).

5. This capacity is rightly distinguished from the historical formation of traditions through enculturation and syncretism that develop over the long course of history.

6. Miller, 6.

7. Miller argues that the phenomenon of bricolage is at the heart of the Christian tradition. The Greek father, Aquinas, and others are celebrated for the way they integrated pagan philosophy and all that seemed antithetical to the Christian worldview. See Miller, 164–178.

8. Michael L. Budde, *The (Magic) Kingdom of God: Christianity and the Global Culture Industries* (Boulder, CO: Westview, 1997). See also, Philip D. Kenneson and James L. Street, *Selling Out the Church: The Dangers of Church Marketing* (Nashville, TN: Abingdon, 1997).

9. William D. Dinges, "The American Cultural Context for Adolescent Catechesis," *Momentum* 38/1 (2007): 52–55. See also Dean R. Hoge, William D. Dinges, Mary Johnson, SND De N, and Juan L. Gonzales Jr., *Young Adult Catholics: Religion in the Culture of Choice* (Notre Dame, IN: University of Notre Dame, 2001).

10. William L. Portier, "Here Come the Evangelical Catholics," *Communio* 31 (Spring 2004): 35–66.

11. Portier, 55.

12. James D. Davidson et al., *The Search for Common Ground: What Unites and Divides Catholic Americans* (Huntington, MO: OSV, 1997), 124–132.

13. Portier, 58.

14. *CIC*, Canon 299 §1.

15. For a study of the experience of "baptism in the Spirit" and its connection to Christian initiation, see Killian McDonnell and George Montague, *Christian Initiation and Baptism in the Holy Spirit* (Collegeville, MN: Liturgical Press, 1991).

16. Davide Rondoni, *Communion and Liberation: A Movement in the Church* (Montreal: McGill-Queens University, 2000).

17. There are many popular accounts of the Community of Sant'Egidio online (see John Allen's interview with the founder of the community, Andrea Riccardi, at http://www.nationalcatholicreporter.org/word/word072304.htm). For an overview of the community's spirituality, see Laurie Johnston, "'To Be Holy in the World': The Influence of Yves Congar on the Spirituality and Practice of the Community of Sant'Egidio," in *Catholic Identity and the Laity*, College Theology Society Annual, vol. 54, Tim Muldoon, ed. (New York: Orbis, 2009), 59–74.

18. For a sympathetic overview of the criticisms and the hopes associated with new ecclesial movements, see Tony Hanna, *New Ecclesial Movements* (New York: Alba House, 2006), 251–282.

19. Leonardo Boff, *The Base Communities Reinvent the Church* (New York: Orbis, 1986).

20. For an excellent overview of emergent probability and history, see Kenneth Melchin, *History, Ethics, and Emergent Probability: Ethics, Society, and History in the Work of Bernard Lonergan* (Lanham, MD: University Press, 1987).

21. Neil Ormerod, *Creation, Grace and Redemption* (New York: Orbis, 2007), 49, n.7.

The Church and Its Liturgical Constitution

The last decades of the twentieth century have witnessed an explosion of interest in alternative forms of Christian worship, and the question of what represents authentic worship has become a controversial topic across denominational divides. The drive to create and experience new liturgical forms and new music poses many challenges and many opportunities for the Church today.

Beneath the surface excitement, though, lies a great deal of anxiety about worship and considerable dissatisfaction with how worship is experienced locally. Reasons for this anxiety and dissatisfaction are ample. It may be the case that there is something inadequate about the church community in which one worships. The lack of hospitality or concrete fellowship in one's home church or parish may leave people feeling alienated and disconnected from worship. It may also be the case that there is something amiss with one's understanding of and approach to worship. And, perhaps, it may be both these factors and others as well. It will be the burden of this chapter to suggest that Christian worship is at the heart of what it means to be Church, of what it means to follow the gospel. Moreover, failures to understand, create, and participate in worship pose serious obstacles for the Church's redemptive mission in the world.

LITURGY AND THE FORMATION OF THE SELF, SOCIETY, AND CULTURE

Worship expresses the values held by a community, and it reinforces those values within that community. Worship, therefore, is serious business, and it has enormous implications for the shape of the life and self-identity of the believer. Formation is not just about the development of the individual, however; it also involves communities whose social structures are established and sustained through various forms of worship. If the world suffers under the reign of sin and death, as Christians claim, and the answer to the problem of sin is given in Christ, then how are these claims manifested in distinctive acts of Christian worship?

Throughout this section, the terms *Christian worship* and *liturgy* will be used interchangeably. Within a Roman Catholic context, a special priority of place must be given to the Eucharist, or the celebration of the Lord's Supper. All other acts of worship, whether they meet the technical definition of liturgy (e.g., Divine Office) or are devotions (e.g., Stations of the Cross), find their meaning and place in the life of the Church in relation to the celebration of the Eucharist. The terms *Christian worship* and *liturgy* have been used in order to (1) make the conversation meaningful to an ecumenical audience (many of the issues related to the place of worship in the life of the Church transcend any specific Christian community or church) and (2) to include the wide variety of forms within the Christian tradition's life of prayer in addition to the Eucharist.

Created for Worship

In the opening book of his *Confessions*, Augustine wrote, "You have made us for yourself Lord, and our hearts are restless until they rest in Thee." For those who attend church services regularly, however, one seldom finds rest. Within contemporary culture, there is an emphasis on movement, multitasking, and production, and many worshippers report being preoccupied with the need to move, to get out, and to get things done during times set aside for worship. Often, worshippers have a general dissatisfaction with the experience of worship, mixed with a resignation that this is an obligation for the serious Christian. Yet for Augustine, and for the Christian tradition in general, worship is more than an obligation and it is more than a time of rest; it is an expression of the heart's deepest longing. Although this conviction may strike some as odd and out of place, Scripture testifies that the human person has been created to have union with God, and this union takes the form of worship. In other words, human beings have been created to worship God.

The first story of creation in Genesis sets forth the origins of the universe from a uniquely cultic point of view. In fact, God is depicted as a priest in Genesis 1 (the story is narrated within the Priestly tradition). God's creation occurs effortlessly through the power of a spoken word. The orderly creation of the universe unfolds over the course of six "days," and the seventh day is declared the day of rest—the Sabbath. From the perspective of Genesis, the very fabric of the universe is ordered by the Sabbath. One must be cautious about such an assertion, since it is often assumed that the Sabbath is really a series of obligations about when to work and how to rest, and this is precisely how it is treated in the context of the controversies regarding the Sabbath in the Gospels (Mark 2:27). It is, however, also the vision of Scripture that the Sabbath, understood as the worship of God, is the goal, the end, the *telos*, of creation.

In other parts of Scripture, the heavenly realm is portrayed as worship. In Isaiah, the angels are perpetually offering worship. In Isaiah 6,

God is present in the Temple of Jerusalem. He is surrounded by seraphim, each of whom cries out, "Holy, holy, holy is the Lord of hosts!"' and in Revelation 4:8b–11 and throughout the visions at the end of the book, it is presupposed that heaven is a temple where the angels and the faithful gather and worship—what else are they to do?

> Day and night they do not stop exclaiming: "Holy, holy, holy is the Lord God almighty, who was, and who is, and who is to come." Whenever the living creatures give glory and honor and thanks to the one who sits on the throne, who lives forever and ever, the twenty-four elders fall down before the one who sits on the throne and worship him, who lives forever and ever. They throw down their crowns before the throne, exclaiming: "Worthy are you, Lord our God, to receive glory and honor and power, for you created all things; because of your will they came to be and were created."
>
> — REVELATION 4:8b–11

If, according to the Christian tradition, humans are created for worship, that is, they are destined to worship God in eternity, then how should one understand worship on Earth?

Consuming Worship

Many Christian theologians today see a resurgence of the ancient Gnostic heresy in the religious sensibilities of contemporary Christians and within the general population as well. Gnosticism tore at the very fabric of the Church for centuries. A religious movement that emerged in the second-century, Gnosticism subtly used elements of the Christian tradition to put forth a disturbing and destructive worldview. Gnostics celebrated the knowledge (the Greek word *gnōsis* means "knowledge") that the created world,

including human bodies, was manufactured by an evil deity who sought to imprison humanity. One's true self, according to Gnostic belief, was pure spirit, and it was by cultivating this knowledge that one could be saved from the prison of this world. Gnosticism, quite understandably, often denied basic tenets of the emerging Christian tradition (particularly the Incarnation and the suffering of Christ). Additionally, Gnosticism placed a greater emphasis on the individual and less emphasis on the believing community or its relationship and responsibility to the world. Although the heresy appeared to die out long ago, different forms of Gnosticism have emerged over the course of the centuries. Many contemporary commentators believe that the Church today is struggling mightily against a new form of this ancient heresy.

One important battlefront in the struggle with Gnosticism is the area of worship or liturgy. Christian worship today has often been reduced to a commodity, a consumer experience in which churchgoers are courted with relevant and uplifting experiences (see especially chapter 5 in this regard). Indeed, within church communities, a musical dividing line often exists between those who prefer the contemporary "praise choruses" (often favored by younger worshippers) and those who prefer traditional music (often older parishioners). Moreover, churches often compete with one another over the most attractive worship times, styles, technology, and relevance. They compete to meet the desires of their consumers—that is the basic principle of the market. Moreover, some would argue that this marketing of the Church represents the new ecumenism in which Christians are no longer tethered to the denomination in which they were raised. They feel free to move between church communities with little concern or fear about alienating family or about moral repercussions. In the end, the needs of the individual often seem to define the discussion of worship, inevitably reinforcing the primacy of the individual and focusing attention on an inner (affective) disposition toward God.

As noted in chapter 6, the expansion of global markets and the advent of media saturation have entrenched a consumerist culture across the globe. Market-driven ideologies create societies organized around consumption. In such societies, everything is for sale, or it has no real value. The intersection of individualism, consumerism, and religion has separated believers from their religious communities and has separated those communities from their histories. The social dimensions of religious belief and worship have increasingly become matters of personal choice, and Christian worship and outreach reflect this development. As young people, particularly those aged 18–35, approach the question of participation in a religious community, they are highly skeptical and often are not committed to a particular religious expression. Increasingly, churches have tried to reach this demographic, self-described as "spiritual but not religious," by constructing appealing worship services in settings that remind one less of a church and more of a coffee shop, nightclub, or even a warehouse. These moves are understandable and often laudable as signs of cultural accommodation and gestures of authentic hospitality and dynamic outreach, elements often missing from traditional parish settings. Yet such moves may also mask a dangerous undertow.

Beth Newman has observed that consumerist culture has had a corrosive impact on Christian worship, particularly by allowing worshippers to observe rather than participate. She argues that contemporary culture trains humans to be spectators—we are constantly watching, observing, taking everything in. Worshippers come to the liturgy already detached from the community, and they often want to be entertained. Pastors and worship teams are compelled to put on a show, to provide music, a message, and above all humor to reach their "audience." The consumer, after all,

is constantly asking, "What am I getting out of this?" The pastor and the worship team, in order to entice people to return week after week, must answer that question in a way that makes sense to the consumer. Traditionalist services (e.g., the Latin Mass), by contrast, are often packaged as a bulwark against the evils of an encroaching corrupt culture. In this context, worship can often become either sentimentalized or ordered to a private communion with God.[1]

Worship for many has become a secondary concern, a matter of style and taste. Perhaps it is important to the extent that it offers support for many people as they go about their daily lives, but it is not seen as really necessary. One does not need church and worship, because God loves each person as an individual; one can feel God's presence apart from the trappings of institutionalized religion. While such sentiments are common in discussions about worship, it is apparent that the communal and sacrificial aspects of church life have been lost in those conversations. While the word *liturgy* (*leitourgia* in Greek) literally means "the work of the people," many Christians tend to neglect the idea that liturgy is *work*!

Within the religious marketplace of salvation, the unseen hand of the market has usurped the mediating role of the religious institution. What once required divine validation via the religious institution now requires validation in the marketplace, and only individuals, cobbled together as demographic groups rather than as communities, matter in the market. Institutionalized individualism grounds the contemporary understanding of religion and worship, and the social and political dimensions of worship are often ignored or vilified by a consumerist Gnosticism that exacerbates the suffering of the world rather than promoting the world's healing. As in the past, the allure of this particular heresy is difficult to resist, and so it permeates one's sensibilities and plays a significant role in Christian self-understanding, worldview, and worship.

The Formation of the Self and a Social Order

The connection between worship and the self need not reinforce the individualism of our age, however. Joseph Komonchak has written clearly about this connection as he reflects on the groundbreaking work of Bernard Lonergan.[2] Fundamental to Lonergan's outlook is that for human beings the world is not simply experienced; rather, the world is mediated by meaning, and meaning is mediated by the community. For example, the human infant is initiated into a world of meaning by his or her interaction with parents, siblings, peers, and environment. Within this context, language is shared and beliefs are imparted. These beliefs concern everything from the ultimate meaning of human existence to matters of geography and history. Infants thus *receive* a world already made and mediated by meanings and values from the communities into which they are born. The world received is governed by certain assumptions, beliefs, and meanings that order the interactions between humans, communities, and institutions, and these relationships produce a common (though not utterly uniform) way of life.

Chapter 5 explored the manner in which meanings and values can be distorted, yielding dysfunction and sinful social and cultural structures (bias). While these structures do not erase the essential freedom that constitutes one's humanity, they do impinge on one's effective exercise of that freedom. For example, whether

An Early Experience of Grace

In Christian worship, values are imparted and reinforced within the community. For example, when I attended a Catholic grade school, we used to gather every Friday during Lent for Stations of the Cross. Stations, as it is often called in Catholic circles, is the ritual whereby one meditates on the journey of Christ from his condemnation by Pilate to the crucifixion and death. There are fourteen stations (marked by small plaques) around the interior perimeter of Roman Catholic Churches that enable the faithful to symbolically reenact Christ's journey to the cross. This ritual, in a technical sense, does not qualify as liturgy but as a devotional practice. However, it can serve as an appropriate example of some dimensions of liturgical worship.

As we filed into church, we were given small booklets that contained brief meditations on each of the fourteen Stations of the Cross. For each station, we were asked to consider Jesus and his sufferings and to tie these sufferings to the pain and alienation our sins had caused. The connections between the suffering of Christ and the suffering of those around us, while not necessarily powerful on any given Lenten Friday, certainly had a powerful cumulative effect in my life. To this day, images and words from that devotion, stories from the Gospels, and images from the celebration of the Eucharist still evoke powerful feelings within me, and despite my selfishness and laziness, I am often compelled to action by the coalescence of these images, the feelings they evoke, and the values they impose on me. I relate this experience to the Christian experience of grace and the furtherance of Christian conversion, the "transformed dying" constitutive of Christian accounts of Christ's saving work and the Church's saving mission.

one can choose to pursue higher education, an exercise of one's effective freedom, is contingent upon the time and place in which one lives, and whether it is a context in which higher education is valued and resources are available. Suppose one belonged to a family and culture that did not value the intellectual development of women. In that context, the effective freedom of young intelligent women would be limited. It would be literally unimaginable for such a woman to go to college or to pursue professional training. So the exercise of freedom is contingent upon the world of meaning and value created and imparted by others; it is a gift, in a sense (or a burden), rather than a right. Humans receive the gift of freedom and learn to be free. Conversely, humans can also become shackled and learn to limit or lose their freedom.

Of course, the world is not defined by a single set of values, but many competing ones. The likelihood that a person will move from one value system to another, however, is affected by the schemes of recurrence discussed in chapter 5. Certain values will become more prevalent, more easily entrenched, and more commonly affirmed even within the marketplace of values. Yet, one must be willing and able to identify the manner in which meanings and values antithetical to the gospel and subversive of the Church's redemptive mission are being imparted. Through liturgical practices, the Church then seeks to form an alternative set of meanings and values that will establish redemptive patterns (schemes of recurrence) within believing communities by opening the minds of worshippers to God through dramatic and practical training.

In reflecting on the dynamics of Christian worship, one might be tempted to simply equate Christian storytelling with other storytelling. For example, the old fairy tales in which medieval values of northern Europe continued to be spun out for children helped to instill a sense of fear

and dread in countless generations. The feelings evoked in children by the retelling of Hansel and Gretel no doubt sent chills down young spines as did the original stories of Cinderella and Little Red Riding Hood. These stories do impart a worldview, they do evoke feelings and help children to apprehend values, much in the same way that Stations did for many Catholic youth during childhood. However, does Christian worship go beyond merely the dramatic and the arousal of feeling? Are the feelings, values, and ethics communicated by the liturgy nothing more than alternative fairy tales?

Liturgy and the Body

Philip Kenneson provocatively delineates the power that human assemblies have in forming one's worldview and values.[3] He compares the power of two assemblies in particular: the amusement park and the boot camp. People gather and form assemblies at each of these locations for very different purposes and with very different expectations. Both assemblies will contribute to the formation of their respective communities by imparting values and establishing relationships. The boot camp impacts the behavior of those assembled more thoroughly than does the amusement park. After all, those gathered at the amusement park are looking for a diversion, an experience that can bring them together and take them away from their cares and concerns, while those gathered in boot camp expect to be shaped in some more lasting way that transcends that place and time. Given culture's insidious capacity to train people to be spectators wanting to be entertained, Kenneson asks the question: should Christian worship be more like a boot camp or an amusement park?

Of course, the image of the boot camp and the violence associated with it are troubling. Kenneson wants nothing to do with images of "Christian soldiers" yelling at the top of their lungs, "Blood makes the grass grow greener!" and he has no desire to connect Christian worship to the militancy of a boot camp. Rather, the illustration simply focuses attention on the assumptions that have come to dominate Christian expectations about and participation in worship. The amusement park image raises problems by diminishing the political and ethical dimensions of Christian worship and ignoring liturgy's formative aspects. The liturgy stands at risk of losing its power when it is understood merely as an opportunity for weary parishioners to recharge their batteries so that they might more happily make it through another week.

M. Therese Lysaught also uses the analogy of the boot camp as well as that of athletes in order to consider the relationship between liturgy, ethics, and the body.[4] Basic training in a military context involves the formation of particular types of bodies. Particularly for those who enter into "combat arms," bodies must be formed in a particular way, and this formation makes such bodies identifiable to outsiders. Veterans are often asked, "Were you in the military? . . . I thought so. I could tell by the way you carried yourself." In the military, particularly in the intensive training periods soldiers undergo at the start of their time in service, bodily actions are

BEST PRACTICES

Foot Washing at Annunciation Monastery

The practice of foot washing goes back to the Gospel of John in which, in chapter 13, Jesus washes the feet of his disciples. The ceremony of reenacting the scene in the Fourth Gospel has been part of Holy Thursday celebrations since as early as the seventh century in Toledo, Spain. In most Catholic and many Protestant parishes today, the scene is enacted with the pastor washing the feet of twelve often uncomfortable parishioners. As the ritual concludes, the twelve participants hurry back to their seats vowing, "I'm never doing that again!"

At the Benedictine Monastery of the Annunciation in Bismarck, North Dakota, the tradition has a sharper edge to it. In this and many other Benedictine communities, the prioress (the woman who is in charge of all the other members of the community) joins the rest of the community to wash the feet of every other member of the monastery. This ceremony often takes some time, but the political significance of it is considerable. The leader of the community, the one to whom a certain obedience is promised and demanded, might kneel before the most junior member of the community to wash her feet!

The prioress in Bismarck is a significant figure. By virtue of her office, she sits on the boards of several major corporations (some of the biggest and most important in the state). The foot washing is a powerful testimony to the nature of Christian leadership, of servant leadership, as the prioress puts her body in a position of humble servitude as a foot is placed in front of her face to be washed. The dominant culture may feel awkward witnessing such an act, as it does not see the prioress's gestures, her bodily position, as indicative of leadership. Imagine, for example, a corporate board meeting beginning with the chair of the board kneeling before each of the board members, or, better yet, kneeling before company employees, to wash their feet?

Liturgical Postures and Gestures

Many gestures occur in the context of the liturgy, and perhaps the most common and one of the most ancient is the Sign of the Cross. In making the sign, Christians call to mind that through the cross God has revealed himself to us, redeemed us, and now calls us to embrace transformation from sin into the life of grace. Through this special gesture, Christians are constantly reminded of the Paschal Mystery and of their vocation to embrace the transformed dying that leads to new life (the Law of the Cross).

In the following chart, a few of the postures used in the liturgy are presented along with a brief synopsis of the meanings these postures convey in the life of the believing and worshipping community.

Posture	Liturgical Context	Meaning
Standing	• Gathering and Dismissal • Prayer (Notice when the celebrant says, "Let us pray" that the congregation stands.) • Proclamation of the Gospel • Receiving Communion	Standing has a range of meanings, but it is surely a sign of respect for the procession and the entrance of the celebrant at the gathering rite as well as respect for the Word of the Lord proclaimed in the Gospel. However, perhaps from the earliest times of the Church, standing was a posture of prayer, a participation in the risen Christ. The congregation stands, it rises with Christ, to offer prayer and praise to God. When worshippers stand for prayer and for the reception of Communion, they are acknowledging the gift of the Resurrection and the participation in God's life that it has given.
Kneeling	• The Eucharistic Prayer • After the fraction of the Host in the Communion Rite (The congregation sings "Lamb of God" as the priest breaks the Host.)	In the early centuries of the Church, Christians were forbidden from kneeling on Sundays and during the Easter season. Writers such as Tertullian and many others insisted that because participants have been raised up with Christ, when they celebrate the Resurrection, their posture should be that of the Risen Christ (standing). However, the penitential sensibilities of the Middle Ages made kneeling a more common penitential posture as well as a posture of adoration and humility.
Sitting	• The first part of the Liturgy of the Word • The Homily • Post-Communion Meditation	While one often thinks of sitting as a position of relaxation and comfort, in the context of the liturgy, sitting is the posture of attentive listening and meditation.
Prostration	• In liturgies of ordination and religious profession, candidates lie prostrate during the Litany of the Saints.	Prostration (lying face down on the ground with the hands and arms out to the side in the shape of a cross) signals utter submission, utter helplessness. In these liturgies the congregation implores intercession so that candidates might be able to carry out the service for which they have been selected. Prostration is a gesture of profound humility. It is begging for divine assistance.

only undertaken at the direction or command of an authority. At times, soldiers hold a position (e.g., the push-up position) until they are physically unable to do so and either collapse or are forced to engage in another posture or activity at the command of a superior. These rituals build one's body in a certain way. It becomes a body that can endure pain and hardship and that will respond to orders rather than the needs or wants of the individual. In short, through basic training, one becomes part of a *corps*, the French word for "body." The individual bodies are trained to become *one* body, ready to endure, sacrifice, and kill at the command of the state.

Lysaught argues that Christian worship produces distinctive bodies as well, and that over time, the regimen of liturgical practices tacitly and implicitly forms bodies capable of distinctive actions whereby the Church may resist and subvert the powers of the world. Maureen Tilley, a scholar of early Christianity, provides Lysaught with some important examples to support her argument.[5] Tilley notes that the ascetic practices of the early Church, practices such as intense fasting, contemplative prayer, and physical mortification, helped to prepare Christians to resist the torture that would precede any execution. The torture was meant to tear believers from their faith and cause them to capitulate to the demands of the state. Through Christian *ascesis* (discipline of the body), always tied to acts of worship, the bodies of the martyrs became

> battlegrounds between God and the demonic. Caesar would not determine their salvation or the meaning of their deaths. For this reason, not just anyone could be a martyr. . . . Those [bodies] not properly produced would not be able to withstand the torture, their failure would both empower the enemy and undermine the morale of the persecuted community, threatening it with dissolution.[6]

The practical formation of such bodies, particularly the production of those bodies necessary for the battlegrounds of contemporary culture, is a difficult issue. However, it seems apparent that the consumerist approaches to Christian worship, as discussed, and the accompanying resurgence of a new form of Gnosticism, require that Christians thoughtfully engage liturgical practices in an effort to promote the redemptive mission of the Church.

The Eucharist as "Counterpolitics"

Echoing some of the insights of the Radical Orthodoxy (RO) movement, many Roman Catholic theologians are increasingly wary of the power of the state. They are also wary of ecclesiastical models that seem to surrender so much to a state that, in turn, does everything it can to marginalize the Church as a private association of the faithful, concerned only with interiority, or "spiritual things." The great American liturgist, Virgil Michel, OSB, was a fervent critic of such privatization, and he argued for a liturgical reform in which the liturgy became the vehicle for enacting a just social order, rather than simply an activity that raised the mind of worshippers to God in heaven. Contemporary theologians like William Cavanaugh have also written provocatively on the subject of the Eucharist as a means by which the Church practices a kind of anarchy in the face of the state's monopoly on power and on discourse about the common good.[7]

For Cavanaugh, one of the most powerfully political dimensions of the Eucharist is the promise of Jesus in John 6:57: "Jesus said to them, 'Amen, amen, I say to you, unless you eat the flesh of the Son of Man and drink his blood, you do not have life within you.'" He also cites Augustine, who comments on this passage in his *Confessions*: "I am the food of the fully grown [the mature]; grow and you will feed on me. And you will not change me into you like the food your flesh eats, but you will be changed into me" (*Confessions* 7. 10).[8]

The Eucharist thus subverts the basic notion of property that is at the heart of the modern state and its politics. Through the self-surrender of Christ, and through the "work" (*leitougia*) of the Eucharist, the Christian does not come to possess Christ; rather, the Christian becomes possessed by God in Christ. For Cavanaugh, the modern liberal democratic state is based on the notion of property (through one's labors one acquires rights over things—these things become a person's property) and the creation of society through contracts that recognize and protect property rights. In the Eucharist, however, Christians move from their status as mere individuals, with their individual rights and their property, to become instead one Body in Christ—living no longer for themselves but for the God revealed in Jesus Christ.[9] The action of the Eucharist thus overcomes the fragmentation that the state seeks to remedy with contracts. However, this Body is constituted both by its union with the Head (Christ) as well as the unity between each of the members of the Body. In other words, the union created by the Eucharist is not simply a union with Christ, a vertical union; it is also a horizontal union.

This horizontal union is what produces the catholicity, the universalism, constitutive of God's Church, and it stands over and against the homogenizing and violent universalism of the globalized market. In the globalized market, transcendent values are co-opted by brands in an effort to make consumption the glue that binds together all those who eat at a particular restaurant chain or who drive a particular car. In the Eucharist, the Church is created in countless local celebrations, and these local celebrations are gathered into one, not through the centralized bureaucracy of Rome, but through the communion of churches whereby the whole Church is present even in the scattered local communities. Thus, the entire Church is gathered "where two or three are gathered" in the name of Jesus to celebrate the Eucharist. Christians believe this to be true precisely because the Church is the Body of Christ, and where the Eucharist is celebrated, Christ exists, not in part, but in what one might describe as an inexhaustible totality.

The political dimensions of the Eucharist (its powers to redeem individuals in their communities and to transform social and cultural orders) are not enacted magically. The celebration of the Eucharist, as well as other liturgical actions, requires attentiveness and deliberation as well as imagination. Certainly, in the words of the Catholic Church, the sacraments work *ex opere operato*; in other words, the sacraments work when they are performed, because God is the agent of the sacrament, God is the one who works in the sacrament. The liturgical reform, however, has also helped to arrest some of the distortions of Christian worship and has helped to reorder the celebration of the liturgy so that its redemptive power may be more fully known. In the next section, the main insights of the liturgical reform articulated at the Second Vatican Council of the Catholic Church will help to round out the discussion of Christian worship and the Church.

THE COUNCIL AND THE PRINCIPLES OF LITURGY

As was noted earlier, the reformation of the liturgy (the celebration of the Eucharist as well the other liturgies of the Church) was one point on which consensus was reached early on at the Second Vatican Council. Even contemporary proponents of the Latin Mass were in favor of major liturgical reforms at the time of the council, and this is evident in the fact that the draft schema on the liturgy, prepared by the conservative Doctrinal Commission and presented to the Central Preparatory Committee, was the only draft document accepted by the council fathers in the first session. In the course of the year that followed, however, the draft document on the liturgy underwent significant revision. Although a variety of topics were debated extensively, certain principles for the reform of

the liturgy were enthusiastically accepted and promulgated in the document. Among these, three deserve special attention: (1) the liturgy as the "source and summit" of Christian life, (2) the centrality of the Paschal Mystery in the liturgy, and (3) the importance of full and active participation of all in the liturgy.

The Return of the Latin Mass?

The pontificate of Benedict XVI has seen the rise of interest (and Vatican approval) for the celebration of the Mass in Latin according to the ritual established prior to the Second Vatican Council. Some groups within the Catholic Church have been interested in a return to the Latin Mass and have seen the overtures by the pope as a sign of hope. These small groups of Catholics view the liturgical reforms of the Second Vatican Council with suspicion. In particular, they regard the implementation of reform by the Consilium (the group appointed by Pope Paul VI to implement liturgical reforms) as heavy-handed, and they believe it did violence to the liturgical life of the Church. They see the so-called new liturgy (Novus Ordo, or Ordinary Form) as a violation of the rich dignity of the tradition. This argument, along with other pertinent arguments favoring better planning, execution, and theological grounding for liturgical practices, are also often accompanied by highly charged invectives against the council itself and even against Popes Paul VI and John Paul II. It must be remembered, however, that the contemporary Latin Mass, the Mass with which some are currently enamored, is itself an innovation, a product of the liturgical renewal and reform.

In the eighteenth and early nineteenth centuries, the celebration of the Mass was often chaotic, rapid, and incoherent. No missals were available with which those not literate in Latin could follow along and participate, and the prayers of the celebrant were often mumbled inaudibly while most of the congregation participated in some quiet personal devotion. Attentiveness to the liturgical arts, careful cultivation of chant, increased education of the laity in the principles of the liturgy, and the expectation of full conscious participation (particularly the emphasis on congregational singing), were all part of the liturgical reform that had its roots in the founding anew of the Benedictine monasteries in the decades after the end of the Napoleonic era. The Latin Mass as it is experienced today, and even as it was experienced by those who remember it from the decades prior to the Second Vatican Council, is an innovation, a construction of the past century and a half.

As Pope Benedict seems to suggest, the traditions of the Latin Mass deserve serious attention in the debates about how to best continue the liturgical reform, but the question with which the Church is wrestling revolves around ongoing reform.[10] The debate cannot revolve around the return to some idealized past that never existed. Additionally, and most importantly, the Church must wrestle with the question of whether a return to the Latin Mass effectively addresses the demands of discipleship within the twenty-first century.

Source and Summit of the Church's Life

Article 10 of *Sacrosanctum concilium* states that "the liturgy is the summit toward which the activity of the Church is directed . . . it is the font from which all her power flows." Such a statement drew criticism from some of the bishops at the council who thought that it was unwise to give the liturgy such a central place in the life of the Church. They argued the Church's mission is to save souls, to bring people to Christ, and to reach out to the poor and the troubled. As such, Christ ought to be recognized as the source and goal of Christian life, and the liturgy ought to be understood as a tool by which Christ is encountered in the Church.[11] However, in the end, the council fathers were clear in refuting the notion that the liturgy is merely instrumental. They affirmed that the actions of Christ and the Holy Spirit are uniquely encountered in the liturgy, and it is from the liturgy that people are sent forth to do other things (works of mercy, preaching, instruction, etc.). Moreover, the goal of these activities is to draw people into authentic worship, because the liturgy is the concrete expression of the fellowship for which human beings are created.

It may seem odd to think of the liturgy as the goal of evangelization and works of love, justice, and mercy, but this thought returns to points made at the opening of this chapter. That is, the Christian belief that humanity has been created to worship God. In *Dei verbum* (Dogmatic Constitution on Divine Revelation), the purpose of divine revelation is articulated:

> In His goodness and wisdom God chose to reveal Himself and to make known to us the hidden purpose of His will by which through Christ, the Word made flesh, [humans] might in the Holy Spirit have access to the Father and come to share in the divine nature. Through this revelation, therefore, the invisible God out of the abundance of His love speaks to [humans] as friends and lives among them (Baruch 3:38), so that He may invite and take them into fellowship with Himself.
>
> — *DEI VERBUM*, 2

Revelation, God's self-communication, has as its goal the fellowship between God and humans, as well as participation in the divine nature—sharing in God's very life. The late Swiss theologian Hans Urs von Balthasar, developing the thought and experiences of his close friend Adrienne von Speyr, expressed the relationship among the persons of the Godhead. He described the relations that constitute God as Trinity (Father, Son, and Holy Spirit) as a relationship of prayer.[12] The *kenosis* (the self-emptying) of God and the *agapē* (the loving self-gift) of God are eternally expressed as worship and prayer. The Father, the Son, and the Holy Spirit worship and glorify one another, and this is what Christians mean when they say that God perfectly expresses and loves God's self. One's participation in the divine nature, one's sharing in God's life, is a sharing in the eternal worship of God. The liturgy, thus, is a proleptic, or anticipatory, participation in the divine life, and this is why in the Christian East the Eucharistic liturgy is called a "window into heaven."

The liturgy not only provides an anticipation of one's participation in the divine life, it also is the source from which the work of the Church flows. In the liturgy, worshippers are called to live in the world as a "kingdom people," and they are supplied with the power and the vision to see the universe in new ways that challenge the assumptions written into the social and cultural order by the counter-liturgy of the various biases (individual bias, group bias, and the general bias of common sense). Heaven erupts into the space and time of a fallen world, renewing human vision, and through the liturgy participants are trained to see the world differently. Indeed, the enacting of the proclamation of the stories of Scripture, and in particular, the story of Jesus, offers a grace-filled alternative to the stories and the vision of the world into which one has been born. This dynamic is at the heart of the "sending," or "missioning," of the Church that will be discussed in greater detail in chapter 7.

Paschal Mystery at the Center

While the liturgy is the anticipation as well as the partial realization of the heavenly kingdom, there is also the recognition that the liturgy promotes that realization within a world under the sway of sin and death. As such, the liturgy functions as a venue for the experience of redemption, of saving transformation. In other words, the liturgy works to foster religious conversion.

As discussed in this chapter, Christian conversion follows the dynamics stated in Lonergan's "Law of the Cross" and is expressed using the traditional language of "the Paschal Mystery." Commentators on *Sacrosanctum concilium* have remarked that the phrase "the Paschal Mystery" was at the heart of the liturgical reform of the nineteenth and early twentieth centuries, and that the council and subsequent papal documents on the liturgy make use of this phrase time and again. It was meant to express the saving work of Christ functioning in the liturgy. This saving work encompasses Christ's life, death, and Resurrection—the entire Christian

story of redemption—and it is made present in the Church through the liturgy.[13]

In *Sacrosanctum concilium*, the Paschal Mystery is at the heart of the Church's life and mission.

> [Christ] achieved His task principally by the Paschal Mystery of His blessed passion, resurrection from the dead, and the glorious ascension, whereby "dying, he destroyed our death and, rising, he restored our life." For it was from the side of Christ as He slept the sleep of death upon the cross that there came forth "the wondrous sacrament of the whole Church."
>
> — *SACROSANCTUM CONCILIUM*, 5

The Church, through its worship, draws humans more deeply into the divine life, which, in a world torn by sin, takes the form of the cross. Through the cross of Christ there is resurrection, new life in God. The Paschal Mystery is a reality in which humanity is called to participate, and it is

PERSON OF INTEREST

Odo Casel, OSB (1886–1948)

Odo Casel was a monk of the German monastery of Maria Laach and one of the most important scholars of the liturgical reform in the twentieth century. Among the most significant achievements of Casel was his cultivation of the Paschal Mystery as the heart of soteriology and the heart of the liturgy. For Casel, the mystery of the liturgy (*Kultmysterium* in German) is made known under the veil of symbols. The liturgy realizes, in the life of the Church and in the life of the world, the saving work of God in Christ. It was Casel who wrote that the liturgy was "the central and essentially necessary activity of the Christian religion" precisely for this reason.

the Church's mission, through the liturgy, to call humans to conversion and full participation in the divine life.

> Thus by baptism [humans] are plunged into the Paschal Mystery of Christ: they die with Him, are buried with Him, and rise with Him; they receive the spirit of adoption as sons "in which we cry: Abba, Father" and thus become true adorers whom the Father seeks.

> — *SACROSANCTUM CONCILIUM*, 6

In the liturgy, through the furtherance of conversion, both the individual Christian and the entire Christian community are drawn more deeply into Christ and, therefore, more deeply into the life of the Trinity. One's worship is transformed so that one offers to the Father the praise and worship that comes from the Son and the Spirit.

This action in the liturgy is not simply the work of liturgists, those who preside, or other ministers who perform various functions in Christian worship; rather, the work is that of Christ who is present in the liturgy.

> To accomplish so great a work, Christ is always present in His Church, especially in her liturgical celebrations. He is present in the sacrifice of the Mass, not only in the person of His minister, "the same now offering, through the ministry of priests, who formerly offered himself on the cross," but especially under the Eucharistic species. By His power He is present in the sacraments, so that when a man baptizes it is really Christ Himself who baptizes. He is present in His word, since it is He Himself who speaks when the holy scriptures are read in the Church. He is present, lastly, when the Church prays and sings, for He promised: "Where two or three are gathered together in my name, there am I in the midst of them."

> — MATTHEW 18:20;
> *SACROSANCTUM CONCILIUM*, 7

The presence of Christ in the Church, in the celebration of the liturgy, is transformative. Through remembering (*anamnēsis*), proclamation, and fellowship, God's life is given over to a world suffering from sin and evil and the world is transformed by this gift. However, God's gift can be abused or neglected, and it can fail to be received through ignorance. This brings forth the third point of focus in the liturgical principles articulated in *Sacrosanctum concilium*—the importance of fully active and fully informed participation in the liturgy.

Full and Active Participation

It was not long ago that Roman Catholics were obliged simply "to hear Mass" on Sundays and Holy Days of Obligation. However, how can such an obligation live up to the lofty purpose of the liturgy set forth previously? At the council, the bishops affirmed that the liturgy itself is formative; it is not merely an obligatory action or simply a matter of church discipline.

> The liturgy in its turn moves the faithful, filled with "the paschal sacraments," to be "one in holiness;" it prays that "they may hold fast in their lives to what they have grasped by their faith;" the renewal in the Eucharist of the covenant between the Lord and [humans] draws the faithful into the compelling love of Christ and sets them on fire. From the liturgy, therefore, and especially from the Eucharist, as from a font, grace is poured forth upon us; and the sanctification of [humans] in Christ and the glorification of God, to which all other activities of the Church are directed

as toward their end, is achieved in the most efficacious possible way.

— *SACROSANCTUM CONCILIUM*, 10

Moreover, the council fathers recognized that in order for the liturgy to be formative, to be fully activated in the lives of the faithful, the liturgy needed to be fully accessible and to invite, even demand, the full and active participation of all.

This emphasis on full and active participation in the liturgy is not new. Pius X (whose pontificate began at the start of the twentieth century) and each of his successors made a point to make changes in the liturgy or in certain practices that would facilitate maximum participation in worship. The council determined that greater instruction in the liturgy itself was in order to facilitate the full and active participation of all participants. Notice too that the council calls for the full and active participation of *all* and not just the laity. Priests, religious, laity, musicians, architects, and artists, everyone must be trained more effectively in order to participate more fully in the liturgy and to summon others to their fullest participation as well.

The ongoing reform of the liturgy was to take into account the growth and proliferation of liturgical practices that had outlived their purpose and were no longer conducive to a proper and fruitful celebration of the Paschal Mystery.

Thus, for well-disposed members of the faithful, the liturgy of the sacraments and sacramentals sanctifies almost every event in their lives; they are given access to the stream of divine grace which flows from the Paschal Mystery of the passion, death, and resurrection of Christ, the font from which all sacraments and sacramentals draw their power. There is hardly any proper use of material things which cannot thus be directed toward the sanctification of [humans] and the praise of God.

With the passage of time, however, there have crept into the rites of the sacraments and sacramentals certain features which have rendered their nature and purpose far from clear to the people of today; hence some changes have become necessary to adapt them to the needs of our own times.

— *SACROSANCTUM CONCILIUM*,
NOS. 61–62

Some elements of the liturgy have become outmoded, not because of their antiquity, but because they do not foster the full and active participation of the faithful in the liturgy. However, almost any proper use of material things can be made suitable for worship and can, therefore, be useful in the liturgy.

An important area of concern for the council fathers was the promotion of an inculturated liturgy. The European, and indeed the "Roman" aspects of the liturgy must not be allowed to dominate or exclude the appropriation of the liturgy within the distinct cultures of non-European and non-Roman cultures that have come to accept the Gospel. The council fathers addressed the issue of inculturation (the adaptation of the liturgy to different cultural settings) and the responsibility of local episcopal conferences to establish and implement reforms necessary for inculturation of the liturgy (*Sacrosanctum concilium*, 37–40). However, the tension remains between a standardized "Roman" form of the liturgy and the need for inculturation, and this tension continues to dominate many debates about the liturgy today. In the end, the continuity of the tradition needs to be measured against the pastoral needs of any given situation—but always with an eye toward the other principles of the liturgy mentioned above.

Saint Peter Claver, New Orleans, Louisiana[14]

The issue of inculturation does not apply only to "overseas territories" in Africa, Asia, and Latin America. The inculturation of the liturgy in the United States within diverse parishes is as appropriate as the inculturation of the liturgy in other parts of the world. Perhaps one of the best examples of this homegrown inculturation can be found at Saint Peter Claver, an African American parish in New Orleans.

At Saint Peter's, Father Michael P. Jacques, a priest of the Society of Saint Edmund, has worked with parishioners for more than twenty-five years to transform the parish and its liturgical life to promote the full and active participation of the faithful. When it came to the liturgy, the pastor (who is white) and other leaders in the parish took it upon themselves to pursue an education in the principles of liturgy in African cultures. This course of study helped to empower the parish to revise the liturgy according to their own needs and their own cultural heritage.

At Saint Peter's the liturgy is still recognizably the Mass, but celebrations regularly include African dance, poetry, liturgical art, and vestments appropriate for an African, rather than a European, context. The pastor approaches his homily using a "call-and-response" format. For example, parishioners are expected to respond at certain points in the homily as the pastor asks questions such as, "Is Jesus here this morning?" Additionally, although silence is still appropriately observed at certain times, at other times the congregation is called upon to applaud or to shout. In all, the liturgy at Saint Peter Claver speaks to the life and developing formation of this African American parish.

The connection between revitalized full participation in liturgy and opportunities for missionary outreach in the parish is obvious. Located in one of New Orleans's most troubled neighborhoods, Saint Peter Claver has managed to fill its school with children from the parish and has made tuition a secondary consideration. In a city where a "conspiracy of silence" empowers drug dealers and others who prey on the weak, the parishioners of Saint Peter Claver have organized a community watch system with the New Orleans Police Department. Moreover, the parish also can mobilize against city officials when injustice is allowed to fester. For example, writer and filmmaker Paul Wilkes narrates the story of one Sunday morning when the New Orleans district attorney was invited to worship at Saint Peter Claver. During the liturgy, a procession was made to a local abandoned property that had become a trouble spot in the neighborhood. The parish was able to successfully lobby for the district attorney's office to prosecute neglectful and absentee property owners. In short, the full and active participation in the liturgy helped to promote redemptive patterns in the living history of this neighborhood (especially true in the wake of Hurricane Katrina). While all is not perfect in New Orleans, the Church of Saint Peter Claver has redemptively engaged the world around it, embracing the cross of Christ and experiencing the gift of new life in God.

The Chinese Rites Controversy

The Jesuit missionary Matteo Ricci (1552–1610) was phenomenally successful in his missionary efforts throughout China in the sixteenth century. The Jesuit missionaries who accompanied him and who succeeded him worked tirelessly to accommodate the Gospel to the customs and world-view of Chinese civilization. Ricci himself was often found wearing garb traditionally associated with a Confucian master and not those of an Italian missionary. A distinct form of Christianity emerged in China among the educated classes, and all seemed well when in 1659 the Vatican's Congregation for Missions (then known by the awkward name, "The Sacred Congregation for Propaganda") encouraged the missionaries in their efforts.

> What could be more absurd than to transport France, Spain, Italy or some other European country among the Chinese? Do not bring them our countries, but our faith—that faith which does not repel or wound the rites or customs of any people, unless they are detestable, but on the contrary, wants them to be kept and protected.[15]

However, for a variety of political, theological, and cultural reasons, Rome's attitude on the matter was reversed, so that Chinese Christians were forced to learn Latin in order to celebrate the liturgy. In fact, one sympathetic missionary noted the cruelty of this when he reported back to his superiors that newly ordained Chinese priests were constantly saying requiem Masses (Masses for the dead) because that was the only text they could muddle through. None of them understood what the words being intoned meant, and no one in the congregation had a clue about what was happening.

As time went on, more and more criticisms were leveled against the Jesuit missionaries, some from within their own order, about their missionary techniques and the inculturation of the Gospel. Within a rather short time, all missionaries were dismissed from China, and the Church has had considerable difficulty reestablishing itself. However, prior to Vatican II, several moves were made by popes as ostensibly conservative as Pius XII to promote inculturation.

CONCLUSION

Christian worship is serious business; however, that seriousness seems often to be absent from conversations about worship and its execution. The seriousness of the liturgy is captured by essayist Annie Dillard as she asks a provocative question concerning Christian worship:

> Why do people in churches seem like cheerful brainless tourists on a pre-packaged tour of the Absolute? . . . On the whole, I do not find Christians, outside of the catacombs, sufficiently sensible of conditions. Does anyone have the foggiest idea what sort of power we so blithely invoke? Or, as I suspect, does no one believe a word of it? The churches are children playing on the floor with their chemistry sets, mixing up a batch of TNT to kill a Sunday morning. It is madness to wear ladies' straw hats and velvet hats to church; we should all be wearing crash helmets. Ushers should issue life

preservers and signal flares; they should lash us to our pews. For the sleeping god [*sic*] may wake someday and take offense, or the waking god [*sic*] may draw us out to where we can never return.

— Annie Dillard, *Teaching a Stone to Talk*, 58–59[16]

Christians contend that humans are created for worship and that they are continually called to encounter and be transformed by the God of Jesus Christ in worship. This call to transformation ought to be daunting; it ought to be overwhelming; it ought to inspire some trepidation.

And this is precisely the point Dillard is making. The forces of the market, powerful, unseen, and insidious, are at work subverting the power of Christian worship and threatening to trivialize it. At the same time, temptations to make the liturgy disconnected from the world and varied cultural situations abound, and these threaten to mute the engaging and transformative power of worship. The Christian commitment to worship is manifest in the creative celebration of the liturgy and the discipline of our bodies and minds. Such commitment holds out promise for the formation of a people who bear witness to the redemptive work of God in Jesus Christ.

Questions for Understanding

1. What is Gnosticism, and how does it affect or threaten Christian worship?
2. Describe Lysaught's comparison of liturgy and boot camp. How are these occasions alike and how are they different?
3. How is the Eucharist a "counterpolitics"?
4. What does it mean to say that the liturgy is "the source and summit" of Christian life?
5. What is the Paschal Mystery, and how is it connected to the liturgy?
6. What is inculturation, and why is it significant for understanding Christian worship?

Questions for Reflection

1. Have you participated in worship where it seemed to be a consumer experience? Describe your own experience with worship.
2. If military boot camp is designed to train the body and the mind to serve the needs of the state, and Christian worship is supposed to form the body and the mind to serve the gospel, can these two "liturgies" coexist in the same person? In other words, can Christians surrender their mind and body to the state without compromising one or the other allegiance? Explain.
3. At many Catholic colleges and universities, worship, particularly the celebration of the Eucharist, is often a contentious issue. Given that almost half of all students and staff are typically not Roman Catholic, and these non-Catholic members of the community are generally prohibited, at least in principle, from receiving Communion, the celebration of the Eucharist is viewed as divisive and is often avoided. How can Roman Catholic colleges, institutions that believe that the

Eucharist is the source and summit of Christian life, celebrate the Eucharist while at the same time allow the full and active participation of those members of the college community who are not Catholic? Test your response by sharing it with both non-Catholic and Catholic colleagues and gauge their reactions to your proposal.

Suggestions for Further Study

Cavanaugh, William T. *Theopolitical Imagination: Christian Practices of Space and Time*. New York: T and T Clark, 2002.

Cavanaugh offers a provocative look at the way in which liturgy reconfigures space and time over and against the demands of the state and the globalized marketplace.

Ferrone, Rita. *Liturgy: Sacrosanctum Concilium*, Rediscovering Vatican II. Mahwah, NJ: Paulist Press, 2007.

Ferrone provides readers with a well-informed and accessible overview of the liturgical principles adopted at the council.

Guardini, Romano. *The Spirit of the Liturgy*. Milestones in Catholic Theology. Translated by A. Lane. New York: Herder and Herder, 1998.

This classic text from the early twentieth century epitomizes the spirit and the insights of the liturgical movement early in the twentieth century.

McKenna, Megan. *Rites of Justice: The Sacraments and Liturgy as Ethical Imperatives*. Maryknoll, NY: Orbis, 1997.

This popular teacher and conference leader offers a general discussion of the seven sacraments in the Catholic Church and discusses the ethical and social implications of the celebration of the sacraments.

Endnotes

1. Beth Newman, *Untamed Hospitality* (Grand Rapids, MI: Brazos, 2007), 41–69.

2. Joseph Komonchak, "The Social Mediation of the Self," in *Foundations in Ecclesiology*, Supplementary Issue of the *Lonergan Workshop Journal*, n. 11 (1995), 97–120.

3. Philip Kenneson, "Gathering: Worship, Formation, and Imagination," in *Blackwell Companion to Christian Ethics*, eds. Stanley Hauerwas and Samuel Wells (Oxford: Blackwell, 2004), 53–67.

4. M. Therese Lysaught, "Eucharist as Basic Training: The Body as Nexus of Liturgy and Ethics," in *Theology and Lived Christianity*, Annual Publication of the College Theology Society, vol. 45 (Mystic, CT: Twenty-third Publications, 2000), 257–286.

5. See Maureen A. Tilley, "The Ascetic Body and the (Un)Making of the World of the Martyr," *Journal of the American Academy of Religion* 59 (1991): 467–479.

6. Lysaught, 267.

7. For most of what follows, see William Cavanaugh, *Theopolitical Imagination: Discovering the Liturgy as a Political Act in an Age of Global Consumerism* (New York: T and T Clark, 2002). See also, William Cavanaugh, *Torture and Eucharist: Theology, Politics, and the Body of Christ* (London: Blackwell, 1998).

8. Augustine, *Confessions*, Oxford World Classics, trans. H. Chadwick (Oxford: Oxford University Press, 1991), 124.

9. For a more diverse treatment of the relationship between liturgy and social justice, see Anne Y. Koester, ed., *Liturgy and Justice: To Worship God in Spirit and Truth* (Collegeville, MN: Liturgical Press, 2002).

10. See Joseph Ratzinger, *Spirit of the Liturgy* (San Francisco: Ignatius Press, 2000).

11. See Rita Ferrone, *Liturgy: Sacrosanctum Concilium*, Rediscovering Vatican II (Mahwah, NJ: Paulist Press, 2007), 25–28.

12. See Adrienne von Speyr, *World of Prayer* (San Francisco: Ignatius Press, 1985), 28–73, for the work that provides the basis for Balthasar's explorations of the Trinity in his *Theo Drama*.

13. Although *Sacrosanctum concilium* and other documents tend to limit the Paschal Mystery to the death and Resurrection of Christ, one cannot separate the Incarnation, life, and ministry of Jesus from his death and Resurrection. In part, that is why the first two chapters of this text were devoted to a presentation and discussion of this expansive understanding of the Paschal Mystery.

14. Material in this section is adapted from the report on Saint Peter Claver Parish found in Paul Wilkes, *Excellent Catholic Parishes: The Guide to Best Places and Practices* (Mahwah, NJ: Paulist Press, 2001), 73–91. More information is available at http://www.spclaver church.org/.

15. The text is translated by Rosemary Sheed in J. Dourne, *God Loves the Pagans* (New York: Herder, 1966), 116, quoted in R. Ferrone, *Liturgy*, 36.

16. Annie Dillard, *Teaching a Stone to Talk* (New York: HarperCollins, 1982). Thanks to Jason King for suggesting this passage to me.

The Church and the Work of Redemption in the World

Although the liturgy, and specifically, the celebration of the Eucharist, is the source and summit of Christian living, "[a] Eucharist which does not pass over into the concrete practice of love is intrinsically fragmented."[1] The Church is called to redemptive communion with God and with a fallen world; it is both called to this communion and sent out to proclaim and promote it. This mission has never been easy, and it has always involved the cross, the vehicle and principle of redemptive transformation. Yet the cultural and societal milieus in which the Church currently finds itself make this mission seem more elusive and troublesome than ever. Christians are tempted to succumb to the pressures of a commodified form of the Church or to embrace a more reclusive and culturally radical form of Christian living, one that refuses to engage the world at all, or does so only hesitantly and with great suspicion.

In this chapter, the political dimensions of the Church itself and the conversation that has taken place in recent years about its voice within the civil order (the realm of government and civil politics) will be examined. The second part of the chapter will be devoted to a brief exploration of the Church's public witness in a few specific areas. This exploration will be limited, but it will help frame a soteriological account of the Church using the framework that has been established throughout the preceding chapters. For in the end, the Church is called to be the instrument of God's redemptive work, and the measure of the Church's authenticity must always be its capacity and commitment to carry out this mission.

THE CHURCH, SOCIAL ETHICS, AND POLITICS

Although one should always be wary of binaries in the world of theology, two distinct alternatives have emerged within Catholic social thought regarding how best to live the Church's mission in the world. These two alternatives do not preclude the existence of subtle variations of each alternative, and they do not exclude the proverbial "third way." For the purposes of introduction, it will be helpful to highlight and contrast these competing accounts of the Church's redemptive encounter with an unjust world.

One alternative represents the mainstream of Roman Catholic thought in the United States and in the Western world in general. According to this approach, secular society and the secular state exist in their own right quite apart from the Church. The Church is thereby free to engage the world and the state, but in order to do so it must adopt the language and practices of the secular world and must cooperate with the state in order to achieve the common good for all members of society. The Church may have unique insights into the human condition, the plight of suffering, and the dignity of the human person, but according to this tradition, these insights must be phrased and pursued on the terms supplied by secular society and with deference to the state.

The other alternative views the emergence of the secular order and the secular state as dangerous to any authentic account of the common good and as powerfully invested in the marginalization of the Church. This marginalization of the Church does not merely involve its visible structures. It also entails a concerted effort to sideline the Church's claims regarding the origins and destiny of humanity, as these claims often threaten the modern understanding of the state and its place in society. According to this view, modern secular culture has employed a variety of strategies to reinforce the primacy of the state for defining "the common good" while at the same time making religion irrelevant, defining it solely as a matter of private or personal significance. The Church's potential to subvert the modern narrative of private religion and public government threatens the state, which relies on that narrative for its power and authority. As a result of this tension, Christians have been taught to privatize their religious convictions or to frame these convictions as universal principles to which all humans of sound reason and good will could agree. While the upshot of all of this is the subtle yet thorough marginalization of the Church in contemporary society, Christians have the ability and the duty to recognize this perversion of the gospel and recapture the political dimension of the Church. The staunchest advocate of this position is the Protestant theologian Stanley Hauerwas, whose work has attracted a significant following among many younger Roman Catholic theologians who have brought the critique of Hauerwas into dialogue with mainstream Catholic social ethics.

Mainstream Catholic Social Ethics in the United States

Perhaps the most influential American theologian of the twentieth century was the Jesuit John Courtney Murray (1904–1968), the one person most responsible for the revision of the Church's teaching on religious freedom at the Second Vatican Council. Although Murray was regularly attacked by conservatives in Rome and in the United States in the years leading up to the council, he nonetheless argued powerfully from a Thomistic perspective for the distinction between the larger society and the state. Murray wrote,

> The purposes of the state are not coextensive with the purposes of society. The state is only one order within society—the order of public law and political administration. The public powers, which are invested with the power of the state, are charged with the performance of certain limited functions for the benefit of society—such functions as can and must be performed by the coercive discipline of law and political power. These functions are defined by constitutional law, in accord with the consent of the people. In general, "society" signifies an area of freedom, personal and corporate, whereas "state" signifies the area in which public powers may legitimately apply their coercive powers. To deny the distinction is to espouse the notion of the government as totalitarian.

— "THE PROBLEM OF RELIGIOUS FREEDOM," 520[2]

Murray's distinction limits the role of the state to maintaining public order and establishing civil administration. For Murray, the state has a circumscribed and limited role in securing the common good of the larger society. The Church and other social entities may debate and pursue the common good, so long as they do not run afoul of the state and its obligations in this regard.

Murray's understanding of the role played by the Church in society is somewhat akin to that of the American philosopher John Rawls. For both Murray and Rawls, the Church (and religion in general) occupies a "free space" in civil society.[3] Within this space, religions are afforded

---

PERSON OF INTEREST

Paul Hanley Furfey (1896–1992)

One of John Courtney Murray's most ardent critics came not from the hyperconservative ultramontanist theologians, but from the sociology department at the Catholic University of America in Washington, D.C. A priest of the Archdiocese of Boston, Paul Hanley Furfey, came to Catholic University as a student and eventually became the chair of the sociology department, serving in that position for more than thirty years. Furfey was a zealous proponent of Catholic Social Teaching (CST) and was determined to bring his practice of sociology into service of social justice. He was an early proponent of interracial communities and even established two houses in Washington, D.C., through which he sought to promote and to understand the social dynamics of interracial living. His association with Dorothy Day and the Catholic Worker Movement animated his work, and it made him a critic of those, like Murray, who adopted neutral scientific language in place of the language of the gospel in order to make CST and its vision of the human and society publicly acceptable. In all, Furfey would not tolerate any discussion of the human that did not include the ultimate end of the person: union with God. For Murray, Furfey's approach was not acceptable in public space and was only applicable within the Church.

the opportunity, free from state interference, to conduct open debate about the common good and would be compelled to do so without making appeals to specific theological or doctrinal language. Of course, conflict will emerge, but these conflicts about the common good will find resolution without recourse to violence, because violence or coercive power is reserved to the state and can only be used by the state in defense of its limited interest.

Murray, and contemporary supporters of his vision, sees the public space in which the Church operates as a place in which it can influence the work of the state. For example, U.S. bishops regularly use their bully pulpit to attempt to influence certain policy discussions (e.g., abortion, euthanasia, immigration, minimum wage, health care). By influencing public opinion, the Church can influence the state and its use of coercive power. Thus, in many ways, the state becomes the observer, the referee, and the target audience of religious discourse in the free space of society so that this free space is really constructed and maintained by the state.

For support of this understanding of the Church's role in public life and in pursuit of justice, many look to the documents of the Second Vatican Council. Of particular interest is the admonition in *Gaudium et spes* that the Church's redemptive mission is bound with politics and government for the common good.

[T]he expectation of a new earth must not weaken but rather stimulate our concern for cultivating this one. . . . Earthly progress can contribute to the better offering of human society, it is of vital concern to the Kingdom of God.

The Church, moreover, acknowledges the good to be found in the social dynamism of today, especially in progress towards unity, healthy socialization, and civil and economic cooperation. The encouragement of unity is

in harmony with the deepest nature of the Church's mission.

— *GAUDIUM ET SPES*, NOS. 39 AND 42

These statements rest on a more positive evaluation of modern culture and society than had been made in the decades leading up to the Second Vatican Council, but Murray and others would contend that the attitude of the council was more in keeping with the ancient tradition of the Church. For within the Thomistic tradition, the goodness of the natural order was affirmed as potentially possessing elements conducive to the formation of human community even apart from the Church.[4]

Murray and his supporters hold an optimistic account of the American political system, often labeled "liberal democracy," in which the state and the larger society are related as described in this section. The role of the Church is to compete within the marketplace of ideas and to make a case for the gospel in terms intelligible to those who do not share Christian convictions. This position is not, however, naive about the shortcomings of liberal democracy; society needs to be redemptively engaged, challenged, and critiqued. However, there is an abiding confidence in the goodness of the social order and its capacity to be engaged. In addition, it is the Church's mission in the modern world to locate the "toothing stones" (to borrow a phrase from Chenu) onto which it can continue to build a social order that reflects the most basic desires common to all humans. To this end, the Church has promoted constructive engagement with the political structures of the state.

The United States Conference of Catholic Bishops (USCCB) has encouraged American Catholics to participate in the electoral process and regularly issues an election-year admonition to this end in a document titled "Faithful Citizenship." The bishops assume the positive

Seven Principles of Catholic Social Teaching

(adapted from www.usccb.org/sdwp/projects/socialteaching/excerpt.shtml)

LIFE AND DIGNITY OF THE HUMAN PERSON

At the heart of CST is the dignity of every human. All things and institutions are rightly ordered only when they promote this dignity and promote fellowship between humans and the Creator.

CALL TO FAMILY, COMMUNITY, AND PARTICIPATION

CST promotes the communal vocation of the person in the family and in larger communal and societal structures. The fellowship of these communities is rightly ordered when they promote the common good with special attention to the poor and the most vulnerable.

RIGHTS AND RESPONSIBILITIES

CST promotes the rights of individuals to life and dignity, yet these rights are correlative to the responsibilities we have for one another in the human community.

OPTION FOR THE POOR AND VULNERABLE

Recognizing the deep divisions between rich and poor in the global economy, CST recalls Matthew's account of the Last Judgment (Matthew 25: 31–46) in which the criterion for judgment is the practice of serving the needs of the poorest among us.

THE DIGNITY AND THE RIGHTS OF WORKERS

CST connects the dignity of the human person with the dignity of work. Part of this dignity is the right to fair wages, the right to organize, the right to private property, the right to economic justice.

SOLIDARITY

From its beginnings, CST has refused to play classes against one another. Instead, CST promotes fellowship among humans and fosters the commandment to love one's neighbor and to be the keeper of one another's welfare.

CARE FOR GOD'S CREATION

The world is God's creation and we are its stewards. CST is grounded in respect for creation and the importance of sustainable economic practices.

role of the government in securing the common good. However, they are also careful to preserve the principle of subsidiarity that maintains that smaller forms of community or voluntary associations have a responsibility and a right to secure the common good and insists that the state not overstep its boundaries by making itself the sole arbiter or architect of the common good. In their advice to citizens of the United States, the bishops reiterate these assumptions and principles and try to apply them to the concrete issues that surface during political campaigns.

> We hope American Catholics, as both believers and citizens, will use the resources of our faith and the opportunities of this democracy to help shape a society more respectful of the life, dignity, and rights of the human person, especially the poor and the vulnerable.
>
> — USCCB, "Political Responsibility," 375[5]

Thus, for the bishops, the Christian faith and the convictions it brings become the means by which the common good may be secured when these convictions are empowered by the structures of the democratic political system.

The experience of democracy and religious freedom in the American context has provided a model for thinking about the relationship between church, state, and the public domain, or the public square for Catholics in general. Many would argue that this situation has produced a far more engaged and socially conscious Catholic electorate and that it vindicates the vision adopted by the fathers at Vatican II. Others, however, take issue with this conclusion and would argue that although the U.S. bishops and the Vatican may occasionally come out with well-crafted policy statements designed to influence public debate, there is no evidence that this course of action is productive or appropriate. Rome and the bishops are concerned that the Roman Catholic Church should not identify itself with any particular political group or agenda, but would rather admonish and exhort Catholic Christians to political action based on the principles of Church teaching and the dictates of individual consciences.[6] However, some have argued that such a position has not yielded any specific results. In fact, "the Catholic vote," as it has come to be known, is broadly representative of the popular culture, with little to distinguish it from other demographic groups. In the end, Christians are increasingly defined by their political or cultural leanings rather than by their affiliation with the Church.

The Church as Social Ethic

Protestant moral theologian Stanley Hauerwas has famously argued that the Church does not *have* a social ethic; rather, the Church *is* a social ethic. The former position, Hauerwas suggests, reflects the correlation approach of Murray and the mainline Roman Catholic position. The latter approach, that the Church *is* a social ethic, is born of Hauerwas's theological mentors: the Reformed theologian Karl Barth and the Mennonite theologian John Howard Yoder. Both the dialectical theology of Barth and the radical Anabaptist thought of Yoder stand in sharp contrast to much of contemporary Roman Catholic theology. The years Hauerwas spent teaching at the University of Notre Dame imbued him with a confidence that while the Catholic tradition possesses elements that make it uniquely able to withstand the larger culture, the mainstream trajectory of Catholic theology was in the process of "selling out" to the ideal of liberal democracy. Over the past several decades, Hauerwas and others have launched an insurgency within Catholic moral theology in an effort to reassess the assumptions that underpin so much of mainline Catholic theology.

Perhaps the most accessible defense of his thesis can be found in his popular book, *The Peaceable Kingdom*, though the book provides only a snapshot of his theology that has come to define an influential movement within both Protestant and Roman Catholic theology over the past several decades. This movement has provoked controversy because Hauerwas's thesis — the Church is a social ethic — challenges and transforms contemporary models of the relationship between ecclesiology and social ethics.[7]

Hauerwas rails against the idea that Christian principles must supply a foundational and universalizing approach to ethics that anyone, Christian or non-Christian, could adopt. Instead, he argues that Christians have a unique story to tell and that this very particular story distinctively forms the lives of Christians and their understanding of the world, or at least it does when they are attentive to it. In order to build the argument, Hauerwas argues against those who assume that Christian ethics is primarily a "personal" matter. He writes,

> Indeed, the notion that one can distinguish between personal and social ethics distorts the nature of Christian convictions, for Christians refuse to admit that a "personal" morality is less a community concern than questions of justice, etc. "Personal" issues may, of course, present different kinds of concern to the community than does justice, but they are no less social for being personal.

— *THE PEACEABLE KINGDOM*, 96

Hauerwas works with the contention, developed in chapter 6 on the liturgy, that the "self" is fundamentally a social self. We are individuals only because we have been formed by a community. Our language, our thinking, our attentiveness, our self-understanding are mediated to us; these things are given to us by the community in which we find ourselves, and those communities are formed and sustained by narrative, by stories.

When addressing the Christian story, Hauerwas is quick to point out that the first words of the Gospel are about a kingdom (see chapter 1), and therefore, the Christian story involves a life together. However, he is also keenly aware of the dangers of constructing an idealized account of the Church that identifies it with the kingdom of God:

The church is not the kingdom but a foretaste of the kingdom. For, it is in the church that the narrative of God is lived in a way that makes the kingdom visible. The church must be the clear manifestation of a people who have learned to be at peace with themselves, one another, the stranger, and, of course, most of all, God. There can be no sanctification of individuals without a sanctified people. We need examples and masters, and if we are without either, the church cannot exist as a people who are pledged to be different from the world.

— *THE PEACEABLE KINGDOM*, 97

The formation of a Christian people who live in between the announcement of the kingdom and its final realization, therefore, requires a community in which certain virtues become paramount.

Thomas Aquinas is famous for admonishing readers that love requires the cultivation of wisdom and courage, among other virtues. In order to love, that is, to "effectively will the good of the other," one must know what "the good" is (wisdom) and one must effectively will that good even in the face of trial (courage).[8] For Hauerwas, in addition to love, patience and hope are two essential Christian virtues, for the absence of these virtues leads to disastrous church practices. Impatience and the temptation to despair ground the violence that masquerades as justice in the world—humans want to make the world safe for democracy, protect the innocent, secure a just future, and each of these statements has been used to legitimate violence as a means:

> The church must learn time and time again that its task is not to make the world the kingdom, but to be faithful to the kingdom by showing to the world what it means to be a community of peace. . . . [W]e must be suspicious of that justice that relies on manipulation of our less than worthy

motives, for God does not rule creation through coercion, but through a cross.

— *THE PEACEABLE KINGDOM*, 103–104

One must learn to be patient in the face of injustice; one must learn to suffer injustice. This is not indifferentism masquerading as virtue. Patience forswears the coercion and violence that are at the root of all injustice and that perpetuate it. Rather, Christians are to be a hopeful people who do not simply identify with the cause of the poor and the suffering—Christians must be like them, poor, powerless, and "out of control," argues Hauerwas.

Dorothy Day and the Catholic Worker Movement

In the early twentieth century, a young socialist and agnostic named Dorothy Day (1897–1980) moved to New York City after abandoning her university studies in Illinois. She had no time for religion or spirituality but was not indifferent to social causes and devoted herself to many. She also had a number of love affairs and fell in love with a man named Forester Batterham, with whom she had a child.

Even before she became a mother, Day's spirit began to moderate, and she increasingly felt the pull of God in her life. Upon the birth of her daughter, she resolved to have the child baptized. She had become attracted to the Catholic Church because of the commitment to the poor she witnessed, particularly in the work of a local group of nuns. Ultimately she entered the Catholic Church.

Day began to integrate her newfound faith with her passion for activism and commitment to the downtrodden. During this time she encountered Peter Maurin (1877–1949), a Frenchman with ties to the Catholic intellectual traditions in Europe, and they began publishing a newspaper in 1933 called *The Catholic Worker*.

The Catholic Worker sought to publicize the fundamental but largely unknown tenets of Catholic Social Teaching. Through *The Catholic Worker*, Maurin and Day challenged the political and economic status quo. In addition to the newspaper, they established a house of hospitality in Day's apartment in Manhattan's lower east side. Through the house of hospitality, Day, Maurin, and others put into practice the demands of Christian discipleship and brought to life the principles that were being articulated in the newspaper.

With the onset of the Spanish Civil War and then World War II, the paper's consistent stand against war and violence in all its forms caused a significant drop in circulation. During those years, many of the Catholic Workers who had joined Maurin and Day were forced into prison or labor camps for their refusal to participate in the war.

Today the Catholic Worker movement includes more than one hundred and fifty houses. It continues to stand as an example of radical discipleship in the face of violence and economic injustice. Catholic Worker Houses encourage volunteers, regardless of religious affiliation, to join them in their work. Those who are committed to the work of Maurin and Day, however, are consistently motivated by a radical commitment to the teachings of Jesus, the documents that comprise contemporary Catholic Social Teaching, and the writings of the early Fathers of the Church.

The desire to control history, or "build the city of God," is a form of idolatry that threatens the gospel by legitimating violence and blinding Christians to radical demands of the Christian life. Says Hauerwas: "The task of the church is not to control history, but to be faithful to the mode of life of the peaceable kingdom. . . . They must endure injustice that might appear to be quickly eliminated through violence." (*The Peaceable Kingdom*, 106)

The Church, therefore, is called by God to be a community of virtue, a community of character in which a people is formed that can resist the temptations to dominate the world. Only then will the Church fulfill its vocation as sacrament of the world because it has received the gift of God's salvation, God's kingdom. A community thus formed cannot help but make all states, all governments, tremble, even those ostensibly constituted by "the people."

Hauerwas's principles have attracted a notable following among Roman Catholic theologians, notably Michael Baxter, David McCarthy, Therese Lysaught, William Cavanaugh, and others who have argued that mainstream Catholic social ethics and its focus on government policy is inadequate to the basic gospel tradition and inappropriate given the contemporary social and political situation. Within a world increasingly defined as post-Christian, the policy proposals of the U.S. bishops' conference mean little to parishioners, and they simply take their place alongside the proposals of various think tanks designed to influence the government on behalf of various constituencies. According to this alternative or radical train of thought, the demands of the gospel ought to revolve around the Church's habits and concrete works of mercy. Through the witness provided by disciples learning to be faithful, learning to be like Christ in their suffering and in their love, the Church manifests and calls the world to account for the loving mercy of God.

Bridging a Divide?

The two alternatives to Catholic social ethics outlined previously no doubt distort and oversimplify a complex landscape.[9] In her award-winning book, *Prophetic and Public: The Social Witness of U.S. Catholicism* Kristin Heyer offers a vision for Catholic social ethics that attempts to overcome some of the divides that exist with these two camps.[10] For Heyer, the demands of the council (Vatican II) and the tradition of Catholic social teaching make this proposal of Hauerwas, Baxter, and others problematic because it seems to withdraw from constructive and cooperative social engagement, and this engagement is precisely what the council sought to encourage and even demand. The refusal to engage the powers of the state and the broader culture stands against the best elements of the Roman Catholic tradition.

Of some concern for Heyer, and critics like her, is the perception that Hauerwas and others offer a sectarian vision of the world, one that demonizes the "natural order" in favor of a more dialectical account of the Church and "the world."[11] Although Hauerwas and others would vehemently disagree with such a characterization, this line of criticism has become somewhat entrenched. At the heart of it is the concern that something like the Anabaptist model of engagement is actually an abandonment of the world to the powers of sin and darkness—a move not in keeping with the teachings and practices of the Church, a move that also compromises the Church's redemptive responsibility in the world. While noting this concern, Heyer also finds value in the prophetic voices of Hauerwas and Baxter and their emphasis on practice, on lived community, on incarnate action on behalf of the marginalized, and on defiance of destructive economic, political, and cultural structure. It is this level of practice that has been at the heart of renewed ecclesiology and church practice such as the Base

Ecclesial Communities and the other ecclesial movements mentioned in chapter 5. The theoretical engagement with the world, the U.S. bishops' conference policy proposals, and the work of academics become eccentric when removed from the liturgy and from the concrete expression of the Church in everyday life. For these reasons, the work of "Hauerwasians" (Hauerwas would bristle at such a term) stands as an important corrective within the Catholic tradition, and it stands in line with figures such as Dorothy Day, Virgil Michael, Paul Hanley Furfey, and others.

For Heyer and many others within the mainstream of Catholic social thought, this radical vision of Christian discipleship, the powerful critique of the world offered in this prophetic account of the Gospel, must not be allowed to demonize the natural order. There is room for a rapprochement between traditional Catholic social teaching and the prophetic tradition, but that rapprochement needs to begin with an affirmation of the natural order and the social structure that arises therein. It must be recognized that

> [Nature] has its own solidity or substance, its own laws, its created autonomy. Sin is what falls short of or contradicts nature, and grace is what heals and transcendentally fulfills nature. This permits one to differentiate the genuine limitations of nature without having to label them as sinful and to affirm the power of grace as the fulfillment and not the destruction of nature.
>
> — JOSEPH KOMONCHAK, "VATICAN II AND THE ENCOUNTER BETWEEN CATHOLICISM AND LIBERALISM," 87[12]

For mainstream Catholic social ethics, relying as it does on the vision of the Second Vatican Council, the affirmation of the basic goodness of the social order and of the natural instruments of that order (the state) is imperative for understanding the Church's redemptive mission in accordance with the long tradition of natural law. Cooperation with the government, promotion of functions proper to the state, are part of the Church's duty to the gospel and are not equivalent to doing the work of Caesar, but rather to granting Caesar his proper due.

Although the Church is not an agent of the state and is not to be identified with the world, it also is not at cross-purposes with the state or with the world properly understood. The common pursuit of truth, of God's truth, necessarily orients the Church toward the world, and Nicholas M. Healy phrases the importance of such an orientation in the following statement:

> [T]ruth is discerned through an engagement with those who are other than "we" are: with the spirit, with those Christians with whom we disagree, and with those outside the Church. To be a disciple and to witness to Jesus Christ requires one to practice engaged inquiry and responsibility to others. . . . The pre-eschatological Church needs the religious and non-religious bodies of the world to be different than itself, and different from one another, in order for it to play its own role in the theodrama [the drama of salvation history] and construct its concrete identity through theological bricolage. But the boundaries between Church and world are never clear. The Church is always sinful and "worldly," and the Spirit acts throughout creation; so Church and world may often be more prescriptive than descriptive categories.
>
> — NICHOLAS M. HEALY, CHURCH, WORLD, AND THE CHRISTIAN LIFE, 170[13]

Healy thus emphasizes that before the eschatological consummation of history (that is, when God will bring history to its end), the Church is entwined with the world, never separate from it, and always something less than what it is called to be. This admonition, commonly called the *eschatological proviso*, makes the search for God's truth a cooperative enterprise in which the Church must look to the religious other as well as the secular other (the world) in order to better secure and understand that truth and thus serve the world as sacrament of God's saving presence. The prophetic practice of the Church cannot override its fundamental commitment to the world or its commitment to engage the world and to learn from it, for this was the vision of the council and is in keeping with the trajectory of the Church's social teaching.

CATHOLIC SOCIAL TEACHING AND REDEMPTIVE ACTION

The Church's redemptive practice demands policy proposals, government engagement, and lived commitment to the radical vision of the Gospel on the local level. However, these dimensions of the Church's mission seem to be rather elusive in many, though not all, parish settings. One issue that bedevils Catholic Christians is the question of the authority, the binding character, of Catholic social teaching. In most instances, CST articulates theological principles from the dogma of the faith and then applies those principles

The Authority of Catholic Social Teaching

Within Roman Catholic circles, Church teaching is always to be given respect and deference. However, some teachings enjoy a level of authority that others do not possess. Richard Gaillardetz provides a helpful discussion of the gradations of teaching authority in his essay "Ecclesiological Foundation of Modern Catholic Social Teaching," in *Modern Catholic Social Teaching: Commentaries and Interpretations*, ed. M. Himes (Washington, DC: Georgetown, 2005), 72–98.

Dogmas are taught infallibly and are, of their nature, not reformable. Dogmas are understood to be divinely revealed and call for the assent of faith.

Definitive doctrines are those teachings that have been definitively taught by the Church, and believers must accept these teachings as true. Definitive doctrines extend the teaching contained in dogmas, or they are logically related to these dogmas.

Authoritative doctrines have been taught by the Magisterium, but they have not been taught as infallible. These doctrines emerge from the interaction between dogmas or definitive doctrines of the Church and the problems and issues specific to some historical context. These teachings, of their very nature, can be reformed.

Doctrinal applications, prudential admonitions, and Church disciplines are not really doctrines, but they reflect the need to apply definitive doctrines (the three categories

Continued

The Authority of Catholic Social Teaching *Continued*

mentioned) to concrete situations. Believers are to respect these applications, admonitions, and disciplinary decrees and they are to implement them so long as they do not violate the conscience of the believer.

While CST is grounded in the dogmas and definitive doctrines of the Church (in the teachings of Jesus and the commandments of Scripture), the teachings are better understood as (1) expressions of authoritative doctrines, (2) an application of doctrine, or (3) prudential admonitions. Gaillardetz spells out the gradations of moral teachings in the life of the Church when specific moral principles, derived from the universal moral teachings of the Gospels (the dignity of the human, respect for human life, respect for the environment) have the status of authoritative doctrine (economic, political, and human rights, preferential option for poor people). Within the tradition of CST, specific moral principles are contextual and open to revision. Other aspects of CST include the concrete application of specific moral principles (e.g., National Conference of Catholic Bishops' [NCCB] pastoral letter "Economic Justice for All") that are tied to very specific contexts and are limited to a specific context.

Additionally, Gaillardetz places significant emphasis on what he calls a *"communio*-model" of the reception of Church teaching and the development of doctrine. The following illustration is adapted from his book, *By What Authority? A Primer on Scripture, the Magisterium, and the Sense of the Faithful* (Collegeville, MN: Liturgical Press, 2003), 115.

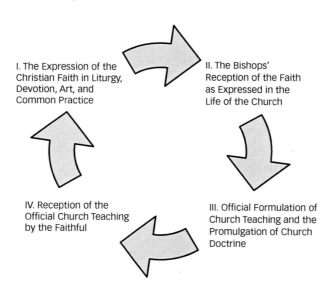

I. The Expression of the Christian Faith in Liturgy, Devotion, Art, and Common Practice

II. The Bishops' Reception of the Faith as Expressed in the Life of the Church

III. Official Formulation of Church Teaching and the Promulgation of Church Doctrine

IV. Reception of the Official Church Teaching by the Faithful

Through this simple diagram, Gaillardetz nicely illustrates the dynamics of reception and the manner in which the reception of official Church teaching helps to shape the teaching.

within concrete social and cultural locations. The applications of those principles, then, seem to leave room for considerable disagreement and debate. However, if the Church is to engage in redemptive practices that do not just save individual souls but that redeem history, then the Church must cultivate both a new understanding of the problems the world faces and consistent action in the face of these problems, even if the world seems reluctant to listen.

There are myriad issues and practices that could be addressed at this point, and a course devoted to the tradition of CST would do greater justice to the complexities of the tradition than can be accomplished here. However, a discussion of the prophetic and public dimensions of CST belongs as part of any ecclesiology, and it is particularly necessary given the soteriological emphasis on ecclesiology taken here. The present section of this chapter will address two issues selected for their proximity and relevance for a significant number of readers and for the impact these issues have on the world: just war and the economic implications of family life.

The Church and War

Before the Second Vatican Council, and even after it, there has been a fundamental (formal) optimism about the Church's relationship to the state. The hostility that developed in the eighteenth and nineteenth centuries was concerned with the nature of the state; the issue had to do with the secularization of the state and its indifference to the Church. With the emergence of the contemporary position on Catholic social ethics articulated by Murray and others, the fundamental assumptions about the state and the common good remained consistent with the long tradition of Catholic thought. Among these assumptions is that the state's recourse to coercive power in defense of itself and the innocent

The Principles of the Just War Theory

The principles of a just war have been articulated with some consistency over the course of the centuries beginning with the work of Augustine at the start of the fifth century. As the tradition developed and specific criteria were enumerated, these criteria began to be distinguished between criteria that lead to a just war (*jus ad bellum*) and the criteria for conducting a just war justly (*jus in bellum*). The criteria in the following outline are drawn from the NCCB's 1983 document "The Challenge of Peace."[14]

Principles or Criteria of *Jus ad Bellum*

Just Cause. A war may be waged in self-defense, in defense of the innocent, and to secure basic rights—in short, to defend the dignity of the human. The desire for glory or the desire for revenge is never a just cause for waging war.

Continued

The Principles of the Just War Theory *Continued*

Legitimate or Competent Authority. War is a function of the state, not a function of individuals. Groups and other individuals may not take up arms for their own causes. "The Challenge of Peace" states, "While the legitimacy of revolution in some circumstances cannot be denied, just war teachings must be applied to revolutionary-counterrevolutionary conflicts as to others. The issue of who constitutes competent authority and how such authority is exercised is essential."

Comparative Justice. Questions concerning the means of waging war today, particularly in view of the destructive potential of weapons, have tended to override questions concerning the comparative justice of the positions of respective adversaries or enemies. In essence: which side is sufficiently "right" in a dispute, and are the values at stake critical enough to override the presumption against war? The question in its most basic form is this: do the rights and values involved justify killing? For whatever the means used, war, by definition, involves violence, destruction, suffering, and death of the innocent along with the combatants.

Right Intention. The ultimate end of a government in waging war must be to establish justice and peace, rather than to use a just war as a pretext for its own gain.

Last Resort. All other diplomatic and nonmilitary options for securing peace and justice must be exhausted before resorting to force.

Reasonable Chance of Success. One may not resort to war unless its prospects for success are good. In this way, lives will not be needlessly wasted in the pursuit of a hopeless cause. Its purpose is to prevent irrational resort to force or hopeless resistance when the outcome of either will clearly be disproportionate or futile, but it also recognizes that the defense of key values, even against great odds, may be a proportionate witness.

Macro-Proportionality. One must respond to aggression with force only when the effects of its defensive actions do not exceed the damage done by the aggression itself. Judgments concerning macroproportionality should not be limited to the temporal order without regard to a spiritual dimension in terms of "damage."

Principles or Criteria of *Jus in Bello*

Proportionality. When confronting choices among specific military options, the criterion of proportionality is concerned with whether the military advantages that will be achieved by using a specific strategy or set of tactics can justify the harm reasonably expected to follow from using it. The exercise of the right and duty of a people to protect their existence and freedom is contingent on the use of proportionate means.

Discrimination. The principle prohibits directly intended attacks on noncombatants and nonmilitary targets. It raises a series of questions about the term *intentional*, the category of *noncombatant*, and the meaning of *military*.

is a moral imperative. The state has a unique, if not exclusive, right to use coercive violence, and in the case of war, no refusal of this power can be made.

Pius XII addressed the issue of "a just war" in a now famous radio address in 1956. At the time, the cold war was extremely tense, and the Soviet Union had invaded Hungary to suppress democratic reforms. In his comments on the possibility of war, the pope reiterated the close connection between the Church and the state and the obligations the faithful have in responding to the needs of the state.

> It is clear that in the present circumstances a situation may arise in a nation wherein, after every effort to avoid war has been expended in vain, war — for effective self-defense and with the hope of a favorable outcome against unjust attack—could not be considered unlawful. If, therefore, a body representative of the people and a government — both having been chosen by free elections — in a moment of extreme danger decide, by legitimate instruments of internal and external policy on defensive precautions, and carry out the plans which they consider necessary, they do not act immorally; so that *a Catholic citizen cannot invoke his own conscience in order to refuse to serve and fulfill those duties the law imposes.* On this matter We feel that we are in perfect harmony with our Predecessors.
>
> — PIUS XII, "CHRISTMAS RADIO MESSAGE," DECEMBER 23, 1956; EMPHASIS ADDED

In these remarks, Pius XII makes two important assumptions that are much at the heart of just war theory. First, he assumes and affirms the capacity of the government to discern the conditions for a just war on its own.[15] Second, he envisions resistance to the government as a matter of individual conscience. Both of these assumptions continue to inform the development of a just war theory within the Church today.

In *Gaudium et spes* (79), although there was now an admonition to governments to accommodate individuals who conscientiously object to participation in military service, the assumptions of Pius XII (assumptions shared by his predecessors) are reaffirmed. More recently, "The Challenge of Peace: God's Promise and Our Response," the 1983 pastoral letter from the NCCB, which marked a significant shift in the approach to the question of war, shares these same assumptions. At the same time, however, even as the long-standing teaching on a just war is consistently defended in Church documents, these more recent statements on the tradition begin to raise serious questions about the applicability of just war criteria (proportionality, possibility for success) within the context of modern warfare — particularly warfare between the major nuclear superpowers. Conversely, the growth of what the military calls "asymmetrical warfare" (war between two highly unequal powers) now involves strategy, tactics, and preemptive strikes in a way that does not allow for the application of many traditional just war criteria. The assumption, and in many cases the presumption, that the state can and will accurately discern when and how to wage a just war has been eroded, yet the just war theory seems to be wedded to a world that no longer exists.

The question of a just war is not remote or hypothetical. Pope Benedict XVI, Pope John Paul II, and countless other Church leaders were concerned and even horrified with the U.S. government's policy of preemptive war in the months leading up to the invasion of Iraq. Church officials viewed the policy as a violation of the Church's teaching on a just war. In fact, in the months leading up to the war, John Paul II gave a particularly pointed evaluation of the push toward war with Iraq:

"NO TO WAR!" War is not always inevitable. It is always a defeat for humanity. International law, honest dialogue, solidarity between States, the noble exercise of diplomacy: these are methods worthy of individuals and nations in resolving their differences. And . . . what are we to say of the threat of a war which could strike the people of Iraq, the land of the Prophets, a people already sorely tried by more than twelve years of embargo? War is never just another means that one can choose to employ for settling differences between nations. . . . [W]ar cannot be decided upon, even when it is a matter of ensuring the common good, except as the very last option and in accordance with very strict conditions, without ignoring the consequences for the civilian population both during and after the military operations. It is therefore possible to change the course of events, once good will, trust in others, fidelity to commitments and cooperation between responsible partners are allowed to prevail.

— JOHN PAUL II, "ADDRESS TO THE DIPLOMATIC CORPS," JANUARY 13, 2003; EMPHASIS ORIGINAL

The bishops of the United States, Canada, France, and even Iraq denounced the U.S. invasion, but only Bishop John Michael Botean of the Romanian Catholic Eparchy of Canton issued a forceful and clear condemnation of the invasion and implored the faithful to resist cooperation with this "grave evil."

[I] must declare to you, my people, for the sake of your salvation as well as my own, that any direct participation and support of this war against the people of Iraq is objectively grave evil, a matter of mortal sin. Beyond a reasonable doubt this war is morally incompatible with the Person and Way of Jesus Christ. With moral certainty I say to you it does not meet even the minimal standards of the Catholic just war theory. Thus, any killing associated with it is unjustified and, in consequence, unequivocally murder. Direct participation in this war is the moral equivalent of direct participation in an abortion. For the Catholics of the Eparchy of St. George, I hereby authoritatively state that such direct participation is intrinsically and gravely evil and therefore absolutely forbidden.

— BISHOP JOHN MICHAEL BOTEAN, "LENTEN PASTORAL LETTER," MARCH 7, 2003[16]

Botean's letter was widely criticized by Church and government officials alike, on the grounds that the bishop overstepped his authority. Of particular interest is the contention (1) that Botean went beyond articulating the general principles of just war and made his own personal application of those principles binding, and (2) that his letter mounted to an intrusion into the conscience of individual believers who alone have the obligation to sort out the morality of any given concrete situation.

In an effort to get at the formal question of how Christians should go about resisting participation in an unjust war, it might be helpful at this point for readers to divest themselves of their specific convictions about the Iraq War or the Bush administration, since these convictions may tend to cloud the discussion one way or the other for political or partisan reasons. Within the framework established by the just war tradition, resistance seems to be first and foremost a matter of public-policy debate and then a matter of *individual* conscience. There seems to be little to no room for corporate discernment and corporate resistance to an unjust war, and there appear to be no structures in place that can begin to systematize resistance to an unjust war. In other words, the Church surrenders to the state the determination of whether or not a war is just, and after weighing in on the question one way or the other, Church officials leave it to individuals to make a decision. The bishops may hope to influence the conscience of the faithful as they make their decisions. War, however, is essentially a communal enterprise; it requires the cooperation and the participation of a significant portion of society (though the professionalization of military forces, and the existence of various "contractors" to engage in warfare often leave the majority of Americans unaware of the ultimate cost of war). It seems utterly odd and dangerous then to assume that individuals are, by themselves, responsible for resisting unjust wars.

The analogy of the Church's position on abortion in the United States might help to illustrate the issue of resistance. Abortion is a legal act, sanctioned and sometimes financed by the state, covered under many forms of health insurance; however, the procedure cannot be performed in Catholic health care facilities. Medical schools, nursing programs, and health care programs in Catholic colleges and universities do not teach students how to execute abortion procedures, and, in fact, these schools quite frequently require coursework that demonstrates the intrinsic evil of these acts. In short, when it comes to the issue of the Church's resistance to abortion, there is a well-ordered regimen in place to resist the state's attempts to carry out these procedures. The procedure may be legal, but the Catholic Church refuses to condone or support it in any way.

Catholic teaching is consistent and unambiguous on the question of abortion. When it comes to the question of an unjust war, however, there are no structures or practices that can help facilitate resistance.[17] Granted, there may be room for legitimate disagreement about the precise application of just war principles, but what practices are in place within Catholic schools, or the Reserve Officers' Training Corps (ROTC)

programs in Catholic colleges and universities, that train students when and how to resist the unjust action of the government and support of the government when it acts to protect justice and the common good? In fact, it seems that the practices of the Church actually move in the opposite direction, teaching the faithful to be obedient to authorities, to swear allegiance to the flag (often making patriotic songs and displays part of Christian worship).

Although good citizenship and even patriotism is not inimical to the gospel, it seems as though the Church must adopt a more robust set of practices and form habits (virtues) that would enable it to play a more decisive role in preventing war. The cost of engaging in these programs, however, may be too much for the Church to bear. The close relationship between Church and state, between cross and sword, goes back to the late classical period and was a principle of medieval ecclesiology. But one might reasonably raise the question as to how the Church can effectively resist or prevent unjust war without adopting a more distinctive posture with regard to the state.

Several years ago, Stanley Hauerwas unleashed his savage wit in an opinion essay for the *Charlotte Observer* in which he attacked conservative Christians who were objecting loudly to President Clinton's attempts to permit gay men and women to serve in the military.[18] In the essay, Hauerwas decried that the military was worried about how homosexual soldiers might have an impact on morale and the fighting capability of the military, whereas the military had every confidence in Christian soldiers. Setting aside his pacifist convictions, Hauerwas adopts the mainstream tradition on a just war but asks the question: Why isn't the military concerned about the Christian soldier's convictions about the gospel and a just war? Hauerwas worries that, in fact, the just war tradition is a theoretical game that has no real bearing on how Christians actually participate in war, because if

BEST PRACTICES

Scottdale Mennonite Church

As a regular part of worship, the people of this small Pennsylvania Mennonite community share their stories, thoughts on the sermon, prayer needs, and family news. Of particular concern for the members of Scottdale Mennonite is the commitment of the youth to the Mennonite tradition as a peace church. To this end, the Church includes as part of the regular worship service, personal accounts of how members of the Church resisted participation in war. Most of the members describe what they went through when they reported to their draft boards during the Vietnam War. Others will recall their resistance to World War II. One member of the congregation, a Canadian, recalled that when he was in England working for Mennonite relief agencies, he was drafted into service. The British magistrate who heard his case was not familiar with the Mennonite tradition, and there was no provision for conscientious objector status. The man was imprisoned and consistently threatened for his refusal to participate, until some form of alternative hospital service was arranged by mutual agreement. The regular retelling of these stories within the setting of Sunday worship sends a powerful message to the assembly, particularly to the youth as they are the main targets for military recruitment, and any effective resistance to military service will be measured in the response of the youth.

it did have a real impact, the government would be worried. What would military training look like if Christian soldiers were obligated to raise questions about the decision to go to war? What if Christian soldiers were taught by the churches and church-sponsored institutions that it is better to die than to take an innocent life? What if Christian soldiers refused to use weapons in a way that would cause civilian casualties?

The Church's redemptive mission in the world calls for prophetic practice as well as constructive cooperation and engagement in public life. The Church's long history of endorsing the just war tradition provides an important test case for its prophetic action: can the Church incorporate its teaching on a just war in such a manner that it informs both participation in a just war and resistance to an unjust war? At this point in the Church's history, most Christians are prepared to endorse the freedom to disagree with

one another over the morality of this or that war, but while disagreements and discussion ought to characterize the believing community, it should also be formed by resolute action that resists cooperation with moral evil.

Such resistance cannot happen overnight. It must be something for which the Church prepares itself, through prayer, worship, and education. When Church members join the military, when they are commissioned after their ROTC programs at graduation, they must be celebrated and charged not only with defending the common good but also with the responsibility to resist those who would attempt to exploit the training and dedication of soldiers in order to make them fight and die for unjust purposes. This resistance will not put an end to war and violence, but it will become part of a scheme of recurring resistance to the unjust use of violence, and the impact of such a scheme cannot help

PERSON OF INTEREST

Franz Jägerstätter (1907–1943)

Franz Jägerstätter was an Austrian farmer of modest means who was conscripted by the German army to fight in World War II. He refused to fight, and German authorities had him arrested. In the torture and interrogations that followed, Jägerstätter suffered greatly but remained resolute in his refusal to fight. At his court martial, the reason for his refusal to fight was recorded:

> . . . due to his religious views, he refused to perform military service with a weapon, that he would be acting against his religious conscience were he to fight for the Nazi State . . . that he could not be both a Nazi and a Catholic . . . that there were some things in which one must obey God more than men; due to the commandment "Thou shalt love thy neighbor as thyself," he said he could not fight with a weapon. However, he was willing to serve as a military paramedic.

— Excerpt from the reason given for the judgment of the Reich Court-Martial, dated July 6, 1943; trans. Catherine Laura Danner in Erna Putz, *Franz Jägerstätter, Martyr: A Shining Example in Dark Times* [Linz: Catholic Church in Austria, 2007]

The German military executed Jägerstätter by decapitation on August 9, 1943. Before his death, he was counseled by his parish priest, family friends, and even his bishop, who all discouraged him and told him that it was not his duty to decide whether or not the war was just; that he had a family and needed to be responsible for their sake. In 2007, Pope Benedict had Jägerstätter declared a martyr.

but be an occasion of God's redeeming love for the world. This is most certainly the lesson of the American civil rights movement, in which the churches and the pastors of the Southern Christian Leadership Conference (SCLC) were the leaders in the nonviolent struggles against legislatures, law enforcement agencies, and even the Supreme Court itself.

Sex, the Family, and Economic Development

Sex, family, and economic development, three topics (or maybe only two) that evoke little interest from most college students, nonetheless pose a major issue for Western Christians, particularly those living in societies of wealth and privilege.

The connection among these three topics has been dramatically underplayed in Western culture, and the world desperately needs the prophetic and public practices of the Church in order to find its way. The Church, particularly the Roman Catholic Church, has been savagely criticized for its teaching on sex and family, yet it has found at least verbal support for its understanding of, and approach to, economic development.

For many Roman Catholics, there is perhaps no more controversial and problematic Church teaching than the prohibition of contraception. The encyclical *Humanae vitae* (On the Regulation of Birth), issued by Pope Paul VI in 1968, reiterated the Church's teaching of the prohibition of artificial contraception. Many Catholics at the time had expected a reversal in this area of teaching. Advances in reproductive technology, the new openness promoted by the Second Vatican Council, and the cultural progress made by women in recent decades all seemed to suggest that contraception was going to be permitted within the context of a fruitful and faithful marriage. In fact, when the discussion of this topic came up at the council, the question was referred to a special commission comprised of cardinals, bishops, and laypeople that included theological, medical, and social science experts (The Pontifical Commission for the Study of Problems of Population, Family, and Birth). In a report that was issued to the pope following the close of the council, the majority of that committee recommended that the Church's teaching allow certain forms of contraception within marriage. However, the pope's decision to side with the minority of the committee and to issue

a reiteration of the Church's prohibition sent shockwaves throughout the laity.

Subsequently, the teaching has been widely ignored at the practical level, with more than 80 percent of Roman Catholic couples using some form of artificial contraception, and many theologians and laypeople alike ask whether the teaching has any currency today. This topic receives some attention when couples are preparing for marriage but little attention in the life of the Church, and it is certainly not regularly connected to other issues such as economic development.

In addition to *Humanae vitae*, Paul VI was responsible for significant contributions to the development of Catholic social teaching. His 1967 social encyclical *Populorum progressio* (On the Development of Peoples) articulated more clearly and earnestly the social demands of the

Populorum progressio

Paul VI made some incredible statements about the connections between market/capitalist economies and the problems that exist in underdeveloped countries. Of particular interest are the pope's statements on private property, capitalism, and revolution in the encyclical *Populorum progressio* (1967):

Private property

23. "He who has the goods of this world and sees his brother in need and closes his heart to him, how does the love of God abide in him?" Everyone knows that the Fathers of the Church laid down the duty of wealthy people toward those in need in no uncertain terms. As Ambrose put it, "You are not making a gift of what is yours to the poor man, but you are giving him back what is his. You have been appropriating things that are meant to be for the common use of everyone. The earth belongs to everyone, not to the rich." These words indicate that the right to private property is not absolute and unconditional.

No one may appropriate surplus goods solely for private use when others lack the bare necessities of life. In short, "as the Fathers of the Church and other eminent theologians tell us, the right of private property may never be exercised to the detriment of the common good." When "private

Continued

Populorum progressio Continued

gain and basic community needs conflict with one another," it is for the public authorities "to seek a solution to these questions, with the active involvement of individual citizens and social groups."

24. If certain landed estates impede the general prosperity because they are extensive, unused or poorly used, or because they bring hardship to peoples or are detrimental to the interests of the country, the common good sometimes demands their expropriation. Vatican II affirms this emphatically. At the same time, it clearly teaches that income thus derived is not for humans' capricious use, and that the exclusive pursuit of personal gain is prohibited. Consequently, it is not permissible for citizens who have garnered sizeable income from the resources and activities of their nation to deposit a large portion of their income in foreign countries for the sake of their private gain alone, taking no account of their country's interests; in doing this, they clearly wrong their country.

Capitalism

26. Certain concepts have somehow arisen out of these new conditions and insinuated themselves into the fabric of human society. These concepts present profit as the chief spur to economic progress, free competition as the guiding norm of economics, and private ownership of the means of production as an absolute right, having no limits nor concomitant social obligations. This unbridled liberalism paves the way for a particular type of tyranny, rightly condemned by Our predecessor Pius XI, for it results in the "international imperialism of money."

Revolution

30. The injustice of certain situations cries out for God's attention. Lacking the bare necessities of life, whole nations are under the thumb of others; they cannot act on their own initiative; they cannot exercise personal responsibility; they cannot work toward a higher degree of cultural refinement or a greater participation in social and public life. They are sorely tempted to redress these insults to their human nature by violent means.

31. Everyone knows, however, that revolutionary uprisings—except where there is manifest, longstanding tyranny which would do great damage to fundamental personal rights and dangerous harm to the common good of the country—engender new injustices, introduce new inequities and bring new disasters. The evil situation that exists, and it surely is evil, may not be dealt with in such a way that an even worse situation results.

Gospel in the midst of the Church's growing rapprochement with modern culture. The pope wanted to extend and clarify the approach to the problems of the modern world taken in *Gaudium et spes*, which was deemed by many to suffer from a "committee approach." The pope also wanted to stress practical plans for developing nations, plans that would unite the quest for authentic justice and peace. This encyclical is what gave Catholics the famous maxim: "If you want peace, work for justice."

Many younger theologians, those who were either born after the council or were infants when the council started, have begun to reconsider the

Church's teaching on sex and family and have moved the locus of the discussion to a more social and global context. David Matzko McCarthy, in particular, has written provocatively about marriage and sex as distinctively Christian practices, and his views are not a "theology of the body" or moralizing about purity or even adherence to Church dogma. Rather, McCarthy's arguments are straightforwardly social and theological.

McCarthy argues "that the framework of *Humanae vitae* is at once social and theological, since it begins with a statement about our cooperation with God and repeatedly turns to concerns about the human community."[19] Those who have read the encyclical and interpreted the Church's contemporary teaching on sex and marriage may be missing the point if they see it as a question of having "the Church in your bedroom." McCarthy argues that *Humanae vitae* and *Populorum progressio* are to be interpreted together, because both documents make arguments about the common life (common good) of the human community centered on the ultimate purpose of human existence.

McCarthy notes that most arguments against *Humanae vitae* begin with an admonition about human rationality's desire to cultivate science and technology in order to improve human living. *Humanae vitae* insists, however, that the use of science and technology to promote human living is good and appropriate so long as it accords with humanity's proper dominion over nature and its role in the perfection of creation in cooperation with God's creative activity, because "[w]hen our answers to human need sever the link between our human good and the Creator, we cannot but fail."[20] The same principle holds true when discussing economic development in *Populorum progressio*, in which the pope makes it clear that the development and progress of a society is false when it is reduced to a merely economic matter. Personal and social growth and economic progress are tied to an authentic

account of the goal of human living—a common fellowship with our Creator, argues the pope. Authentic progress necessarily involves an account of the entire human person (on the individual level) and the whole human community (on the social and cultural levels).

In *Populorum progressio*, Paul VI asserts a number of points as indicative of major social problems in the modern world, which, if not addressed, will lead to violence and the breakdown of societies:

- poverty (including inadequate resources such as food, education, and health care)
- colonialism and dysfunctional economic structures
- inadequate distribution of wealth
- inequity in power
- conflict between industrialization and traditional ways of life

Remedies to these social problems will require, above all, a developed sense of solidarity between wealthy and developing nations, and a willingness to restructure the economic and political systems of developed nations as well as those still developing.

Marriage, family life, and sexual practices are often viewed as intensely personal, while the social and ecclesial dimensions of these areas are overlooked. However, only in the nineteenth and twentieth centuries has sex been seen as an intensely intimate and private act. The systematic attempt to separate sex from procreation is of great concern in *Humanae vitae*, and the document does not allow an argument for the intimacy or unitive dimension of sex to be divided from the procreative dimension. Such a division, the encyclical argues, does violence to the meaning of sex and to our eschatological destiny. As McCarthy provocatively observes, what used to be called "making babies" is now "making love," and only in the twentieth century does intercourse become a means of producing love.[21] The meaning of the sex act is circumscribed by the duty to welcome the stranger—the child. Only in the cultivation of such hospitality can the true meaning, the sacramentality of sex be rightly understood. Otherwise, the sex act becomes burdened with wildly overwrought meanings and values it cannot bear, and one's sex life becomes cause for concern and frustration. Sex becomes an experience that one consumes, and experience that brings a range of satisfactions is soon lost in the boredom and monotony of a marriage. Like the shopper, one becomes obsessed with desire, and the fulfillment of that desire becomes alienating. For McCarthy, the real meaning of sexual intercourse in marriage is, ironically, that *by itself*, it does not have to mean very much.

If sex and child-rearing practices are at the heart of *Humanae vitae*, these practices also say a great deal about how one understands human solidarity and development. Whether one accepts the morality of artificial contraceptives in any given instance is not necessarily the issue. A good reading of *Humanae vitae* shows the social dimensions of the argument and moves beyond the identification of children (or people in general) as a burden to be managed or overcome. The development of peoples in *Populorum progressio* demands that developed nations understand and accept their fundamental solidarity with the people of developing nations. If a "contraceptive economy" sets economic advancement against childbearing, then the economic and social status of women is defined in terms of the nonprocreative activity of men. Increasingly, there has been a rather healthy backlash against this pseudoequality as working mothers and fathers insist upon interrupting their careers and work schedules in order to attend to the responsibilities of parenting. Such insistence has significant economic and social demands, as many employers (including churches) have noted. If *Humanae vitae* calls both men and women to the mission of raising children, then *Populorum progressio* calls all nations to the mission of development through attentiveness to the dignity of the human person and the ultimate end of human existence. One's economic activity and sense of prosperity must be governed by an authentic account of the human good, and such an

BEST PRACTICES

Parenting for Peace and Justice Network

The connection between "doing family," "doing church," and living redemptively is often obscured within our culture. In an effort to counteract the effects of the culture, a Saint Louis, Missouri, couple has created an institute and a network of families committed to the integration of family life, church, and social justice. Jim and Kathy McGinnis are the cofounders of The Parenting for Peace and Justice Network (PPJN), which was established in 1981. The network of diverse families of various cultural and faith backgrounds are committed to peace and justice within the family and the broader community and see the two as intimately connected. The network establishes local chapters and local coordinators who work with family support groups on a wide range of issues pertinent to the neighborhoods and social contexts in which families find themselves. The network also creates and makes available a wide range of resources, including parenting books, program guides, and workshops (http://www.ipj-ppj.org/).

Adelphoi Village

In the early 1970s, Latrobe, Pennsylvania, was going through a significant period of economic and social transition, and, as is often the case, children suffered from these transitions. The Benedictine community of Saint Vincent had long been a force of economic and social stability and strength in the community and, as the need to assist troubled children became increasingly apparent, one young monk of the community stepped forward to address the problem. In 1971, Paschal Morlino, OSB, undertook remarkable challenges and established a home for abused, neglected, and troubled boys. Through this initial experience, and with the help of many friends and coworkers, he helped to establish a movement on behalf of children. The movement became known as Adelphoi, and over the years of failures and frustrations, more and more homes were established with more services provided. Under the direction of Jim Bendel, and with the continuing support of the Saint Vincent community, Adelphoi worked with the state of Pennsylvania and several other states to provide services and therapy for thousands of young people. Adelphoi currently provides services to more than eight hundred children and families through a variety of programs, including foster care, group homes, a charter school, education services, therapy, and even "secure care" services for troubled youth. These programs are remarkably successful, with more than 70 percent of the clients who are discharged from them reporting success after one year.

Adelphoi stands out as an example of the Church welcoming children under troubled circumstances and promoting redemptive recovery within the local community. Welcoming children, welcoming strangers, these are practices that transform one's way of living and economic activity, and one does not need to be a biological parent in order to cultivate the practices envisioned in *Humanae vitae* and *Populorum progressio*. (http://www.adelphoivillage.org/)

account may radically challenge one's assumptions about what one is doing when having sex, buying a pair of pants, or going to work.

CONCLUSION

The people of God have been called together in Christ to make available the redeeming love of God in a world haunted by sin and violence. The issues presented and discussed in the last part of this chapter are by no means the most important issues in the life of the Church (though they are certainly of great importance), and there are many other issues that could be presented that would offer compelling challenges (racist and sexist culture and social arrangements, interreligious intolerance, labor, and so on). It is hoped, however, that one or both of the topics raised at the end of the chapter help to spark a discussion about what Christians are doing when they "do church." Are the practices of parish life sufficient to help shape a people redemptively so that they might have an impact in history and become God's sacramental agent, through Jesus Christ and the work of the Sprit, and help to shape newly emerging patterns of redemptive recovery in history? Has the Church been trained by its leaders simply to wait for policy papers on important issues to the point that the Church neglects the importance of prophetic practice in the world? Are small church communities, new ecclesial movements, and radical Christians engaging in prophetic practices in a way that separates them from the world and from the larger Church, making them susceptible to the labels *sectarian* and *irrelevant*, or is this the future of the Church? At the close of this chapter, and at the end of this brief text on the Church, these questions should animate further discussion on what it means for Christians to "be" church. Through such a discussion, perhaps Christians might reconnect to the Church and understand it as the essential expression of God's work in Christ for the salvation of the world, for as Scripture says, God sent his Son so that all of us might have life and have it in abundance (John 10:10).

Questions for Understanding

1. Describe Murray's understanding of the relationship between Church, state, and society.

2. What does Hauerwas mean when he says that the Church must "be" a social ethic rather than "have" a social ethic, and why is he so critical of Murray's approach to "public theology"?

3. What are the essential virtues of the Church according to Hauerwas? Why are these virtues so important to his ecclesiology?

4. What are the basic criticisms of Hauerwas's position? What are some important affirmations of Hauerwas's position?

5. What are the criteria for a just war in the Catholic tradition? Who has the responsibility for determining whether a war is just or unjust?

6. According to David McCarthy, how are the encyclicals *Humanae vitae* and *Populorum progressio* linked?

7. According to *Populorum progressio*, why is solidarity so important for understanding authentic development?

Questions for Reflection

1. What role should religious convictions play in public discourse? Do you find yourself identifying with Murray or with Hauerwas? Why?

2. Approach a relative, a friend, or an acquaintance in the military or one who has had experience in the military and ask him or her about the possibility of an unjust war. How would that person react if ordered to serve in a war that person strongly believed to be unjust? Would resistance be an alternative? If the answer is yes, how would resistance be expressed? Would it be acceptable to go to jail or even die? If the answer is no, why not?

3. If collaboration and resistance are both part of the Christian ethos, inasmuch as Christians are called both to enact the gospel within an alien culture that is troubled by sin and violence and to cooperatively engage all that is good within that culture, then how are Christians to be formed for this task? In other words, what are the practices that will help form people who balance the goals of collaboration and prophetic witness effectively?

Suggestions for Further Study

Allman, Mark. *Who Would Jesus Kill? War, Peace, and the Christian Tradition*. Winona, MN: Anselm Academic, 2008.

This award-winning book provides an engaging and provocative overview of the theory and practice of "just war," its origins, and the controversies that surround the theory today.

Healy, Nicholas M. *The Church, World and the Christian Life: Practical-Prophetic Ecclesiology*, Cambridge Studies in Christian Doctrine. Cambridge: Cambridge University Press, 2000.

This slender but demanding text offers an ecclesiology that moderates between the Hauerwasian and Murrayite approaches to the Church's prophetic mission in the world.

Heyer, Kristin. *Prophetic and Public: The Social Witness of U.S. Catholicism*. Washington, DC: Georgetown, 2006.

Heyer contrasts Roman Catholic versions of Hauerwas's program with those of Murray and his supporters and charts a middle course between the two alternatives.

Martin, Stephen L. *Healing and Creativity in Economic Ethics: The Contribution of Bernard Lonergan's Economic Thought to Catholic Social Teaching*. Lanham, MD: University Press of America, 2008.

This demanding book unlocks the economic writings of Lonergan and integrates Lonergan's economic writings with Catholic social thought.

McCarthy, David M. *Sex and Love in the Home*. London: SCM, 2001.

McCarthy offers a thoroughgoing reassessment of the sacramentality of Christian marriage and its role in the Church and the world.

Rubio, Julie H. *A Christian Theology of Marriage and Family*. New York: Paulist, 2003.

This text examines what it means to live marriage prophetically within the present cultural and social context.

Endnotes

1. Benedict XVI, *Deus caritas est*, n. 14.

2. John Courtney Murray, "The Problem of Religious Freedom," *Theological Studies* 25 (1964): 503–575.

3. See John Rawls, *Political Liberalism* (New York: Columbia University Press, 1993).

4. Richard Gaillardetz, "The Ecclesiological Foundations of Modern Catholic Social Teaching," in *Modern Catholic Social Teaching: Commentaries and Interpretations*, ed. Michael Himes (Washington, DC: Georgetown University Press, 2005), 80.

5. United States Conference of Catholic Bishops, "Political Responsibility: Proclaiming the Gospel of Life, Protecting the Least Among Us, and Pursuing the Common Good," *Origins* 25, no. 22 (1995): 369–383.

6. See John Sniegocki, "The Social Teaching of Pope Benedict XVI: Clergy, Laity, and the Church's Mission

for Justice," in *Catholic Identity and the Laity*, College Theology Society Annual, vol., 54, Tim Muldoon, ed. (New York: Orbis, 2009), 120–133.

7. Stanley Hauerwas, *The Peaceable Kingdom: A Primer in Christian Ethics* (Notre Dame, IN: University of Notre Dame Press, 1983).

8. STh I–II, 26, 4.

9. For example, see Jonathan Malesic, *Secret Faith in the Public Square: An Argument for the Concealment of Christian Identity* (Grand Rapids, MI: Brazos, 2009).

10. Kristin Heyer, *Prophetic and Public: The Social Witness of U.S. Catholicism* (Washington, DC: Georgetown, 2006).

11. Michael H. Barnes, "Community, Clannishness, and the Common Good," in J. Donohue and M. T. Moser, *Religion, Ethics, and the Common Good*, vol. 41, Annual Publication of the College Theology Society (Mystic, CT: Twenty-third, 1996), 27–52.

12. Joseph Komonchak, "Vatican II and the Encounter between Catholicism and Liberalism," in *Catholicism and Liberalism: Contributions to American Public Philosophy*, R. B. Douglass and D. Hollenbach, eds. (Cambridge: Cambridge University Press, 1994), 76–99.

13. Nicholas M. Healy, *The Church, World and the Christian Life: Practical-Prophetic Ecclesiology*, Cambridge Studies in Christian Doctrine (Cambridge: Cambridge University Press, 2000).

14. For a succinct but helpful discussion of the criteria and the history of the just war tradition, see Mark Allman, *Who Would Jesus Kill? War, Peace, and the Christian Tradition* (Winona, MN: Anselm Academic, 2008), 158–206

15. See *Catechism of the Catholic Church*, §2309: "The evaluation of these conditions (the conditions pertaining to whether a war is just or not) for moral legitimacy belongs to the prudential judgment of those who have responsibility for the common good."

16. The letter is available at http://www.centerforchristiannonviolence.org/data/Media/Pastoral_Letter_Iraq_War.pdf (accessed 2/1/10).

17. This is precisely the point made in Daniel Bell, *Just War as Christian Discipleship: Recentering the Tradition in the Church rather than the State* (Grand Rapids, MI: Brazos, 2009).

18. Stanley Hauerwas, "Why Gays (as a Group) are Morally Superior to Christians (as a Group)," reprinted in *The Hauerwas Reader*, J. Berkman and M. Cartwright eds. (Durham, NC: Duke University Press: 2001), 519–521; originally published as "Christian Soldiers," *Charlotte Observer*, May 31, 1993.

19. David Matzko McCarthy, "Procreation, the Development of Peoples, and the Eschatological Destiny of Man," *Communio* 26 (1999): 698–721, at 699.

20. Ibid., 701.

21. Ibid., 709.

Index